Advance Praise for

REACHING GOD SPEED

"Another inspiring and insightful book and resource on the Bible by Joe Kovacs."

—Chuck Norris

"Even though there's nothing more important in this life than discerning God's direction and meaning for our lives, it's easy to miss in a world that always seems headed in the other direction. Fortunately, in *Reaching God Speed*, author Joe Kovacs, in a disarmingly lighthearted yet earnest and penetrating way, coaches the reader in how to detect God's transcendent and redemptive message in every area of life, even the most improbable."

–David Kupelian, journalist and author of *The Marketing of Evil*

"Joe Kovacs has done it again! Forget *Shocked by the Bible* and *Shocked by the Bible 2*, though they are masterful books about Scripture. Now he unlocks the hidden principles of God to help you understand every jot and tittle."

–Joseph Farah, author of *The Gospel in Every Book of the Old Testament* and chief executive officer of WND

"Everyone understands the enemy's message permeates our world. Even in the classic comedy film *Oh, God!*, George Burns noted how 'Nobody had any problem believing that the devil took over and existed in a little girl. All she had to do was wet the rug, throw up some pea soup and everybody believed. The devil you could believe, but not God?' This is so true because few ministers or people of faith realize God is actually everywhere and involved in every single thing. That includes the books we read, the music we listen to, and the movies we watch. We witness a spectacular dawn and we thank God for it. We understand the Creator made the clear, beautiful morning, but often don't realize the same God inspired some author, even those who hate or reject God, to deliver His messages of hope and warning in popular movies. Joe Kovacs' new book, *Reaching God Speed*, explains what most of us do not know about the real God. It's an eye-opening work that will make us better understand that in everything we do, God is present with HIS MESSAGE! So even though the devil may be embedded in music, God is also there, and deeper still!"

–Bob Barney, editor of ThePlainTruth.com

REACHING GOD SPEED

UNLOCKING *the* SECRET BROADCAST REVEALING *the* MYSTERY *of* EVERYTHING

JOE KOVACS

FIDELIS
BOOKS

A FIDELIS BOOKS BOOK
An Imprint of Post Hill Press
ISBN: 978-1-63758-122-3
ISBN (eBook): 978-1-63758-123-0

Reaching God Speed:
Unlocking the Secret Broadcast Revealing the Mystery of Everything
© 2022 by Joe Kovacs
All Rights Reserved

Cover Design by Cody Corcoran

Although every effort has been made to ensure that the personal and professional advice present within this book is useful and appropriate, the author and publisher do not assume and hereby disclaim any liability to any person, business, or organization choosing to employ the guidance offered in this book.

Unless otherwise indicated, all Scripture quotations are from the King James Version of the Holy Bible. Public domain.
Scripture quotations marked "NKJV" are taken from the New King James Version. Copyright © 1982 by Thomas Nelson. Used by permission. All rights reserved.
Scripture quotations marked (NLT) are taken from the Holy Bible, New Living Translation, copyright © 1996, 2004, 2007. Used by permission of Tyndale House Publishers Inc., Carol Stream, Illinois 60188. All rights reserved.
Scripture quotations marked CSB have been taken from the Christian Standard Bible®, Copyright © 2017 by Holman Bible Publishers. Used by permission. Christian Standard Bible® and CSB® are federally registered trademarks of Holman Bible Publishers.
Scripture quotations marked (NIV) are taken from The Holy Bible, New International Version® NIV® Copyright © 1973 1978 1984 2011 by Biblica, Inc. TM Used by permission. All rights reserved worldwide.
Scripture quotations marked ESV are from the Holy Bible, English Standard Version, copyright © 2001, 2007, 2011, 2016 by Crossway Bibles, a division of Good News Publishers. Used by permission. All rights reserved.

Post Hill Press
New York • Nashville
posthillpress.com

Published in the United States of America
3 4 5 6 7 8 9 10

TABLE OF CONTENTS

1ST GEAR:
The Secret Message Hidden *in* Everything

WHAT DO *Back to the Future* and "Stairway to Heaven" have in common with making love, our solar system, and the coronavirus pandemic? And what do *Raiders of the Lost Ark* and *The Wizard of Oz* have in common with the sinking of the Titanic, 9/11, the structure of atoms, and popular ad campaigns like "I've fallen and I can't get up!"? And what do all these seemingly unrelated items have to do with your personal life and future? The answer is a stunning surprise, as we're about to probe a subject that is simply astonishing.

Is it possible we have all been missing something extremely important and wonderful? Perhaps something that holds the key to life, success, happiness, peace of mind, and understanding? The answer is yes, and what we're about to explore is life-changing. It's truly amazing.

I wish to share with you perhaps the best-kept secret in the history of mankind. Ironically, it's also the most open secret of all time; yet people remain unaware of it because they simply aren't paying attention to what they should be—to what truly matters. We're so consumed with our day-to-day work, paying bills, getting or staying healthy, spending time with friends and families, pets, personal hobbies, entertainment, and looking for love, that we're missing out on a staggering, invigorating message about our own lives and futures that's being broadcast on all frequencies. All we have to do is open our eyes and ears. And I'd like to help with that.

"I'm going to tell you a story. It's going to sound ridiculous. But the longer I talk, the more rational it's going to appear." That statement is a movie line uttered by Tom Cruise in the 2014 film *Edge of Tomorrow*. You know, the action flick with the tag line of "Live. Die. Repeat." I'm quoting

Cruise because the story I am going to tell you is completely true. It may initially sound ridiculous, but the longer you read what I say, the more rational it's going to appear.

What I'm about to share with you is so astonishing, so seemingly unbelievable, that I, myself, may not have believed it until I lived a certain amount of years, gaining enough solid knowledge and life experience to discern truth from lies, fact from fantasy. And yet these facts are so fantastical, they may seem preposterous at first. But again, the longer you keep reading, the more rational they're going to appear. So please bear with me, since this information can change your life for the better. If you apply it properly, it can even help you live without a single moment of anxiety and worry and may actually help extend your living years indefinitely. I'm not kidding.

This life-altering information is based on the idea that everything we see, hear, and experience on a daily basis is broadcasting a message—a single, positively inspiring message. It's a message that's virtually hidden to untrained eyes and ears but one that can be clearly understood when we recognize the source of the broadcast, which I shall explain in great detail in this book.

We hear and see the message all the time, although most of us don't recognize it. It's embedded inside our favorite songs on the radio, whether they be sung by the Beatles, Elvis, Madonna, Frank Sinatra, Johnny Cash, Aerosmith, Queen, U2, Adele, Pink, or Pink Floyd.

The message is the underlying theme in famous children's stories, from "Hansel and Gretel" to "Cinderella," and "Sleeping Beauty" to "Snow White."

It's featured in famous advertising campaigns including "You deserve a break today" from McDonald's; "I've fallen and I can't get up!" from LifeCall; "I'd like to teach the world to sing in perfect harmony" from Coca-Cola; and "He likes it! Hey Mikey!" from Life cereal.

The same wondrous message is displayed in popular movies like *Die Hard, I Am Legend, Groundhog Day, A Christmas Story* and *National Treasure.*

It's found in news headlines, even if the news is bad, such as the worldwide coronavirus pandemic, the sinking of the Titanic, or the collapse of the World Trade Center in New York on 9/11.

The message is present in everyday sayings including "rise and shine," "cleanup needed in produce," "runaway bride," "plenty of fish in the sea," "you are what you eat," "I give you my word," "don't soil yourself," and "man up."

It's found in typical life activities such as breathing, getting married and changing one's name, sleeping, waking up, getting sick, traveling, teaching, learning, and having sex.

The message is even prominent in nature, coming to light on a higher level when we examine our solar system, black holes in deep space, atoms, plants, and animals.

The reason most people remain unaware of the message is because our minds are operating at typical human speed. We experience everything through our five senses of sight, hearing, smell, taste, and touch. That's only natural, since those are the senses we've been given in our physical bodies. But there's another factor involved that most of us don't take into account or we outright dismiss. This element brings to life that which is unseen and that which is unheard by countless millions.

It is the means by which we can truly decipher virtually everything with which we're presented in life. It provides the ability to make the unseen visible, the unheard audible, and the complex simple. It is the speed of thought that carries the secret message on every frequency and every wavelength. It is a level of understanding that operates much faster than human speed. It's infinitely quick and alive. It's what I call "God speed."

Now before I write another word, I wish to make it clear this book is not about religion. It's about unseen truth, explaining the real reason everything in life is the way it is. I have no interest in your personal belief when it comes to matters of faith. What we're about to discover goes beyond what's presented in churches, schools, or government. In simple fashion, we're going to unlock the mystery of how everything in our world operates, as we wake up to truth that is often unrecognized.

"God speed" is a term I'm coining to reveal the way the Creator of the universe thinks, operates, and teaches, having a mind that runs above and beyond the human speed at which all of us regular folk in the flesh naturally think. It is the divine velocity at which everything actually runs in our world, be it seen or invisible, heard or inaudible. It is the higher speed or spirit level at which God broadcasts to us, embedding His message in everything. It is different from the single word *Godspeed*, which the dictionary defines as success or a prosperous journey, though you can certainly experience the success and prosperity of Godspeed if your mind gets up to speed, reaching God speed.

As you continue to read, it will become obvious there is a common theme coursing through everything that we know. It is this masterful connection that contains the hidden message broadcast at all times in all places.

We'll learn how to recognize this message so our lives can be enriched with what we've been missing. All of our minds in their present forms operate at human speed. If compared to the movements of a car, our thoughts are running in low gear, creeping along at a slow speed on a highway intended for high-speed travel. Perhaps they're even stuck in park or merely idling in neutral, going nowhere. Sadly, some of us may actually have our mind in reverse, proceeding in the wrong direction. But that's about to change for the better. I'll explain how to rev up the vehicle of your mind and shift it into high gear, so it's no longer sitting in idle or moving sluggishly.

In outer-space adventures in movies or on TV, interstellar vehicles make the jump from regular speed to light speed, warp speed, or hyperspace all the time. You can do something similar, as your mind can make the jump from human speed to God speed. This awesome level of understanding can be reached with just a tiny bit of effort, and I'll coach you how to get there. It's so tremendous, it needs to be shared with others. Once you grasp the very simple concept, you'll be able to comprehend things you never understood before, greatly reducing or even eradicating any fear and anxiety festering inside. You can have true peace of mind and be confident for your personal future when you realize there's a certain reason everything is the way it is.

I'll start by showing you the unrecognized message in things you already know, mostly fun things with which you're already very familiar. I shall present and examine popular songs, movies, children's stories, famous sayings, news events, daily life activities, and objects in the natural world to help open your eyes and unplug your ears to what you've been missing. Because it's a lot.

As I unveil to you this stunning secret, it's important to pay close attention, because you'll come to find out there is not just an apparent, physical meaning to what's being said. There is a secondary meaning, a higher or spirit connotation of which most people are not aware initially. It is this higher meaning on the spirit level that is the key to accelerating our thoughts and making the jump to God speed. Don't worry if you have no idea what I'm talking about yet. This is the reason I'm selecting your favorite songs, movies, and sayings, so we can slowly step on the gas pedal and bring you up to speed. You'll come to realize that virtually everything we know is some sort of a metaphor, analogy, or allegory, another way of saying the hidden message. This journey is going to be a fun ride, as all your personal favorites suddenly take on new meaning as your mind awakens to new life and greater understanding.

We all have been asleep at the wheel to some extent, but once we acknowledge this missing element in our lives, we can move forward with clarity and purpose most of us have never experienced. We can do this when we acknowledge the existence of something and someone greater than us. It will allow us to grasp the higher meaning of every single thing in all places. It will allow us to exceed the posted speed limit of human speed and reach our intended understanding at God speed.

By the time you finish reading this book, I hope you have a brand-new awareness, seeing things you've never seen before. You should hear spoken sentences and songs with a startling new comprehension. Even the Word of God will have a new meaning, as the Scriptures themselves are broadcasting at God speed, in addition to physical, human speed.

2ND GEAR:

If You Listen Very Hard,
the Songs Remain *the* Same

PERHAPS THE best way to begin this trip of revving us up to speed is with music, since virtually everyone loves listening to the radio. So let's focus on some of the most famous tunes ever recorded, and a pattern will emerge that may surprise you. It is this pattern that will begin to get the wheels turning inside your noggin. Because, as we're about to see, the message that's hidden in everything is, amazingly enough, the same message embedded in the ancient Scriptures of the Bible. Let's have a look.

The song "Stairway to Heaven" by the British rock band Led Zeppelin is considered by many music lovers to be among the greatest rock songs of all time, if not *the* greatest. In 2000, it was actually voted as No. 3 on VH1's list of "100 Greatest Rock Songs." Don't worry, this is not a best-song contest or an episode of "Name That Tune." I'm starting with this classic hit solely because of its enormous popularity, since millions know its words by heart. And what you're about to learn about this musical smash should certainly make you wonder, as the lyrics declare.

While any song can certainly mean different things to different people, amazingly "Stairway to Heaven" is actually proclaiming—both directly and metaphorically—the message of God in the Bible, and most likely without the conscious knowledge of band members Jimmy Page and Robert Plant, who wrote the ballad. I'm fully aware such a claim could blow a gasket in the minds of countless rock fans, especially all the dudes and dudettes who smoked plenty of weed listening to this number that's still aired countless times a day on radio stations worldwide. But the assertion is true, and I'll explain it now as clearly as I possibly can.

First of all, the song's title is outright declaring the path to get to heaven, the way to ascend to the next level, with the destination being the heavenly paradise of eternal life with God. I mean…*hello*! Its very name is "Stairway to Heaven" for goodness' sake, just in case you weren't paying attention.

But beyond the obvious title, there's plenty more. One lyric toward the end of the tune provides a defining clue in decoding the message of God—not just in "Stairway to Heaven," but in all songs, in all films, in commercials and in nature. That line says that you "must listen very hard."

This lyric actually contains two extremely important concepts. The first is something I've already mentioned, and that is to pay attention. To listen very hard means to listen to the words with purpose and intent as if you really want to learn something, because a hidden message is being broadcast on a higher level you're probably not aware of if you're not putting your mind to it. It takes some effort to focus and chew on what's really being said in the words.

The second concept, as strange as this may sound to some, is precisely the same directive God often states in a variety of phrases throughout Scripture. We're meant to listen very hard, as in listen to and obey God's instructions.

For those not familiar with the Old or New Testaments, the Creator actually tells people numerous times to "pay attention," "take heed," "listen to my words," and "incline your ear." Jesus Himself says seven times in the book of Revelation: "He who has an ear, let him hear what the Spirit says." And all these phrases imply more than just listening but actually following the instructions that are given, like when a mother tells her children: "Listen to your father."

If I may paraphrase Jesus in today's street language when it comes to the instructions to pay attention and take heed, here's what He's saying: "Hey, you doofuses! Take the crud out of your ears and listen up!" I'm not kidding, nor am I trying to sound silly, because there is, in fact, a Bible verse conveying the same idea. Open your eyes for this sparkling gem from the mind of God Himself:

> "Pay attention, you stupid people! Fools, when will you be wise?"
> (Psalm 94:8 CSB).

Clearing the garbage out of our ears to listen very hard is just the beginning of shifting to God speed. God also talks about us opening our eyes, to see and understand messages otherwise invisible to the naked eye.

For instance, Scripture says, "Open my eyes so that I may contemplate wondrous things from your instruction" (Psalm 119:18 CSB). And God Himself complains about defiant people who are not using their eyes and ears properly. "They have eyes to see but do not see, and ears to hear but do not hear, for they are a rebellious house" (Ezekiel 12:2 CSB).

Thus, if we open our eyes to see more than the obvious, physical level, and if we focus our ears to listen very hard, closely tuning in to follow God's directions and hear the additional communication, that secret message the Maker of us all is broadcasting at God speed, then the meaning of "Stairway to Heaven" and every other tune becomes clear.

In case you never noticed it before, Led Zeppelin's signature song itself slaps us across the face to inform us there is indeed a secondary meaning to the lyrics, reminding us that we already know sometimes words have more than one meaning.

To further this point of the higher, secondary meaning, it's well-known that Jesus taught people using metaphors and allegories, stories that hide the true meaning from the general population but were intended to be understood only by those with a higher level of spiritual understanding. Scripture breaks out the P-word for these riddles, calling them "parables." But what many people may have missed is that Jesus spoke to crowds in this mysterious, metaphorical fashion all the time.

> "Jesus spoke all these things to the crowd in parables; he did not say anything to them without using a parable" (Matthew 13:34 NIV).

He also explained the parables are intended to **hide** His secret message:

> "The secret of the kingdom of God has been given to you. But to those on the outside everything is said in parables so that, 'they may be ever seeing but never perceiving, and ever hearing but never understanding...'" (Mark 4:11–12 NIV).

With this in mind, examining more of Led Zeppelin's composition makes it obvious the entire song is a divine message from the One who inspired the lyrics to begin with. Incidentally, musicians and songwriters speak constantly about being inspired to write a certain lyric or rhyme. To remind you, words such as *inspire* and *inspiration* literally mean having the spirit or breath of God being blown into someone. Here's how the Merriam-Webster dictionary describes *inspire*: "The meaning is a metaphorical extension of the word's Latin root: *inspirare* means 'to breathe or blow into.' The metaphor is a powerful one, with the very breath of a divine or supernatural force asserted as being at work."

"Stairway to Heaven" discusses two paths that people can choose to go by, but there's time still available to change the road folks have chosen to travel on. If that's not the message of the Bible condensed into a line or two of a song, I don't know what is. All throughout Scripture, God says He has presented people two paths to choose, the way of everlasting life or the way of eternal death:

> "See, I have set before you today life and good, death and evil"
> (Deuteronomy 30:15 NKJV).

> "...I have set before you life and death, blessing and cursing; therefore choose life, that both you and your descendants may live"
> (Deuteronomy 30:19 NKJV).

Led Zeppelin is merely echoing the fact that God is presenting us with two choices to go by: the path of obedience to His instructions or the road of resistance, disobedience, and rebellion, also known as sin. We can either follow the way of God or the way of the devil. We can pursue the light or remain stuck in the darkness.

The more we study it, the more it becomes clear that every portion of "Stairway to Heaven" can be correlated to the Bible at God speed, with some lines quite easy to understand. Here are a few that everyone should be able to grasp.

When the song mentions a piper who is calling people to join him, the piper is a reference to God, the One playing the true music. And when it says he's calling people to join him, it means the Creator Himself is **calling** individuals to **join themselves** to their Maker:

> "He has saved us and **called** us with a holy **calling**..."
> (2 Timothy 1:9 CSB).

"Many nations will **join themselves** to the LORD on that day and become my people. I will dwell among you..." (Zechariah 2:11 CSB).

The song also talks about a new day to dawn in the future for people who stand long. That new day is tomorrow, the dawn of eternal life for those who heard the call from above and hopped on board the Messiah train. The apostle Paul referred to this current time period in which we dwell as "the night," and he told people the new "day" is about to arrive:

"The night is nearly over; the day is almost here. So let us put aside the deeds of darkness and put on the armor of light"
(Romans 13:12 NIV).

And this business in the song about standing long means to stand firm in one's faith in the face of every evil challenge:

"For this reason take up the full armor of God, so that you may be able to resist in the evil day, and having prepared everything, to take your **stand**"
(Ephesians 6:13 CSB).

The beginning of "Stairway to Heaven" mentions a lady who's buying a stairway to heaven, which simply means she's buying into or agreeing with the pathway to God's dwelling place. It also explains that she can get what she's come for with "a word."

At God speed, the "word" is not just any word. It is The Word, as in God Himself. The first sentence in the gospel of John plainly says "the Word was God" (John 1:1).

The Word is the master key—or that could be phrased "The Master's Key"—the key that unlocks everything about everything and helps us all make the jump from human speed to God speed, as we'll see.

The lady about whom Led Zeppelin is singing represents all of us, humanity as a whole, and the band knowingly or unknowingly is stating poetically that when we make use of the Word (which is God), we can "get" what we came for. In other words, we can understand as well as obtain the reason we're all here, our reason for being, which, of course, is God. The word "get" does not just mean to obtain or gain possession of something. It also means to understand. Remember, the lyrics indicate that words sometimes have two meanings, and the dictionary lists more than a dozen different senses for "get."

This is an important concept to keep in mind as we continue, remembering that any word or phrase can have more than a single meaning. Sometimes a word can even mean the opposite of itself. For example, the word "cleave" is a contronym, as it not only means to cling, like a wife cleaves to her husband; but it also means the exact opposite, to split apart, as in the sentence, "The man cleaved the firewood with his ax."

The final portion of "Stairway to Heaven" reveals what will happen if we listen very hard. It explains that the tune will finally come to us when all are united as one, so that we all become a rock and don't roll away. A lot is being said here, and I'll try to keep it simple as I translate the stunning news using God's eyeglasses and bring you up to speed.

When we listen very hard to the Word—with purpose, intent, and obedience—the tune that comes to us is God Himself. Yes, the Spirit of Jesus, the God who created you and everything else, is described in Scripture as a "song" (Exodus 15:2, Isaiah 12:2). (No wonder God can be heard in song lyrics, because He Himself is a song.) He is a song that will come to us and personally take up residence inside our physical bodies.

This might be a new idea for you, but Scripture talks about "the coming of Jesus Christ in the flesh" (2 John 1:7 CSB) and reveals that "this is the secret: Christ lives in you. This gives you assurance of sharing his glory" (Colossians 1:27 NLT).

This sharing of Christ's glory is what Led Zeppelin's song means when it talks about you and me becoming a rock and not to roll away, as in not departing from God. Many folks already know that Jesus is called a Rock many times in the Bible, including:

> "They remembered that God was their Rock, that God Most High was their Redeemer" (Psalm 78:35 NIV).

> "And who is a rock, except our God?" (Psalm 18:31 NKJV).

But just like the song says, we become one with God, uniting with the Rock. The Bible describes this notion of becoming one with God in many different ways. The Creator says: "I am married unto you" (Jeremiah 3:14).

And other Scriptures indicate:

> "The LORD our God, the LORD is one!" (Deuteronomy 6:4 NKJV).

"I said, 'You are gods; you are all sons of the Most High'"
(Psalm 82:6 CSB).

"Christ, who fills all things everywhere with himself"
(Ephesians 1:23 NLT).

"On that day you will know that I am in my Father, you are in me, and
I am in you"
(John 14:20 CSB).

Thus, using the Bible as the template, the words put into one of the most famous tunes ever, "Stairway to Heaven," are actually voicing at God speed the same message that God has written in His own Good Book. And the human writers of this song, just like the writers of most other songs, probably have no idea they're spreading the Good News.

But this is far from the only song that follows this pattern. Once we begin investigating, it's easy to see that countless songs keep this sacred beat. I can't possibly examine all of them in this writing, but I'd like to look at some of the most famous titles so you realize it's not a one-and-done situation. And I strongly encourage you to put YouTube to good use, to watch the official videos of these songs and really pay attention to everything you see and hear, since they follow the scriptural template.

HAPPY BIRTHDAY

Let's try a simple song that most everyone knows by heart, even if you never listen to the radio. It's called "Happy Birthday to You," and if you don't know these lyrics by heart, you've obviously been living under a rock. Guinness World Records calls it the most recognized song in the English language. The lyrics to this song are now in the public domain, so here they are in all their glory in case you forgot them:

Happy birthday to you

Happy birthday to you

Happy birthday dear [name of the birthday boy or girl here]

Happy birthday to you.

That's short and sweet, with a whole lot of repetition, but this is exactly how God works: quickly, sweetly, with the same message repeated over and over.

Now you may be wondering, "How on earth does the Happy Birthday song reflect the hidden message of God?"

It's actually quite simple. The song is telling you at this very moment in time your personal past, which is your original birthday, and your future, the day of your rebirth, your second birth. In other words, it's declaring the end from the beginning. This concept is spoken by God Himself, as He says, "I declare the end from the beginning" (Isaiah 46:10 CSB).

So when people tell you Happy Birthday or sing the song to you at a party, they're actually telling you the intended "end" to your personal story, announcing the day of your happy future birth into the coming kingdom of God, while at the same time recalling the beginning of your personal story, your original day of birth.

We all need to remember there's not just a beginning to everything, there's an endgame as well. And the end is the reason we're all here, our intended destiny with God. All of us have been born a first time as human beings, and we're intended to be born again at some point in the future, as Jesus said, to have a second birth. Our initial birthday was the day we emerged from the womb of our mother in our physical bodies made of flesh. But our ultimate future birthday, our second birth when we're born again, will be a birth into our new bodies composed of spirit as children of God. As you may have seen plastered on highway billboards, Jesus famously noted: "unless one is born again, he cannot see the kingdom of God" (John 3:3 NKJV).

Thus, the ultimate end of everyone's story is designed to be an extremely happy birthday, the happiest birthday you'll ever have. Because we'll no longer be shackled in our physical, human bodies that are dying and decaying every moment that we draw breath. We'll be alive forevermore, being born into the real world, the spirit world to join God and the angels on a higher plane of existence. So remember this concept the next time there's a birthday celebration. Whenever you sing or say "Happy Birthday" to someone, you're actually declaring the end, the biggest and happiest celebration of all time, from the beginning.

LIKE A VIRGIN

Let's get back to the radio now, because it's astonishing to see how many popular tunes are based on Scripture irrespective of the songwriters' awareness or intent. When listening to the opening lines of Madonna's "Like a Virgin," the legendary pop singer is amazed that she somehow made it through the wilderness and didn't know how lost she was until she found you. She explains she was beat and incomplete, feeling very sad, but you made her feel "shiny and new" as if she were a virgin. Yes, folks, this is the message of the Bible, even if Madonna or her writers Tom Kelly and Billy Steinberg never knew it.

As the singer here, Madonna represents all of humanity, just like the woman in "Stairway to Heaven." The "you" to whom she's singing is God. The wilderness represents this physical world in which we dwell. Thus, when we connect the dots to Scripture, the song is saying at God speed that people in the wilderness of our world don't realize how lost they are until they find God. We all feel beaten down and incomplete, sad and blue, until we come to God who will make us shiny and new in all respects, like a virgin. In fact, this is really a song about our spectacular future, once we're resurrected from the dead and start living eternal life in our glorious, new spirit-composed bodies. Just like "Happy Birthday," it's declaring the end from the beginning, because in becoming born again at the end of this age in which we presently exist, God will actually re-create people, regenerating them as members of His own spirit family, the literal children of God, re-forming us to be shiny and new, shining like the sun:

> "Then the righteous will **shine like the sun** in their Father's kingdom. Let anyone who has ears listen" (Matthew 13:43 CSB).

> "Behold, I make all things **new**" (Revelation 21:5).

> "Blessed are the peacemakers, for they will be called **children of God**" (Matthew 5:9 NIV).

And, yes, we'll all be like a virgin. The Bible talks about virgins quite a bit, with both men and women getting that label. Anyone who truly follows God and gets saved by Jesus, the Lamb of God, is called a virgin:

> "They are **virgins**. These are they which follow the Lamb whithersoever
> he goeth. These were redeemed from among men, being the firstfruits
> unto God and to the Lamb" (Revelation 14:4).

So Madonna gets it correct when we listen at God speed. It is our loving Creator who rescues us from being lost in this wilderness, saves us from feeling beat and incomplete, sad and blue, and transforms our spiritually dead bodies into ones that are shiny and new, like a virgin.

ROLLING IN THE DEEP

It's simply stunning when we look at songs from the higher perspective and realize that most, if not all of them, are packed with biblical references, either plain, in-your-face quotes, or hidden allusions.

Take the popular song "Rolling in the Deep" by British superstar Adele. Regardless of what this songstress and her co-writer Paul Epworth might think it means, the song is full of Bible references, both obvious and metaphorical ones. One lyric that's unquestionably scriptural speaks of being paid back in kind and reaping just what you sow.

This notion of reaping what you sow is found in the Old Testament, in the book of Job, to be specific:

> "As I have observed, those who plow evil and those who sow trouble reap it"
> (Job 4:8 NIV).

And this "Rolling in the Deep" business is a biblical metaphor for living here on Planet Earth, what the Bible actually calls "the deep." The exact phrase "the deep" occurs twenty-seven times in a King James Bible and initially appears extremely early in the second verse of Genesis.

> "And the earth was without form, and void; and darkness was upon the
> face of **the deep**" (Genesis 1:2).

On a physical level, it can refer to the deep waters of our oceans and seas, reminiscent of the 1977 movie *The Deep* starring Nick Nolte and Jacqueline Bisset.

Scripture blatantly equates the deep with the sea, saying of God: "Wasn't it you who dried up the **sea**, the waters of the great **deep**...?" (Isaiah 51:10 CSB).

But there's so much more at God speed.

"The deep" is the abyss. It's this low place where we currently dwell on our planet, the physical dimension located below the higher spirit dimension of heaven above. The deep is the place where spiritually dead people are walking around—seemingly alive but actually dead in the eyes of God. (Think of *The Walking Dead* TV series.) The deep refers to people who think they're alive but are actually infected with a terminal disease called mortality that allows them to continue walking around even though they are, for all intents and purposes, dead. We all live in a state that's deep, the "Deep State," as some in politics might say.

So, now you can understand what the apostle Paul is talking about when he wrote: "Who shall descend into **the deep**? (that is, to bring up Christ again from **the dead**)" (Romans 10:7). He's merely saying that "the deep" is the place where dead people are located. It's here. It's this watery Earth. It's our temporary home. It's where we roll. Rolling in the deep.

TAKE ON ME

In 1984, the Norwegian band A-ha became an international sensation with its song and groundbreaking video titled "Take On Me." The translation of the title is simple. The "Me" in the song is God, and He is urging all of us to take Him into our lives, to "put on Christ" in the same way we put on clothing (Galatians 3:27).

The sensational video for "Take On Me" became one of the most instantly recognizable videos in history, winning many awards as it featured a technique known as rotoscoping, where pencil-sketch animation was combined with live action. It has more than a billion views on YouTube today. This may sound like a complete shocker, but the characters in the popular video metaphorically act out the storyline of the Bible.

Here's the plot at human speed: A kind man is seen extending his hand outward from another dimension, actually out of a book, beckoning to the object of his love, a beautiful woman, asking her to come and join him for a life of love.

Here's the translation at God speed: The kind man from the other dimension is obviously God, and He is extending His hand out of the Book (the Bible), reaching for the object of His love, human beings who are His bride or wife in the spiritual story, to draw near and be united to Him in love. All of these elements are found in Scripture:

"But it is good for me to draw near to God" (Psalm 73:28).

"The marriage of the Lamb has come, and His wife has made herself ready" (Revelation 19:7 NKJV).

"And the Spirit and the bride say, Come" (Revelation 22:17).

"You hold me by my right hand" (Psalm 73:23 NKJV).

But as the story portrays, all does not remain sunshine and butterflies for the happy couple. Through the course of the video, the backdrop of which is a motorcycle race, the lovers are relentlessly pursued by enemies seeking to kill the couple. Here's how Scripture describes it:

"Those who chased us were swifter than eagles in the sky; they relent-lessly pursued us" (Lamentations 4:19 CSB).

"For the enemy has pursued me, crushing me to the ground" (Psalm 143:3 CSB).

In fact, the evil men in the video pursuing the couple are successful in killing the man, as he's shown lying dead on the floor. But as his woman cries a tear and raises her eyes toward heaven for help, her deceased man is miraculously, instantaneously raised back to life from the dead.

This is precisely what the Bible depicts. Disobedient people not only pursued and killed Jesus some two thousand years ago, but they've also been relentlessly chasing and persecuting those who worship Him:

"Since you have also suffered the same things from people of your own country, just as they did from the Jews who killed the Lord Jesus and the prophets and persecuted us. They displease God and are hos-tile to everyone...they are constantly filling up their sins to the limit" (1 Thessalonians 2:14–16 CSB).

Jesus, too, was miraculously raised from death: "Christ was raised up from the dead by the glory of the Father..." (Romans 6:4).

In the video's climax, the man is depicted in a fierce struggle, exerting tremendous energy to break through the dimensional barrier that had been keeping the pair from consummating their relationship. He is shown breaking out of his two-dimensional body, his penciled "image," to join the love of his life on equal footing in the real, three-dimensional world. The ferocious struggle alludes to the lifelong fight endured by both Jesus and every believer as they wrestle against every dark power, everything that is evil:

> "For our struggle is not against flesh and blood, but against the rulers, against the authorities, against the powers of this dark world and against the spiritual forces of evil in the heavenly realms" (Ephesians 6:12 NIV).

> "Fight the good fight of faith, lay hold on eternal life" (1 Timothy 6:12).

Thus, when we suffer for God in the years we're given here and faithfully endure our struggles, overcoming the forces of evil looking to destroy us, then we're finally able to "Take On Me," the Me being the Spirit Person known as God, and grab hold of eternal life.

LET 'EM IN

One of the most prolific and successful songwriters of our time is Paul McCartney. Not only did this Liverpool, England, native become a household name across the globe as a member of the Beatles in the 1960s, he also enjoyed huge success with his wife Linda in their band called Wings and as a solo artist. If we take even a cursory glance at some of his work, it becomes clear who is speaking through him.

In 1976, Wings—a band whose name poetically alludes to biblical messengers famously known as angels—released a song titled "Let 'Em In."

The first thing it tells us is that someone is knocking at the door.

Take one stab at where this comes from, folks. You guessed it. The Bible. In the last book of the New Testament, Jesus voiced that very thought in an unforgettable way.

> "Here I am! I stand at the door and knock. If anyone hears my voice and opens the door, I will come in and eat with that person, and they with me" (Revelation 3:20 NIV).

As you can see, Jesus Himself is not only standing at the door and knocking, He agrees with McCartney's suggestion to open the door and "Let 'Em In," as the title urges, explaining that people will be dining with God. In other words, open the door to your heart to let God in, and He'll actually dwell inside you.

In another well-known McCartney song, Paul asks people to "Listen to What the Man Said."

"The Man" in the lyric is God, and in the spiritual song that the Bible is, God is the Ultimate Man. We need to remember that "God created man in his own image" (Genesis 1:27) and the Maker even became a human man named Jesus, the Spirit who was made into flesh "and dwelt among us" (John 1:14) for some three decades back in the first century.

McCartney's instruction to "Listen to What the Man Said" sums up every command of the Bible, to listen closely to what the Man (who is God) said, to pay attention to Him and closely follow the instructions of the Creator. It's repeating Led Zeppelin's instruction to "listen very hard." Like Scripture says:

> "Come closer and **listen** to the words of the LORD your God"
> (Joshua 3:9 CSB).

> "I will **listen** to what God will say; surely the LORD will declare peace to
> his people, his faithful ones, and not let them go back to foolish ways"
> (Psalm 85:8 CSB).

> "If you want to enter life, keep the commandments" (Matthew 19:17 NIV).

And Jesus's own mother told us to listen to what the Man said, as she instructed moments before her Son turned water into wine: "Do whatever he tells you" (John 2:5 CSB).

Even in McCartney's early years with the Beatles, he and his co-writer John Lennon were scripting songs at God speed, echoing the voice of the Almighty. For instance, when the Fab Four sings, "I Want to Hold Your Hand," that's like God singing:

> "For I the LORD thy God will hold thy right hand" (Isaiah 41:13).

When they repeat, "you're coming home," in the song "It Won't Be Long," it reminds us that Jesus has temporarily left His home on our planet but will be coming home again soon:

> "For the goodman is not at home, he is gone a long journey: He...will **come
> home** at the day appointed" (Proverbs 7:19–20).

"I am **coming soon**" (Revelation 22:20 CSB).

THE EDGE OF GLORY

In the song "The Edge of Glory," Lady Gaga is, in fact, broadcasting at God speed that we human beings are on the verge of glory, that we'll receive glory when we reach the final goal, which is eternal life. One lyric in the song tells us quite plainly that the singer is on the edge of "something final" that we call life. This is precisely how the Bible describes eternal life, that we receive glory:

> "When Christ who is our **life** appears, then you also will appear with Him in **glory**" (Colossians 3:4 NKJV).

> "He will give eternal life to those who keep on doing good, seeking after the **glory** and honor and **immortality** that God offers" (Romans 2:7 NLT).

In the song "A Million Dreams" from Hugh Jackman's movie, *The Greatest Showman*, when Pink sings about there being "a house we can build," it's based on the biblical foundation that we human beings are God's building, that His dwelling place is inside us:

> "I tell you that the LORD will build you a house" (1 Chronicles 17:10 NKJV).

> "Build the house; and I will take pleasure in it, and I will be glorified, saith the LORD" (Haggai 1:8).

> "Don't you yourselves know that you are God's temple and that the Spirit of God lives in you?" (1 Corinthians 3:16 CSB).

> "The kingdom of God is within you" (Luke 17:21).

THE DAY THAT I DIE

One of the most beloved songs of all time is Don McClean's "American Pie," and it's packed with a large number of biblical references. For now, I wish to focus on one of the most repeated lyrics in the chorus, which is also the final line of the song, where McClean sings this will be the day "that I die."

This single statement is one of the most profound thoughts ever, because it encompasses something both good and bad at the same time, specifically this being the day that we die. What does it really mean? You don't need to wonder any longer because the explanation comes right now as we make the jump to God speed.

Let's start with the bad aspect. A long time ago in the garden of Eden, God told the first man and woman, Adam and Eve, that they would "live forever" if they ate from the tree of life (Genesis 3:22). But He also gave them explicit instructions not to eat from the tree of the knowledge of good and evil, "for on the day you eat from it, you will certainly die" (Genesis 2:17 CSB).

You probably already know the rest of the story, as Eve took the first bite from the forbidden fruit, then shared it with her husband. This is "the day that I die," as the song goes, in the bad sense. Human beings died that very day—that is to say, they and their descendants all became mortal. Had they been obedient to God, Adam and Eve would have remained alive forever. But because they rebelled and did not follow the one, simple instruction not to eat from the tree of the knowledge of good and evil, they committed spiritual suicide on that day, even though their actual physical deaths came many years later. To put it in modern terminology, they became "dead to God" that day. As a result, all of us are mortal to "this day." Since we're mortal in the present time, this is the day that we die.

But the Bible is a book filled "Good News," which is what the word "gospel" means. It's about overcoming death and learning the way to get eternal life in spite of our rebellion against God's instructions. Most of Scripture is showing us the right way of thinking and personal conduct, so that we can live forever, as intended by the Creator.

That's why the Bible also talks in a good sense about dying. For instance:

> "And the day you die is better than the day you are born" (Ecclesiastes 7:1 NLT).

Now why in the world is the day we die better than the day we're born? It certainly does not suggest going out and killing yourself. We have to remember the Bible is not just a physical book about physical things in this physical life. It's a book about Spirit beings who are offering an everlasting, spirit-based existence to spiritual minds who are initially dwelling in physical bodies, if we'd just take the crud out of our ears and "listen very hard," as Led Zeppelin sang. Here are a couple of New Testament verses to shed light on this:

> "Though our bodies are dying, our spirits are being renewed every day"
> (2 Corinthians 4:16 NLT).

> "So, you too consider yourselves dead to sin and alive to God in Christ Jesus" (Romans 6:11 CSB).

Scripture is telling us quite a bit in these two verses. First, our physical bodies are dying. We all know that already. Every human being is mortal. But it also talks about our spirits being renewed every day. In other words, the spirit inside our minds and hearts is being renewed, refreshed, invigorated every single day by God, leading toward the end goal of eternal life, so we have no reason to fear our physical death.

The second instruction tells us to consider ourselves "dead to sin and alive to God." This means that we have to make the conscious decision in our minds to put to death any disobedience against our Maker. Because when we choose to stop rebelling and instead obey our Creator, that's when we're on the path to being alive forever, which, again, is the intended destiny for everyone. That's why the day that you die is better than the day you are born. Because the day that you put your sinful, disobedient, rebellious way of existence permanently behind you, that's the day you're truly on the way to eternal life with God. So, we all should want to sing "this'll be the day" that we die, as Don McLean famously wrote, so we, too, can live forever with God.

MYSTERIOUS WAYS

By now, you might be thinking this musical secret of how God operates, hiding Himself in song lyrics, is somewhat strange and mysterious. That's because it is, and the Bible states outright that God works in mysterious ways.

> "Truly, O God of Israel, our Savior, you work in **mysterious ways**"
> (Isaiah 45:15 NLT).

This prophecy manifested on the pop charts in the 1990s when the Irish rock band U2 had a smash hit with "Mysterious Ways." Like "Stairway to Heaven," U2's song gives pointers on how we can obtain eternal life with God. For example, one lyric suggests that if we wish to "kiss the sky," we should actually learn "how to kneel."

In other words, if we wish to kiss the sky, that is, have an intimate, loving relationship with the God who dwells in the sky (heaven), then we should become humble and meek, submitting ourselves to God's will, learning to kneel before the Creator. Like Scripture says: "…let us **kneel** before the LORD our maker" (Psalm 95:6).

The song also notes that to touch people is like healing them. The Bible is filled with many examples of people being instantly healed by the touch of God:

> "And he touched her hand, and the fever left her" (Matthew 8:15).

> "So Jesus had compassion on them, and touched their eyes: and immediately their eyes received sight" (Matthew 20:34).

> "Then he came up and touched the open coffin, and the pallbearers stopped. And he said, 'Young man, I tell you, get up!' The dead man sat up and began to speak" (Luke 7:14–15 CSB).

There's another interesting note about this U2 song. It mentions that people have been living "underground." This statement may be overlooked or not understood by millions, but it's extremely important. What it refers to at God speed is the state of existence of human beings, what we're made from and where we dwell. And that, of course, is the ground, the land, the dirt, mud, clay, sand, or dust of the earth, as Scripture says in a variety of ways. It's the real reason we call ourselves "earthlings." We all live under the ground, because the dust of the ground covers us, even as we walk around on top of the earth.

> "And the LORD God formed man of the dust of the ground" (Genesis 2:7).

> "I also am formed out of the clay" (Job 33:6).

> "He brought me up from a desolate pit, out of the muddy clay" (Psalm 40:2 CSB).

To put it simply, earth is equated with people in Scripture:

"Listen, all you **peoples**; pay attention, **earth** and **everyone in it**!"
(Micah 1:2 CSB).

When we feel our own skin, we all have to realize we're touching soft clay, the same substance that makes up the ground. But we also know there's more to a person than mere dirt and minerals from the earth. There's also a spirit inside us that gives us our mind, intelligence, emotions, and understanding.

"But it is the spirit in a person, the breath of the Almighty, that gives them understanding" (Job 32:8 NIV).

"The human spirit is the lamp of the LORD that sheds light on one's inmost being" (Proverbs 20:27 NIV).

Understanding this concept that human beings consist of a spirit that is wrapped, covered, and masked by an exterior face of muddy clay made from the dust of the earth will help you understand not only who and what you are at this moment but also your intended destiny. More on that later.

The mysterious ways in which God works are all part of the fascinating Word puzzle we've been given, the riddle in the scriptural song God has composed, concealing the truth and prompting us to investigate it. The Maker, in fact, tells us outright to solve the divine mystery, to connect all the dots inked in the Bible, to completely uncover and understand the incredible message hidden before our very eyes and ears.

"It is the glory of God to conceal a matter and the glory of kings to investigate a matter" (Proverbs 25:2 CSB).

It is when our minds approach God speed that we can truly begin to uncover and solve the mystery.

THE REPETITION

As we continue our investigation, you may notice that often times there's more than a single song on the radio that broadcasts the same exact message. Here's a simple example. In 1983, John Cougar Mellencamp released an album that featured the "Authority Song," which told us that when you fight authority, "authority always wins." If that sounds familiar, it's because another lyric from another famous tune broadcast the very same idea. That other song is "I Fought the Law," recorded by many artists, including the Bobby Fuller Four, Roy Orbison, the Clash, the Stray Cats, Green Day, Bryan Adams, Steve Earle, the Nitty Gritty Dirt Band and Hank Williams Jr.

In case you haven't figured it out by now, fighting authority or fighting the law means, at the higher level of God speed, fighting against the ultimate Authority and Law, which is God. And since we can't defeat God, "Authority always wins," and "the Law won," as the songs declare. What may stun you is that this very idea was penned thousands of years ago in the Bible, both Old and New Testaments:

> "Do not fight against the LORD, the God of your ancestors, for you will not succeed" (2 Chronicles 13:12 NIV).

> "But if it is of God, you cannot overthrow it—lest you even be found to fight against God" (Acts 5:39 NKJV).

It's strange how intriguing stuff like this never gets mentioned in church or Sunday school, because it might actually make those places much more interesting.

CAN YOU HEAR ME NOW?

The repetition of ideas can be heard across different media, as God tries to capture people's attention. One fun example of this is: "Can you hear me now?"

This theme became a popular catchphrase in the early 2000s when Verizon launched a commercial campaign with ads featuring a cell-phone technician named Paul holding a phone to his ear as he was seen treading through dead zones, remote and barren areas, asking someone we're never shown on the other end of the call, "Can you hear me now?"

But Verizon wasn't the first to use this famous question. The thought has been repeated many times in well-known radio hits spanning the decades.

In July 1969, David Bowie released "Space Oddity," the cosmic tune repopularized in 2013 by actress Kristen Wiig as she sang it to Ben Stiller in the film, *The Secret Life of Walter Mitty*. In Bowie's original, Major Tom is repeatedly asked: "Can you hear me?"

Just two months earlier in 1969, The Who released its famous rock opera "Tommy," featuring the same exact question with a person who, interestingly, also had the name of Tom, which literally means "twin." In the song "Tommy Can You Hear Me?" Tom's name was placed in front of the question, while Bowie placed the name after the question. In the 1975 film version, Ann-Margret, as Tommy's parent, asks her son (Roger Daltrey) the same question: "Tommy Can You Hear Me?"

In 1979, Pink Floyd built *The Wall* album, and on its popular hit "Comfortably Numb," the singer says to simply "nod if you can hear me."

In 1985, Mike + The Mechanics released a highly popular song and video titled "Silent Running (On Dangerous Ground)" and kept repeating the lyric: "Can you hear me calling you?"

And in Adele's uber-popular 2015 smash "Hello," which has more than a quarter of a trillion views on YouTube, after the word "Hello," Adele sings, "can you hear me?"

All these songs and Verizon commercials are broadcasting the same question—"Can you hear me?"—because, at God speed, it's actually the Creator who is the One asking people if they can hear Him. He is calling out to people, asking if they can hear Him, to listen to His words, to be obedient instead of rebellious:

> "Hear me now" (Proverbs 5:7).

> "Hear, my children, the instruction of a father, And give attention to know understanding" (Proverbs 4:1 NKJV).

> "Hear me, you heavens! Listen, earth! For the LORD has spoken: 'I reared children and brought them up, but they have rebelled against me.'" (Isaiah 1:2 NIV).

Incidentally, if you ever wondered why some people actually hear God while others don't, Jesus answered that question in a succinct, yet powerful, way:

> "Whoever belongs to God hears what God says. The reason you do not hear is that you do not belong to God" (John 8:47 NIV).

Thus, we might want to incline our ears, to get our minds in tune with what God has been broadcasting for thousands of years on all frequencies if we wish to enjoy life without end.

I could go on all day with popular songs and their true meanings at God speed. Here are a few more, and remember to think on the higher, spirit level at God speed, not merely the physical level, to grasp the true meaning.

In "New York, New York," when Frank Sinatra says he wishes to wake up in a big city that never really sleeps to become "king of the hill," he's saying that he wants to be awakened, as in being resurrected from the sleep of death, in a city where there is no more sleep, what the Bible calls "no more death" (Revelation 21:4). That city is "the city of God" (Psalm 46:4) where he himself will be a king of the hill, just like God says: "I set my king upon my holy hill" (Psalm 2:6).

When Dire Straits tells everyone to do the "Walk of Life," they are telling people "to walk before God in the light of life" (Psalm 56:13 CSB) because "obedience would have given them life" (Ezekiel 20:13, 21 NLT). And when they sing that you're "So Far Away," that's the voice of God lamenting how most everyone's "heart is far from me" (Matthew 15:8).

In Rush's "Spirit of Radio" song, the Spirit that Canadian superstar Geddy Lee is singing about is God, because "God is a Spirit" (John 4:24), and when he sings of invisible airwaves crackling with life, he's talking about radio airwaves that are invisible. We can't see them with our eyes, but we can hear them when we tune into the correct frequency. The radio analogy is instructing us to tune our minds into the correct spirit frequency to hear God—in other words, reach God speed. The invisible airwaves crackle with life, because God Himself is an airwave that's "invisible" (1 Timothy 1:17). He crackles with life, because God is life. He says, "I am the resurrection, and the life" (John 11:25), and He is willing to give us His "everlasting life" (John 3:16).

MELT WITH YOU

When members of Modern English sing that they'll stop the world and "melt with you," they're actually speaking for the Creator, who's saying two things at God speed.

First, He'll stop the world, meaning He'll put an end to the evil ways of this world, and separate the good people from the bad ones:

> "That is the way it will be at the end of the world. The angels will come and separate the wicked people from the righteous, throwing the wicked into the fiery furnace, where there will be weeping and gnashing of teeth" (Matthew 13:49–50 NLT).

Second, He'll melt together with you, as in unite with you like in a melting pot, always being one with you, even at "the end of the world" (Matthew 28:20).

You may have never noticed it before, but "I Melt with You" has a line clearly alluding to Jesus, the true Spirit who inspired this song, as it sums up His divine mission for human beings. The singer has made a pilgrimage, he says, "to save this humans race."

And in Scripture, Jesus said the same thing about His pilgrimage to Planet Earth: "For the Son of man is **come to seek and to save** that which was lost" (Luke 19:10).

When the Goo Goo Dolls sing their popular song "Iris," written for the 1998 film *City of Angels* with Meg Ryan and Nicolas Cage, they note when everything has been made to be broken, they simply want the listener "to know who I am."

God Himself is actually voicing that sentiment. One of God's names is "I AM WHO I AM" (Exodus 3:14).

It's reminiscent of Neil Diamond's song "I Am...I Said." God is telling everyone His name, and "no one heard" because, as God says, "my people did not listen to my voice" (Psalm 81:11 CSB).

And, yes, God wants His followers to "know Him," even if the people of the world don't want that: "He is the Spirit of truth. The world is unable to receive him because it doesn't see him or know him. But you do know him, because he remains with you and will be in you" (John 14:17 CSB).

And the Goo Goo Dolls' line about everything being made to be broken sums up how God is breaking our spirit of rebellion, in the same way a cowboy breaks an unruly horse into submission.

> "The sacrifice pleasing to God is a **broken** spirit. You will not despise a **broken** and humbled heart, God" (Psalm 51:17 CSB).

Incidentally, John Rzeznik, lead vocalist of the Goo Goo Dolls, told Songfacts in 2013 that when he wrote this song, he was thinking about a heavenly being "completely willing to give up his own immortality.... And

I think, 'Wow! What an amazing thing it must be like to love someone so much that you give up everything to be with them.' That's a pretty heavy thought." That does sound pretty heavy, because Rzeznik summarized the entire plan of God, the Most High Heavenly Being who gave up His immortality for a time to be with the ones He loves so He can rescue them.

WE GOTTA GET OUT OF THIS PLACE

When The Animals sing "We Gotta Get Out of This Place," they're not merely singing about getting out of the death-packed hellhole of Vietnam during the 1960s war. The place we ultimately want to get out of is this human body of flesh where we're constantly tormented in this scorching realm of the walking dead. At God speed, the Bible uses the destruction of fiery Sodom as an example of the deadly danger zone from which we should remove all our loved ones: "**Get them out of this place**—your sons-in-law, sons, daughters, or anyone else" (Genesis 19:12 NLT).

The song even provides the reason we've got to get out of this place: because there's "*a better life* for me and you."

This is actually a promise from the New Testament, which proclaims our "hope in **a better life** after the resurrection" (Hebrews 11:35 NLT).

It's also fascinating that the group that sings this song is called The Animals, because in our current bodies of flesh, we human beings are, at least metaphorically, the animals, especially when compared to God, who is a divine Spirit. We're the beasts who are made of flesh. So, when the animals (humans) declare we've got to get out of this place, we're saying we've got to exit this body of the beast, this body of man. Much more on this later.

ANOTHER BRICK IN THE WALL

One of the most frequently played songs on the radio is "Another Brick in the Wall, Pt. 2" by British supergroup Pink Floyd, and it's one of the most biblical songs ever.

This well-known anthem of rebellion against improper teaching opens with the famous line of not needing "no education," immediately adding that people don't need "no" thought control.

What's ironic about the statement is that it's a double negative, meaning it can be taken in the very opposite sense from which people initially hear the lyric. So, when it declares what we don't need is "*no* education," it actually is saying, "We *do* need education"—that we need to be taught properly. If we don't need *no* thought control, it means we really do need to be in control of our thoughts.

This, of course, is based on the template of the Bible, which is our guide for proper education, teaching us to control our thoughts so we can be alive forever:

> "Teach me good judgment and knowledge: for I have believed thy commandments" (Psalm 119:66).

> "But I will be merciful only if you stop your evil thoughts and deeds and start treating each other with justice" (Jeremiah 7:5 NLT).

> "God, you have taught me from my youth, and I still proclaim your wondrous works" (Psalm 71:17 CSB).

> "I have taught you in the way of wisdom" (Proverbs 4:11 NKJV).

But "Another Brick in the Wall, Pt. 2" rails against overcontrolling, wicked teachers, as Pink Floyd repeatedly and passionately warns teachers to leave those kids alone. If people are following the teachings of this world, instead of those in Scripture, we're actually being taught wrongly by our teachers, no matter how well intentioned they may seem. The Bible constantly warns against false teachers who provide wrong instruction, while pretending to be doing it right:

> "I know that false teachers, like vicious wolves, will come in among you after I leave, not sparing the flock" (Acts 20:29 NLT).

> "Those false teachers are so eager to win your favor, but their intentions are not good. They are trying to shut you off from me so that you will pay attention only to them" (Galatians 4:17 NLT).

> "There were indeed false prophets among the people, just as there will be false teachers among you. They will bring in destructive heresies, even denying the Master who bought them, and will bring swift destruction on themselves" (2 Peter 2:1 CSB).

This song was part of Pink Floyd's 1979 album *The Wall*, which was made into a 1982 movie starring Bob Geldof. If you watch the film clip of the song on YouTube, schoolchildren with what appear to be melted faces are shown marching in lockstep, as they're methodically hammered and brainwashed by their oppressive teachers. They end up falling into a meat grinder where they die and get processed into ground beef. This follows the biblical template that we human beings, if we march in lockstep to the false teachings of this world and keep rebelling against God, we fall and end up spiritually dead, becoming nothing more than piles of worthless flesh. Jesus famously said: "And you will perish, too, unless you repent of your sins and turn to God" (Luke 13:3 NLT).

The title "Another Brick in the Wall" reminds people of their divine destiny, since everyone is just a single brick, a single stone in the wall, the united structure of precious stones mentioned in the book of Revelation, which describes this bejeweled wall of faithful believers in detail.

The wall is described as part of "the city," "the bride of God," and "the Lamb's wife" (Revelation 21:9).

The wall's foundations are the apostles of Jesus:

> "And **the wall** of the city had twelve foundations, and in them the names of the twelve apostles of the Lamb" (Revelation 21:14).

The author of the book of Revelation, the apostle John, had an angel displaying to him the wall of the future city, even taking its measurements:

> "And he that talked with me had a golden reed to measure the city, and the gates thereof, and **the wall** thereof" (Revelation 21:15).

This glorious wall of your own intended future is shown gleaming with the brightness of not only pure gold but also a large variety of precious stones, including diamonds, emeralds, jasper, sapphires, and amethyst:

> "And the building of **the wall** of it was of jasper: and the city was pure gold, like unto clear glass" (Revelation 21:18).

> "And the foundations of **the wall** of the city were garnished with all manner of precious stones" (Revelation 21:19).

The Old Testament prophet Isaiah also foresaw the future eternal city, as God said through him: "Behold, I will lay your stones with colorful gems, And lay your foundations with sapphires" (Isaiah 54:11 NKJV).

The key to understanding all this is that when the Bible and Pink Floyd talk about a precious stone or another brick in the wall, the ultimate meaning is about individual *people*, who are all united as one in spirit, because "he that is joined unto the Lord is one spirit" (1 Corinthians 6:17).

So when you hear that you're just "Another Brick in the Wall," the statement is saying, at God speed, that you, yourself, are another brick, another individual and precious stone in the wall, which, when joined together with other precious stones, comprises the single, united wall, the divine Spirit called God.

The end of the song features a couple of spoken lines from a teacher repeatedly telling a student that he's wrong, and he should do his task again, in hopes of finally learning to do it right, learning to do good, as Scripture states: "Learn to do good; Seek justice, Rebuke the oppressor" (Isaiah 1:17 NKJV).

The teacher also famously hollers that if students don't eat their meat, they can't have any pudding. After all, how can any of us have our pudding if we don't eat our meat? If you ever wondered what that means, here's the explanation.

Biblically speaking, "meat" is not merely physical nourishment, it also refers to obedience to God's will, and doing His work. Jesus noted: "My meat is to do the will of him that sent me, and to finish his work" (John 4:34).

Pudding, as we all know, is a delicious, sweet dessert. It's a reward for eating the main course of a meal, which is often some type of meat. So once we eat the meat, once we do the will of God and finish His work, that's when we can fully enjoy the sweet reward of the pudding, the delicious dessert. And what is the reward? It's God. It's salvation. It's an eternal life with our own Maker.

"I am thy shield, and thy **exceeding great reward**" (Genesis 15:1).

"I will **reward** them with a **long life** and give them my **salvation**" (Psalm 91:16 NLT).

"I come quickly; and my **reward** is with me, to give every man according as his work shall be" (Revelation 22:12).

And, fascinatingly, as we connect more dots, pudding can actually be made out of milk and honey. There are actually recipes on the internet for pudding using milk and honey. I mention this because the phrase "milk and honey" is mentioned twenty times in Scripture, referring to the Promised Land. And by the Promised Land, I'm not referring only to the geographic land in the Middle East where the ancient Israelites booted out wicked inhabitants. I'm speaking at God speed, referring to the spiritual Promised Land, the coming kingdom of God, in which obedient people will be alive for a very long time, as in forever:

> "**If you obey, you will enjoy a long life** in the land the LORD swore to give to your ancestors and to you, their descendants—a land flowing with **milk and honey**!" (Deuteronomy 11:9 NLT).

Yes, folks, the land flowing with milk and honey is the ultimate Promised Land. It's where the pudding is. It's the place of that sweet reward, the ultimate dessert known as eternal life with God. But we all have to eat our meat before we can have any pudding. We have to obey God's instructions to finish His work before we are given the reward of eternal life, becoming an immortal, precious stone because, all in all, we individual human beings are just another brick in The Wall.

Want more songs? Here you go.

When Captain & Tennille sing Neil Sedaka's song "Love Will Keep Us Together," they're broadcasting at God speed: "Above all, clothe yourselves with **love**, which **binds us all together** in perfect harmony" (Colossians 3:14 NLT).

When they sing not to mess around, and just be strong, they're telling us to be strong and resist sin:

> "Be strong in the Lord, and in the power of his might" (Ephesians 6:10).

> "Resist the devil, and he will flee from you" (James 4:7).

When The Police sing "Every Breath You Take," Sting makes it quite clear that he'll be watching you. This is what God is doing, as He monitors every step we take and every move we make.

> "His eyes are on the ways of mortals; he sees their every step" (Job 34:21 NIV).

"He...watches my every move" (Job 33:11 NLT).

"For the LORD watches over the way of the righteous" (Psalm 1:6 CSB).

"Yet he watches over both individuals and nations" (Job 34:29 CSB).

When Roy Orbison sings about watching the song's subject walk down the street in "Oh, Pretty Woman," it's God taking note of His beautiful future bride, humanity, as she's walking down the street: "O most beautiful woman, follow the trail of my flock" (Song of Songs 1:8 NLT).

When Elvis Presley sings "Suspicious Minds," he complains to his suspicious loved one that she doesn't believe a word he says. Jesus complained of the same problem with suspicious-minded people refusing to believe a word He said: "But **you don't believe me** because you are not my sheep" (John 10:26 NLT).

When the Bee Gees sing "Stayin' Alive," the Brothers Gibb are discussing the main goal of our existence, which is to stay alive, to live forever as is described countless times in the Bible, including "I am the living bread that came down from heaven. If anyone eats of this bread he will **live forever**" (John 6:51 CSB).

When Rod Stewart sings "Forever Young," he's proclaiming a message similar to that of the Bee Gees, and that is being young forever, youthfully alive for all eternity. His opening lyric quotes the Bible from numerous places, including "may the LORD be with you" (1 Chronicles 22:11 CSB), and his song even sums up the Golden Rule of Jesus (Matthew 7:12) as Stewart suggests we "do unto others" as we'd have done to us.

When Carl Carlton sings "Everlasting Love," he's singing a direct quote from God Himself, who says, "I have loved you, my people, with an **everlasting love**" (Jeremiah 31:3 NLT).

When Aerosmith tells us to "Walk This Way," Steven Tyler and his bandmates are giving us God's instruction: "This is the way; walk in it" (Isaiah 30:21 NIV).

When American Breed sings "Bend Me, Shape Me" any way you happen to want me, they're proclaiming a person's desire to have God bend and shape his or her character properly, just as a potter bends and shapes clay into a beautiful vessel. "We are the clay, and You our potter; And all we are the work of Your hand" (Isaiah 64:8 NKJV).

When Bonnie Raitt sings "Something to Talk About," she calls that something a "mystery to figure out." This is exactly what God is doing with us, as He has given us a mystery to figure out. As mentioned previously:

> **"It is the glory of God to conceal a matter and the glory of kings to investigate a matter" (Proverbs 25:2 CSB).**

And the Bible makes no secret what this "mystery" actually is, saying openly, "this mystery...which is Christ in you, the hope of glory" (Colossians 1:27).

When Huey Lewis and the News sing about "The Power of Love," they mention changing a hawk into a little white dove. The translation is: Change your heart from that of a warlike hawk into that of a humble (little), pure (white) Spirit (dove). The Bible says: "I saw the Spirit come down from heaven as a dove and remain on him" (John 1:32 NIV).

When Gloria Estefan sings "Get on Your Feet," she tells us to get up and to "make it happen." This is precisely what God is instructing everyone to do, and Jesus used almost those exact words to the apostle Paul: "Now get up and stand on your feet" (Acts 26:16 NIV).

When Soul Asylum sings "Runaway Train," they talk about leading oneself astray and going the wrong direction "on a one-way track." This is exactly how Scripture describes running away from God, who is the "right way."

> **"They have forsaken the right way and gone astray" (2 Peter 2:15 NKJV).**

Soul Asylum's runaway-train analogy is also prominent in Ozzy Osbourne's line about going off the rails on a "Crazy Train." We're all going off the rails when we're disobedient to the Maker's instructions. We're all riding a crazy train because we're all enemies of each other. There are millions of people, as the song explains, "living as foes." King David of ancient Israel noted the same problem: "LORD, how my foes increase!" (Psalm 3:1 CSB).

In the song "We Will Rock You" by Queen, the band indicates you have "mud on your face," noting it's a big disgrace. This is a reminder of our corruptible, disgraceful, human form in the flesh, as we all have mud on our face, being currently composed of mud, the miry clay and dust of the earth:

> **"He has thrown me into the mud. I'm nothing more than dust and ashes" (Job 30:19 NLT).**

"He lifted me out of the pit of despair, out of the **mud** and the mire"
(Psalm 40:2 NLT).

In U2's "Where the Streets Have No Name," when Bono sings that he observes the dust cloud disappearing "without a trace," he's voicing God's message that obedient human beings who are currently dust clouds will be completely transformed from flesh to spirit when God returns, as the flesh disappears without a trace:

"We will all be **transformed**! It will happen in a moment, in the blink of an eye, when the last trumpet is blown. For when the trumpet sounds, those who have died will be raised to live forever. And we who are living will also be **transformed**" (1 Corinthians 15:51–52 NLT).

When U2 sings "Running to Stand Still," the title recalls the car analogy I mentioned early on. We're running in our physical lives, but we're actually standing still when it comes to making any progress toward the destination of eternal life. Another U2 song, "Beautiful Day," stresses that same point as Bono sings that the listener is "not moving anywhere" stuck in the traffic. He also notes that we may be on the road, but we've got no destination.

When Dido sings "Here With Me," she identifies God as the true vocalist, noting a thought similar to "I am that I am" (Exodus 3:14) and that God won't sleep "until you're resting here" alongside Him. Scripture indicates the Creator "does not slumber or sleep" (Psalm 121:4 CSB) and that "God will provide **rest** for you who are being persecuted and also for us when the Lord Jesus appears from heaven" (2 Thessalonians 1:7 NLT).

When disco-queen Gloria Gaynor sings "I Will Survive," she begins her song by noting, "At first I was afraid." She's actually quoting the very first man, as Adam told God at first, "I was afraid" (Genesis 3:10). Her title "I Will Survive" is similar to the Bee Gees' "Stayin' Alive," which, of course, is our main objective, to survive forever, inheriting eternal life. The Bible talks often about surviving, including: "This is what the LORD says: 'Those who survive the coming destruction will find blessings...'" (Jeremiah 31:2 NLT).

When Van Halen sings "Hot for Teacher," they're not merely lusting for a gorgeous instructor in the classroom, as their video depicts. They're actually, on the spirit level of God speed, talking about being hot, as in passionate and zealous, for the ultimate Teacher, who is God.

"You call me 'Teacher' and 'Lord,' and rightly so, for that is what I am"
(John 13:13 NIV).

All of us should be hot for our divine Teacher, and the Bible says so in different ways:

"Love the LORD your God with all your heart, with all your soul, and with all your strength" (Deuteronomy 6:5 CSB).

"A scribe approached him and said, 'Teacher, I will follow you wherever you go'" (Matthew 8:19 CSB).

When The Verve sings "Bitter Sweet Symphony," the singer repeatedly says that he can change.

This is significant in more than one way. First, the Bible talks many times about us changing our hearts for the better, including:

"Change your hearts and stop being stubborn" (Deuteronomy 10:16 NLT).

"Let the wicked change their ways and banish the very thought of doing wrong" (Isaiah 55:7 NLT).

Secondly, on another level, Scripture is shouting our final destiny, our ultimate change, when our physical bodies of flesh are completely transformed into glorious, Spirit bodies. Yes, folks, we can change to a glorified state!

"He will take our weak mortal bodies and **change** them into glorious bodies like his own" (Philippians 3:21 NLT).

This theme of a phenomenal change that's coming is also demonstrated in The Who's classic-rock hit, "Won't Get Fooled Again." When Roger Daltrey sings that the change had to come and that we should all be smiling and grinning at the change all around us, he's ultimately singing at God speed about the instant transformation of our bodies into Spirit when Jesus returns and we're raised from death. Here it is: "We shall all be **changed**, In a moment, in the twinkling of an eye…the dead shall be raised incorruptible, and we shall be **changed**" (1 Corinthians 15:51–52).

And in case you never noticed, the end of "Won't Get Fooled Again" tells everyone they'll be meeting the new boss, who just happens to be the same as the previous boss. This refers to the coming day when our new and highest Boss—Jesus, who is always the same—returns to Earth, and everyone will finally know that He is, and always has been, their Boss, their God:

> "Jesus Christ is the **same** yesterday, today, and forever" (Hebrews 13:8 CSB).

> "Then you will know that I am the LORD" (Ezekiel 20:38 CSB).

Meeting the new boss also refers to our own transformation to becoming God's own divine helpers, when we will actually become like God:

> "When he (Jesus) shall appear, we shall be like him" (1 John 3:2).

Thus, the new boss, the folks newly put in charge by God, will be the same as the old Boss. We'll be the same type of divine, eternal Being that God is.

In Bonnie Tyler's smash hit "Total Eclipse of the Heart," the singer keeps urging people to turn around. This is the message of our Creator, telling us to turn around from our sinful ways. The command to turn around is simply another way of saying, "repent," just as Scripture urges: "repent of your sins and **turn** to God, so that your sins may be wiped away" (Acts 3:19 NLT). The title "Total Eclipse of the Heart" refers to people eclipsing out God, not letting His light of life shine inside our heart.

When Petula Clark sings "Downtown," she indicates things will be great when we go to the city where the lights are much brighter, letting you "forget all your troubles" and all your cares. The city that causes people to forget their troubles is none other than the "city of God" (Psalm 46:4, 87:3), as "God has made me **forget all my troubles**" (Genesis 41:51 NLT). And Petula is absolutely correct because things will be fantastic when we're living downtown in God's own city, which is called "the paradise of God" (Revelation 2:7).

When Nick Lowe sings you have to be "Cruel to Be Kind" in just the right measure, he is voicing what God says about disciplining His rebellious people, to prompt them to repent: "Lashes and wounds purge away evil, and beatings cleanse the innermost parts" (Proverbs 20:30 CSB).

When Cheap Trick sings "I Want You to Want Me," it's virtually identical to what God says: "I want you to know me" (Hosea 6:6 NLT). The song proclaims how God is begging people to desire and obey Him. "If only they had such a heart to fear me and keep all my commands always, so that they and their children would prosper forever" (Deuteronomy 5:29 CSB).

When The Cranberries sing "Linger," vocalist Dolores O'Riordan explains that if the subject of the song "could get by" and try not to lie, then things in life wouldn't be so confused. Scripture has the same warning about not lying to people: "Do not act deceptively or lie to one another" (Leviticus 19:11 CSB). The result of all our lying is confusion—what the Bible calls "Babylon."

> **"Therefore it is called Babylon, for there the LORD confused the language of the whole earth" (Genesis 11:9 CSB).**

Speaking of The Cranberries, when they sing "Dreams," there's a lyric referring to someone's beloved who has a totally amazing mind, who is understanding and kind. These character descriptors—understanding and kindness—are also mentioned together in a single lyric of Scripture: "We prove ourselves by our purity, our **understanding**, our patience, our **kindness**, by the Holy Spirit within us, and by our sincere love" (2 Corinthians 6:6 NLT).

When Johnny Cash sings "I Walk the Line," the famous man in black is reminding people at God speed that because we belong to God, our Creator is walking the straight path, living the godly way, and so should we.

> **"Mark out a straight path for your feet; stay on the safe path" (Proverbs 4:26 NLT).**

> **"Thus you will walk in the ways of the good and keep to the paths of the righteous" (Proverbs 2:20 NIV).**

When Katrina and the Waves sing "Walking on Sunshine," they're talking about being powered by God, the brightest light we can imagine:

> **"So now I can walk in your presence, O God, in your life-giving light" (Psalm 56:13 NLT).**

> **"Happy are those who hear the joyful call to worship, for they will walk in the light of your presence, LORD" (Psalm 89:15 NLT).**

In this song, Katrina says she feels alive, feels the love, and feels "the love that's really real." Scripture actually defines what is the love that's really real:

"This is real love—not that we loved God, but that he loved us and sent his Son as a sacrifice to take away our sins" (1 John 4:10 NLT).

While Katrina is walking on sunshine, many other songs proclaim the sun's brightness, including "Brighter Than the Sun" by Colbie Caillat. What most people don't know is that the exact phrase "brighter than the sun" is found in the Bible, referring to the divine light of God: "I saw a light from heaven **brighter than the sun**, shining around me and those traveling with me" (Acts 26:13 CSB).

When The Doors sing "Riders on the Storm," they warn there's a killer waiting on the road, and if we happen to give this guy a ride, then sweet family members will end up dead. The killer on the road Jim Morrison is warning about at God speed is none other than Satan the devil, whom Jesus said "was a murderer from the beginning" (John 8:44). And if we give the devil a ride, that is, if we allow him to ride inside our minds, then the result is certain death.

"If you ever forget the LORD your God and follow other gods to serve them and bow in worship to them, I testify against you today that you will perish" (Deuteronomy 8:19 CSB).

When The Cars sing "Drive" to a woman in an insane asylum in their famous video, they tell the woman, portrayed by supermodel Paulina Porizkova, that she can't go on thinking that nothing's wrong. This is the message of God to all people who disobey Him—that we cannot go on, we cannot live forever—if we think nothing is wrong with our adulterous rebellion against our own Divine Spouse.

"This is the way of an adulterous woman: She eats and wipes her mouth and says, 'I've done nothing wrong'" (Proverbs 30:20 NIV).

Thus, humanity as a whole is represented by the nutcase gal in the loony bin, all because we think there's nothing wrong with the way we currently think and act.

When Simple Minds sings "Don't You (Forget About Me)" from *The Breakfast Club* movie, it's really the Most Simple (Humble) Mind, which is God, telling us not to forget about Him: "Repent, all of you who **forget me**, or I will tear you apart" (Psalm 50:22 NLT).

This is astonishing, because in the Simple Minds song, lead vocalist Jim Kerr sings that he will "take you apart." And in the very next line, he says he'll be putting us back together at heart. This is God saying that despite the fact He has torn us apart because we forget about Him, He will still reunite with human beings, putting us all back together with Him to live as one: "I have given them the glory you have given me, so that they may be one as we are one" (John 17:22 CSB).

So now you know. The songs remain the same, as Led Zeppelin might say, as Jesus and His message remain the same. The Word, which is God, is secretly embedded in countless songs, even if the human songwriters had no intention of including any message from their Maker. But this is just the very beginning. You're about to see how omnipresent the message is as your mind shifts into higher gear and begins to gain speed.

3RD GEAR:
Children's Stories *at* God Speed

IT'S NOT just songs on the radio that are broadcasting the Good News from above, the words in children's stories are packed with the same messages for those who have eyes to see and ears to hear. The pattern becomes obvious once we realize the underlying themes come from the Spirit known as God.

For instance, we've all heard the common phrase at the end of many fairy-tale love stories that says, "And they lived happily ever after." This, folks, sums up the conclusion of the Bible, as God is coming back to marry His bride, His obedient followers, and they will all *live* happily ever after, all being alive forever in the happiest, most loving existence one could ever imagine. Here are a few Scriptures describing the happy, everlasting life:

> "You will **live in joy** and peace. The mountains and hills will burst into song, and the trees of the field will clap their hands!" (Isaiah 55:12 NLT).

> "**Happy** are you, O Israel! Who is like you, a people saved by the LORD?" (Deuteronomy 33:29 NKJV).

> "Turn from evil and do good, and you will **live** in the land forever" (Psalm 37:27 NLT).

> "What **joy** for those who can **live** in your house, always singing your praises" (Psalm 84:4 NLT).

Let's get specific now and take a glance at some of the most beloved children's tales to recognize their true inspiration and bring you up to God speed.

HANSEL AND GRETEL

"Hansel and Gretel" is the story of two young kids who become lost in the wilderness, and despite having left a trail of breadcrumbs to find their way home, they end up being tricked and kidnapped by a witch looking to cook and eat the pair. The witch had lured the brother and sister by constructing her home from junk food, such as cake, candy, and all kinds of unimaginable yet extremely desirable treats. The children were then held prisoner by the evil one, with Hansel locked in a cage.

But once the kids became wise to the witch's evil plan, Gretel stepped up to the plate with courage and fearlessness, pushing the wicked witch into a blazing oven, leaving "the ungodly creature to be burned to ashes," as some versions put it.

"Hansel, we are saved. The old witch is dead," declares the young girl at the climax. The story's conclusion notes, "Then all anxiety was at an end, and they lived together in perfect happiness."

By now, you may be able to make some connections at God speed to the True Author of this parable, but I'll spell it out for you, just so there's no confusion. Let's start with the obvious. The witch represents Satan the devil, often spoken of in Scripture as "the evil one" or simply "the wicked."

"The wicked shall be turned into hell" (Psalm 9:17).

"We know that we are of God, and the whole world is under the sway of the evil one" (1 John 5:19 CSB).

The children, Hansel and Gretel, represent God's own offspring, humanity, starving in the wilderness, facing certain death because they cannot find their way back home. The wilderness is this place where we all presently reside, Planet Earth, as we struggle to survive. We all need food and shelter to live, and if we try to exist without God, we face certain death.

The wicked one, whether it's the evil witch in the story or the devil himself, is extremely tricky. Satan uses every desirable temptation to lure people into his house, to lure folks into his way of thinking, so that, just like Hansel and Gretel, we "eat" the unclean "junk" food of disobedience to God's commands. Like the house made out of candy, whatever our eyes lust for may seem attractive at first. But when we consume the junk and avoid eating the **real food**, which is God Himself, then we face certain destruction.

As Jesus said,

> "For my flesh is real food and my blood is real drink"(John 6:55 NIV).

Like the witch in the tale, the devil also keeps everyone locked up as prisoners:

> "...the devil shall cast some of you into prison, that ye may be tried"
> (Revelation 2:10).

When the petrified children finally overcome their fear and fight the good fight of faith (1 Timothy 6:12) against the wicked one, it's then that they're victorious. The Bible has countless reminders to be courageous and unafraid, including:

> "Be strong and of a good courage; be not afraid" (Joshua 1:9).

> "Be of good courage, and he shall strengthen your heart" (Psalm 31:24).

And what happens to the deceptive, evil character at the end of the story? "Hansel and Gretel" broadcasts the same message recorded in Scripture: the wicked one gets tossed into a ferocious blaze, an unquenchable fire.

> "The devil who deceived them was thrown into the lake of fire"
> (Revelation 20:10 CSB).

> "You will make them burn like a fiery furnace when you appear; the LORD
> will engulf them in his wrath, and fire will devour them" (Psalm 21:9 CSB).

> "He will burn up the chaff with unquenchable fire" (Matthew 3:12).

As the young girl Gretel told Hansel, "We are saved." This is the salvation the Bible speaks of from beginning to end.

> "But the one who endures to the end will be saved" (Matthew 24:13 CSB).

"Then all anxiety was at an end, and they lived together in perfect happiness." In other words, on the spirit level of God speed, they **lived** happily ever after without any fear or stress. They received the reward of eternal life.

THE WIZARD OF OZ

The Wizard of Oz is not merely a beloved children's story by L. Frank Baum, it's actually the most seen film in movie history, so that makes it perfect for analysis here.

The basic plot centers on a girl named Dorothy, famously played by Judy Garland in the 1939 film, who leaves home to save her beloved animal, a dog named Toto, from certain death by euthanasia.

She becomes injured in a tornado, enters a fantastical dreamworld filled with little people called Munchkins and is confronted by the Wicked Witch of the West, who seeks Dorothy's demise while trying to steal her ruby slippers. The girl is instructed by a Good Witch of the North named Glinda to follow the yellow-brick road to her destination, the Emerald City.

During her journey, Dorothy does her best to help a "brainless" Scarecrow, a "heartless" Tin Man, and a "cowardly" Lion seeking courage. She faces fierce, relentless persecution from the wicked witch, who at one point sends minions of flying monkeys to chase Dorothy and her dog.

Dorothy is finally able to defeat the evil one by dousing her with water, causing the evil one's body to literally melt away.

Her friends are ultimately given gifts of honor, helping them realize they already possess the attributes they were seeking—a working brain, a compassionate heart, and courage.

In the end, Dorothy awakes in her bed, surrounded by loved ones, who dismiss her experience as merely a dream. The girl insists it was real, and says she'll never go away from home again, as she lovingly declares, "There's no place like home!"

You probably know the story better than this brief summary. But what you don't know is that this well-known tale is actually an outstanding parable for the message of the Creator when understood at God speed.

Again, let's start with the obvious. The Wicked Witch of the West represents the wicked one, Satan the devil, just like the evil character in "Hansel and Gretel." She is the obsessed-with-death, havoc-minded destroyer in the story, since God has "created the destroyer to cause havoc." (Isaiah 54:16 CSB)

Her wicked minions, the flying monkeys, represent demons, servants of the evil one, whose mission is to "possess" people, holding them captive in fear as they coax people to follow evil instead of good.

"Now the Holy Spirit tells us clearly that in the last times some will turn away from the true faith; they will follow deceptive spirits and teachings that come from demons." (1 Timothy 4:1 NLT)

The Wicked Witch's righteous enemy is Glinda, the Good Witch of the North, a beautiful, powerful, divine figure dressed in white whose name derives from the Welsh language and means pure, holy, clean, and good. Glinda represents God, who, of course, is pure, holy, clean, and good, whose "clothes were white as snow" (Matthew 28:3 NIV) and who just happens to live "on the mount of the gods' assembly, in the remotest parts of the North" (Isaiah 14:13 CSB).

Glinda is a righteous figure who instructs Dorothy to follow the yellow-brick road to reach her destination of the Emerald City. Another way of saying this is to stay on God's path to get your ultimate reward, and the Bible openly says that very thought:

"Stay on the path that the LORD your God has commanded you to follow. Then you will live long and prosperous lives in the land you are about to enter and occupy" (Deuteronomy 5:33 NLT).

The phrase "prosperous lives" refers to the ultimate prosperity, which is the eternal life of which the Bible constantly speaks. The yellow-brick road is the color yellow because it resembles gold, and Scripture says regarding the place we're meant to go: "the street of the city was pure gold" (Revelation 21:21).

The Emerald City is our destination, the "city of God" (Psalm 46:4, 87:3), the place of God's own throne, which, believe it or not, is glowing like an emerald rainbow! "There was a rainbow round about the throne, in sight like unto an **emerald**" (Revelation 4:3).

Dorothy, whose name means "gift of God," represents Jesus. She is the one who went on a long journey, leaving her home, as Jesus left His original home in heaven.

"The coming of the Son of Man can be illustrated by the story of a man going on a long trip. When he left home, he gave each of his slaves instructions about the work they were to do, and he told the gatekeeper to watch for his return" (Mark 13:34 NLT).

The hidden message of God is broadcast constantly in *The Wizard of Oz*. For instance, when Dorothy arrives in Munchkinland, her house crushes and kills the Wicked Witch of the East.

> "You come out to save your people, to save your anointed. You crush the
> leader of the house of the wicked" (Habakkuk 3:13 CSB).

Glinda, the pure and holy one, announces that the little (humble) people are rejoicing because they are no longer fearful prisoners of the devil, as she tells Dorothy: "The Munchkins are happy because you have freed them from the Wicked Witch of the East."

> "He gives justice to the oppressed...The LORD frees the prisoners"
> (Psalm 146:7 NLT).

When Dorothy confronts the Wicked Witch, she destroys the evil one by melting her.

> "As wax melts before the fire, so the wicked are destroyed before God"
> (Psalm 68:2 CSB).

> "Their flesh will rot while they are still standing on their feet, their eyes
> will rot in their sockets, and their tongues will rot in their mouths"
> (Zechariah 14:12 NIV).

The specific agent that causes the instant rotting and dissolving of the evil one is water, which is equated with God's Spirit in Scripture:

> "For I will pour **water** upon him that is thirsty, and floods upon the dry
> ground: I will pour **my spirit** upon thy seed, and my blessing upon
> thine offspring" (Isaiah 44:3).

Not coincidentally, water is the exact same weapon used by Mel Gibson in his film *Signs* to dissolve the evil destroyers from outer space because God is telling the same story over and over again.

Dorothy's friends, the Cowardly Lion, the Tin Man, and the Scarecrow represent ordinary people who are all fearful, heartless, and brainless at times. The Cowardly Lion wanted to be powerfully courageous. The Tin Man sought a loving heart. And the brainless Scarecrow wanted a sound mind.

Near the end of the story the characters realize they are already in possession of all these traits, and the Bible nicely mentions all three of them in a single verse, because people filled with God's spirit have all these attributes present inside them:

> "For God has not given us a spirit of fear, but of **power** and of **love** and of a **sound mind**" (2 Timothy 1:7 NKJV).

And at the conclusion of the tale, when Dorothy declares, "There's no place like home," she is voicing what God says about His own home:

> "For the LORD has chosen Zion; he has desired it for his home: This is my resting place forever; I will make my home here because I have desired it" (Psalm 132:13–14 CSB).

CINDERELLA

Cinderella is one of the most well-known and beloved children's stories of all time, with numerous variations over many years and cultures. I'll stick with the version that became a Walt Disney movie classic in 1950, since that's probably the most famous.

To summarize the plot, Cinderella is a kind-hearted, young woman who is forced by her wicked stepmother and cruel, jealous stepsisters to dwell in captivity and become the family slave, doing endless chores for her relatives while she dreams of having a better life someday.

Meanwhile, there is a king who wants to see his son, the handsome Prince Charming, marry a suitable bride and provide plenty of grandchildren. An invitation is sent out to all the maidens in the kingdom to attend a royal ball, and Cinderella does, with help from friends, including mice and a fairy godmother, who provide the young lady some assistance in fighting off the stepmother's equally demonic cat so she can attend the dance, with the caveat that she leave the event before midnight.

Though Cinderella hits it off with Prince Charming, whose singing voice is provided by none other than TV's legendary Mike Douglas, she dashes away as the clock strikes midnight, accidentally leaving her glass slipper behind. A search then commences to locate this mysterious beauty to whom the slipper belongs so she can marry the prince and live happily ever after, which is the glorious ending to the story that began as one of intense persecution and captivity.

Hopefully you now recognize the pattern, because it shouts Bible from every angle.

Let's start with the wicked stepmother, Lady Tremaine. She obviously represents Satan the devil, as she's the evil character who has trapped her stepchild, forcing her to live in captivity as a servant to her own wicked children while she ferociously persecutes the kind girl. And just in case you couldn't figure out for yourself that the wicked stepmother represents the devil, her cat is named "Lucifer," a name for the devil in the Old Testament: "How art thou fallen from heaven, O Lucifer" (Isaiah 14:12).

The beautiful Cinderella represents God-fearing humanity, the "captive daughter" (Isaiah 52:2) the Bible speaks of, who desperately wants to escape the trap of her wicked and controlling stepparent, or as the Bible puts it, "escape the trap of the devil, who has taken them captive to do his will" (2 Timothy 2:26 CSB).

Cinderella's name comes from the French name Cendrillon, meaning "little ashes," and is a reminder that all of us human beings are, in fact, composed of ashes and dust. Abraham of the Bible affirms this fact: "I am dust and ashes" (Genesis 18:27 CSB).

The jealous stepsisters represent fallen angels, who are actually jealous of God's pure and obedient bride that He truly loves. You may have never heard this before, but God is actually making the wicked, rebellious angels jealous by having them watch the righteous behavior of His beautiful bride, as Scripture explains: "But he wanted his own people to become jealous" (Romans 11:11 NLT).

The handsome Prince Charming represents Jesus, the Son of the ultimate King, God the Father, who is searching for His bride (obedient people) so He can unite with her (them) at a glorious wedding feast. This notion of God marrying humanity cannot be overstated, as it's a major theme of Scripture, with God telling His people in advance:

"I am married unto you" (Jeremiah 3:14).

"Let us be glad, rejoice, and give him glory, because the marriage of the Lamb has come, and his bride has prepared herself" (Revelation 19:7 CSB).

"Blessed are those who are invited to the wedding feast of the Lamb" (Revelation 19:9 NLT).

As for being the prince in the tale, Jesus is called in Scripture both the "Prince of Peace" (Isaiah 9:6) and "the prince of the kings of the earth" (Revelation 1:5).

And not only is Jesus a prince, this beloved Husband of humanity is fittingly described in Scripture as being both handsome and **charming**: "How handsome you are, my beloved! Oh, how charming!" (Song of Songs 1:16 NIV).

In the end, the beautiful and pure-hearted Cinderella, the little (humble) woman of ashes, overcomes her wicked controller and is able to finally unite with her beloved and presumably expand the family, as in produce more children of God. The New Testament looks forward to that consummated marriage and future offspring, when it is said: "Here I am with the children God gave me" (Hebrews 2:13 CSB).

As mentioned before, the end is merely the beginning, as the conclusion of this parable depicts the commencement of an eternal life of wondrous joy for the Prince of Peace and His bride, just as the fairy tale says, "and they lived happily ever after."

SLEEPING BEAUTY

Sleeping Beauty is another classic fairy tale that, when viewed with our spiritual eyes and ears open, becomes obvious it's yet another metaphor for the Bible.

The tale features a beautiful princess named Aurora (meaning dawn) who is cursed to sleep for a hundred years by an evil fairy and eventually would be awakened by a handsome prince. Not only is the princess supernaturally put to sleep, so is every living person and animal in the palace until the princess awakes.

The evil character in the story is a wicked supernatural being called Maleficent, whose name means "evilmaker," obviously referring to the devil, the one responsible for having put all of humanity into the "sleep of death" (Psalm 13:3).

Maleficent actually transforms into a gigantic dragon just before getting killed near the end of the story, reminding us what was written about the deceptive maker of evil in Scripture: "So the great dragon was thrown out—the ancient serpent, who is called the devil and Satan, the one who deceives the whole world" (Revelation 12:9 CSB).

In modern English, another way of referring to death is "the big sleep." And the handsome prince in Sleeping Beauty is, once again, the handsome Prince of Peace, Jesus, who awakens His bride (His obedient followers) from the sleep of death:

> "And many of them that sleep in the dust of the earth shall awake, some to everlasting life" (Daniel 12:2).

> "But those who die in the LORD will live; their bodies will rise again! Those who sleep in the earth will rise up and sing for joy!" (Isaiah 26:19 NLT).

And what brings people out of their death sleep? A kiss of love, because "God is love" (1 John 4:16).

> "Let him kiss me with the kisses of his mouth: for thy love is better than wine" (Song of Songs 1:2).

And they lived happily ever after, as Jesus and His bride are alive and happy with their everlasting life together.

SNOW WHITE

Sleeping Beauty is similar to another famous tale, *Snow White*, which features a beautiful princess whose enemy is an evil queen, a vain and jealous stepmother who keeps asking a magic mirror, "Who is the fairest one of all?" When the wicked queen is no longer considered the most beautiful because Snow White has replaced her, the evil stepmother plots the killing of the young princess.

At one point in the story, the wicked queen creates a poison apple that will put whomever eats it into a state of "sleeping death," a curse she learns can only be broken by "love's first kiss," but is certain Snow White will be buried alive. The evil queen fools Snow White into biting into the toxic apple by pretending it's a magic apple that grants wishes.

With Snow White seemingly dead, she's placed in a glass coffin, remaining in a death-like slumber courtesy of the poison. In the end, the wicked queen is put to death, and a handsome prince who had previously met and fallen in love with Snow White learns of her eternal sleep and visits her coffin. Saddened by her apparent death, he kisses her, breaking the spell and awakening her with his love. There's a massive celebration at the end, with everyone rejoicing as the prince takes Snow White to his kingdom, which just happens to be headquartered in heaven.

By now, you can see the biblical template clearly. The vain and jealous stepmother infatuated with her own looks is Satan the devil, whom the Bible notes "was the seal of perfection, full of wisdom and perfect in beauty" (Ezekiel 28:12 NIV) and had "arrogant eyes, a lying tongue, hands that shed innocent blood" (Proverbs 6:17 CSB). The devil is also called "a murderer from the beginning" (John 8:44).

This business about tricking the beautiful princess (who, once again, represents God's people) into eating a dangerous fruit that causes a death-like sleep is precisely what happened in the Garden of Eden. It was the devil who tricked Eve, "the mother of all living" (Genesis 3:20), into eating a forbidden fruit that put humanity into a death sleep just like Snow White, all with promises that were extremely tempting. It was God who had warned Eve: "you must not eat from the tree of the knowledge of good and evil, for on the day you eat from it, you will certainly die" (Genesis 2:17 CSB).

And once humanity was placed in its state of sleeping death, the only way to be awakened was what we saw in *Sleeping Beauty*, the kiss of love from the handsome prince. The rejoicing concerning this resurrection from the dead is reflected countless times in Scripture, including: "What a joyful and enthusiastic procession as they enter the king's palace!" (Psalm 45:15 NLT).

And with the wicked one put to death in both Snow White and the Bible, that's when the kingdom of God arrives in all its glory:

> "Then I heard a loud voice in heaven say, The salvation and the power and the kingdom of our God and the authority of his Christ have now come, because the accuser of our brothers and sisters, who accuses them before our God day and night, has been thrown down" (Revelation 12:10 CSB).

And, as you know well by now, they **lived** happily ever after, as the marriage of God and His faithful followers is consummated, and people are finally granted eternal, joyful life.

4TH GEAR:

Advertising: Spot-On *at* God Speed

NOW THAT you're familiar with the basics of how the Word of God is present in songs and children's stories, it's time to get a bit more advanced and see how divine messages are being broadcast in the modern world of commercial advertising. You may be surprised to learn that some of the best-known campaigns in history are based on the contents of the Bible.

HE LIKES IT! HEY MIKEY!

One of the most memorable commercials in the history of television is a 1970s campaign for Life cereal. It featured a hard-to-please, three-and-a-half-year-old boy named Mikey, who tasted Life and was thrilled to enjoy it, even though his own brothers were originally afraid to sample the food. The ad was so popular, Quaker Oats even rebooted the spot almost half a century later in 2019, with a young girl playing the role of Mikey.

But in the original '70s spot featuring John Gilchrist as little Mikey, here's the classic dialogue between the brothers as they debate whether they should eat Life:

"What's this stuff?"

"Some cereal. Supposed to be good for ya."

"Did you try it?"

"I'm not gonna try it. You try it!"

"I'm not gonna try it."

"Let's get Mikey!"

"Yeah."

"He won't eat it. He hates everything."

Then, upon watching their younger brother thoroughly enjoy eating Life, one astonished brother exclaims the famous catchphrase: "He likes it! Hey Mikey!"

Now, you might be wondering, "How on earth does this ad for Life cereal have any connection to the Bible?"

Here's the answer, and, at God speed, it's all embedded in the word. In this case, the word to focus on is "Life." The ad shows young children debating whether or not they should even try sampling Life. The children in the commercial represent God's obstinate children, better known as humanity in general. And what they're debating about sampling is, in effect, God, since God has declared that He Himself *is* life:

"I am...**LIFE**" (John 11:25).

In fact, Jesus points out that He Himself is food, the true food, that is actually called "life":

"My flesh is true food" (John 6:55 CSB).

"I am the bread of **LIFE**!" (John 6:48 NLT).

In case you never connected the dots, Jesus was born in the town of Bethlehem, a Hebrew word meaning "house of bread" or "house of food," and He was placed in a manger, which is a **feeding** box for animals, because He is the true food meant to be spiritually consumed by us, since we're a kind of animal in our flesh when compared to the Spirit entity who is God.

And what many people don't realize is that just as was depicted in the Life cereal ad, Scripture actually encourages people to **taste** God, to sample His word, because once they do get a taste of God, they'll realize He is good:

"**Taste** and see that the LORD is good" (Psalm 34:8).

"How sweet your **word** is to my **taste**" (Psalm 119:103 CSB).

Thus, if people would only try the word of God, instead of acting like the fearful brothers in the ad who refused to consume Life until they witnessed the smallest, meekest one in the family enjoy it, they would find out how good the Lord really is.

One final note on this commercial, when you learn what the name "Mikey" means, it makes the catchphrase of "He likes it! Hey Mikey!" even more fun and inspiring. Mikey, of course, is a shortened, endearing form of Michael. And in Hebrew, Michael means one "who is like God."

So, if we're saying that "Mikey likes Life," that can also be translated as "One who is like God likes Life," or "One who is like God likes God," since, God **is** Life! And since God is Life, the statement could also be understood as "One who is like Life likes Life!" Isn't this delicious?

I'VE FALLEN AND I CAN'T GET UP!

Among the most famous catchphrases in advertising history is: "I've fallen, and I can't get up!"

It has been used by products such as LifeCall and Life Alert, both of which are devices worn around the neck by senior citizens and disabled people to call for help in case they fall. The electronic pendants allow people to remotely contact someone who can provide whatever help is needed.

In a 1980s commercial, an elderly woman is shown lying helplessly on her bathroom floor. Unable to stand on her feet, she shouts into her LifeCall: "I've fallen, and I can't get up!"

This ad captures the spirit of the Bible in just seven words, as it broadcasts the important message that we as human beings have fallen away from God by our sinful behavior:

"For all have sinned and **fall** short of the glory of God"
(Romans 3:23 CSB).

The ad's catchphrase even sounds like a direct lyric from one of King David's songs: "they **cannot get up**; they **fall**..." (Psalm 18:38 CSB).

In other words, because we have fallen away from God, we cannot get up on our own. We need help, God's help, actually, to be able to "stand perfect and complete in all the will of God" (Colossians 4:12).

Notice, too, that the products associated with the phrase "I've fallen, and I can't get up" have the word "Life" in their name, just like Life cereal. Because when we fall away, we're spiritually dead and need to call on Life, who is God, to rescue us.

While Bible fans should have little problem grasping this basic concept, there's also a hidden message as well. And it deals with Satan the devil, who also is fallen and can't get up.

In the New Testament, Jesus noted, "I beheld Satan as lightning **fall from heaven**" (Luke 10:18).

What many people don't realize is that this infamous fall that happened way back in ancient times is also recorded at the end of the Bible in its final book:

> "I saw a star **fall from heaven** unto the earth: and to him was given the key of the bottomless pit" (Revelation 9:1).

The star that had fallen from heaven is the fallen angel Satan, whom Jesus saw falling like lightning from heaven. He can't "get up" because he's come to the "bottomless pit," also known as "the Abyss" in some Bibles.

This important verse about the star falling from heaven to earth in Revelation 9:1 immediately follows six verses in Revelation 8:7–12 in which the exact same event is recorded and repeated over and over. Remember, God constantly repeats things to get the message through our thick skulls. This section mentions numerous times that a great fiery object is **fallen** from heaven, and it destroys a third part of anything that had life in it. That fiery object (like lightning, as Jesus stated) is none other than the fiery dragon known as Satan, who prompted a third of the angels to leave God and fall to the Earth along with the evil one:

> "There was a great fiery red dragon.... Its tail swept away a third of the stars in heaven and hurled them to the earth" (Revelation 12:3–4 CSB).

So, the next time you hear the famous phrase: "I've fallen, and I can't get up," you now can understand its true significance on the spirit level. It pertains to anyone and everyone who has rebelled against their Creator and sinned, be they human beings, angels, or even Satan the devil. Unless and until we turn to God, we've all fallen, and we can't get up!

I'D LIKE TO TEACH THE WORLD TO SING IN PERFECT HARMONY

In 1971, a groundbreaking commercial for Coca-Cola assembled young people from all over the world on a hilltop in Italy to sing one of the greatest TV jingles of all time. It contained the words, "I'd Like to Buy the World a Coke." This "Hilltop" ad featured the famous lyric that was later recorded as a song in its own right by two different groups—The New Seekers and The Hillside Singers—titled, "I'd Like to Teach the World to Sing (in Perfect Harmony)."

The song became so popular that many people today, half a century after its release, can sing the lyrics verbatim at the drop of a hat.

And what could be behind its success and instant recognition? How about Scripture? The Bible is, in effect, one giant love song from God to His people, and the Creator actually tells people to teach the song to each other so they comprehend the tune He's singing:

> "So write down the words of this **song**, and **teach** it to the people.... Help them learn it..." (Deuteronomy 31:19 NLT).

As the Coke jingle declares, it's all the people of the world who are meant to sing the song:

> "Let the whole earth **sing** to the LORD!" (Psalm 96:1 NLT).

And, yes, the Bible even mentions "perfect harmony," saying it's love that joins us all in perfect harmony:

> "Above all, clothe yourselves with love, which binds us all together in **perfect harmony**" (Colossians 3:14 NLT).

Coca-Cola calls this commercial "Hilltop," and Jesus said of His followers:

> "You are the light of the world—like a city on a hilltop that cannot be hidden" (Matthew 5:14 NLT).

Of course, Coca-Cola, one of the most popular drinks in the world for many years, has billed itself as "the Real Thing." And wouldn't you know it?

Jesus let everyone know that He, Himself—His own blood, specifically—is the "real drink" (John 6:55 NIV).

In later years, Coca-Cola has employed many other well-known slogans, including "Coke Adds Life."

If we combine the slogans with Scripture, we find: The Real Thing (Jesus) adds life. And the Bible says something resoundingly familiar:

> **"I will reward them with a long life"** (Psalm 91:16 NLT).

> **"The fear of the LORD adds length to life"** (Proverbs 10:27 NIV).

> **"The one who has the Son has life"** (1 John 5:12 CSB).

YOU DESERVE A BREAK TODAY

McDonald's is perhaps the most successful fast-food chain in history, serving about sixty-nine million customers daily in more than one hundred countries.

In 1971, the same year as Coke's "Hilltop" commercial, McDonald's launched what is arguably the chain's most-remembered ad, "You Deserve a Break Today." It featured actors Anson Williams, who went on to fame playing Potsie Weber on TV's *Happy Days*, as well as John Amos, who portrayed popular dads in *Good Times* and *Coming to America*. They were among the crew at McDonald's singing the praises of how impeccably clean they kept the restaurants. Ad Age actually rated "You Deserve a Break Today" as the top advertising jingle of the twentieth century.

The final line of the song is what sticks with people nearly five decades after its debut, as the crew sang: "You deserve a break today," prompting people to get up and get away to their local McDonald's restaurant.

In case you haven't guessed by now, this famous spot is broadcasting a major portion of Scripture. How? Let's take a bite and chew on this with our spiritual senses open.

We'll start with "You deserve a break today." It's simply another way of saying you deserve a rest and tasty reward for all that you've done today.

In the New Testament, Jesus made no secret that upon His return, He would be rewarding His obedient followers for all that they've done: "For the Son of Man is going to come with his angels in the glory of his Father, and then he will **reward** each according to what he has done" (Matthew 16:27 CSB).

And though it may surprise you, the idea that believers actually deserve to enter God's rest, or God's break, today has been inked in the Bible for thousands of years:

> "For only we who believe can enter his rest.... So God set another time for entering his rest, and that time is today" (Hebrews 4:3–7 NLT).

McDonald's suggestion to get up and get away is voiced many times in Scripture, including:

> "Get up and go on your way. Your faith has saved you" (Luke 17:19 CSB).

> "Get up; let's leave this place" (John 14:31 CSB).

> "Get up and walk!" (Acts 3:6 CSB).

Beyond the jingle, the meaning of the word "McDonald's" carries huge spiritual significance. This ubiquitous Scottish family name literally means "belonging to the son of the world ruler." Of course, this makes perfect sense, because Jesus is the well-known Son of the ultimate World Ruler, who is God the Father, and believers belong to Him.

The company's pitchman, Ronald McDonald, sports an outfit of brilliantly bright colors, reminiscent of the coat of many colors worn by the biblical patriarch Joseph (Genesis 37:3). Interestingly, the name Ronald means "Having the Gods' Power." So his first and last name together indicate: "The Son of the World Ruler has the Gods' Power."

McDonald's is well known for its slogans, and a couple of others over the years have included "We do it all for you" and "Food, folks, and fun." Regarding the former, if we capitalize that last word "You," the motto reads as, "We do it all for You," as in "We do it all for God." That sounds an awful lot like a couple of statements by the apostle Paul:

> "So whether you eat or drink or whatever you do, do it all for the glory of God" (1 Corinthians 10:31 NIV).

> "And whatever you do, whether in word or deed, do it all in the name of the Lord Jesus, giving thanks to God the Father through him" (Colossians 3:17 NIV).

If we don't capitalize "you," the slogan could be understood, at God speed, as meaning We (God the Father and Jesus) do it all for you, as in They do everything for the benefit of humanity. They created us, They sustain us, and They are our destiny.

Concerning the latter slogan, one of the wisest men who ever lived, King Solomon, said pretty much the same thing as "Food, folks, and fun," but he used a few more words: "So I recommend having **fun**, because there is nothing better for **people** in this world than to **eat**, **drink**, and **enjoy life**" (Ecclesiastes 8:15 NLT).

Perhaps the most visual symbol of McDonald's, the Golden Arches, is also a metaphor for God's kingdom. The word "arch" when combined with other words means "ruler" or "leader," as we all recognize in words such as monarch or matriarch.

The kingdom of God is not a monarchy with just one king but is based on a system of more than one ruler, as Jesus is called King of **kings** (Revelation 17:14) and He said: "To all who are victorious, who obey me to the very end, To them I will give authority over all the nations. They will rule the nations...." (Revelation 2:26–27 NLT) So the Golden Arches refer to us, as we are the future kings of the kingdom.

And, like the Golden Arches, the central message of Christianity is summed up in a maxim known as the Golden Rule:

> "Do to others whatever you would like them to do to you. This is the essence
> of all that is taught in the law and the prophets (Matthew 7:12 NLT).

As we can see, virtually everything about McDonald's screams the glory of the kingdom of God, from its universal presence and popularity to its well-known slogans and characters, its intriguing name, and even its famous Golden Arches. I'm lovin' it!

MORE IS BETTER

In 2013, AT&T broadcast one of the most memorable commercial campaigns in recent history, with the tagline: "It's not complicated. More is better."

One of the ads featured *Saturday Night Live* comedian Beck Bennett portraying a deadpan moderator of a focus group consisting of kindergarten-age children.

"Who thinks more is better than less?" asks Bennett to the kids seated in a circle on the floor.

All the kids raise their hands.

"OK. Why?" asks Bennett.

An adorable young girl stumbles through her own tongue to openly declare: "More is better than less because if stuff is not [less]—if there's more less stuff, then you might, you might wanna have some more, and your parents just don't let you because there's only a little."

"Right," says Bennett in a dry, matter-of-fact manner.

"We want more! We want more! Like, you really like it. You want more!" the young girl exclaims.

"I follow you," Bennett concludes.

An announcer then declares at the end of the commercial: "It's not complicated. More is better."

The concept that "more is better" is found many times in Scripture concerning blessings for obedient servants of God. Jesus famously broadcast this notion in the parable of the talents, as He rewarded an industrious worker with more duties:

> "Well done, my good and faithful servant. You have been faithful in handling this small amount, so now I will give you **many more** responsibilities. Let's celebrate together!" (Matthew 25:21 NLT).

And He clearly explained that having more is better, especially when it comes to life itself:

> "I am come that they might have life, and that they might have it **more abundantly**" (John 10:10).

> "And everyone who has left houses or brothers or sisters or father or mother or children or fields because of my name will receive a hundred times **more** and will inherit eternal life" (Matthew 19:29 CSB).

Thus, AT&T is absolutely correct. "It's not complicated. More is better."

These are just a handful of memorable commercial campaigns, but there are countless others that voice similar messages from God. Here are some obvious examples that will get you thinking about advertisements on a whole new level:

When Prudential life insurance urges us to "Get a piece of the rock," we're being told to get a hold of God and make him our portion, as in unite with

Him, because "He is the **Rock**, his work is perfect," (Deuteronomy 32:4) and "God is the strength of my heart, and my **portion** for ever" (Psalm 73:26).

When Arby's restaurant says, "We have the meats," it's like Scripture saying: "the LORD Almighty will prepare a feast of rich food for all peoples…the best of meats" (Isaiah 25:6 NIV).

It's akin to Clara Peller shouting "where's the *beef?*!" in Wendy's ads or actor Sam Elliott declaring, "Beef. It's what's for dinner." The answer to Clara's question is that God Himself is the beef, as Jesus said: "Whoso eateth my flesh…hath eternal life; and I will raise him up at the last day. For my flesh is meat indeed" (John 6:54–55).

And lest we forget, all the folks who departed Egypt in the famous Exodus all ate "the same spiritual meat; And did all drink the same spiritual drink: for they drank of that spiritual Rock that followed them: and that Rock was Christ" (1 Corinthians 10:3–4).

When actor Jeff Goldblum makes the pitch for Apartments.com to "change your apartment, change your universe," he is broadcasting a message from God about our ultimate change, when we're raised from the grave, and our dwelling place, our body, is changed instantly: "We shall all be changed, In a moment, in the twinkling of an eye…the dead shall be raised incorruptible, and we shall be changed" (1 Corinthians 15:51–52). It's what The Who alluded to when they sang that the change had to come in "Won't Get Fooled Again."

The same theme is found with Bounty paper towels, which bills itself as the "The Quicker Picker Upper." The words "quick" and "quicken" in Scripture mean to raise from death and make the human body immortally alive, as in:

> "He that raised up Christ from the dead shall also **quicken** your mortal bodies by his Spirit that dwelleth in you" (Romans 8:11).

> "Thou, which hast shewed me great and sore troubles, shalt **quicken** me again, and shalt bring me up again from the depths of the earth" (Psalm 71:20).

So the word "quicker" can mean the Person who makes people quick, as in the One who makes people alive.

And, of course, a "picker upper" is merely the One who does the picking up or raising, who is God Himself: "God raised up the Lord and will also raise us up by his power" (1 Corinthians 6:14 CSB).

Thus, "The Quicker Picker Upper" is actually saying the same thing twice: "The Quicker" is "The One who makes us alive." "Picker Upper" is the "One who raises us." Fittingly, the item that does all this goes by the name of Bounty, as in: "the best products of the ancient mountains and the **bounty** of the eternal hills" (Deuteronomy 33:15 CSB).

And what precisely does a Bounty paper towel do? It cleans up messes. This, of course, is what God does, cleaning up all of us messes known as human beings.

When the vitamin product Emergen-C says, "Emerge and see," it's announcing our future emergence from the grave, enabling us to "see" everything, even God, with complete clarity:

> "When he [Jesus] shall appear, we shall be like him; for we shall **see** him as he is" (1 John 3:2).

In one 2018 ad for Emergen-C, a man is shown vivaciously bursting out of his tent, with an announcer stating: "Emerge restored. Replenished. Fortified…Emerge and see."

The language in this campaign is amazingly close to what has been in prophecy for thousands of years:

> "When he has tested me, I will **emerge** as pure gold" (Job 23:10 CSB).

> "I have **replenished** every sorrowful soul" (Jeremiah 31:25).

> "I will make you a **fortified** wall" (Jeremiah 15:20 CSB).

> "He was **restored**, and **saw**" (Mark 8:25).

When Skittles candy encourages us to "Taste the Rainbow," it's telling us to taste God, as in sample God, since the rainbow signifies the presence of God, as we learned earlier:

> "The appearance of the brilliant light all around was like that of a **rainbow** in a cloud on a rainy day. This was the appearance of the likeness of the LORD's glory" (Ezekiel 1:28 CSB).

> "**Taste** and see that the LORD is good" (Psalm 34:8).

When Lexus says, "Experience Amazing," it reminds us that we all can and should experience amazing, wondrous works by God: "Everyone was gripped with great wonder and awe, and they praised God, exclaiming, 'We have seen **amazing** things today!'" (Luke 5:26 NLT).

In ads for Energizer batteries featuring the Energizer Bunny, we're repeatedly told, "They keep going and going and going and going...." The Bible says something quite similar: "Those who trust in the LORD...will endure forever" (Psalm 125:1 NLT).

When Motel 6 says, "We'll leave the light on for you," we're reminded that God, who is our ultimate resting place (even better than a Motel 6) is leaving the light on for us, because "God is light, and in him is no darkness at all" (1 John 1:5).

Leaving the light on for **us** may also be a veiled prophecy for our future, as God will make our bodies completely brilliant, totally illuminated with light.

> "If then your whole body is full of light, having no part dark, the whole body will be full of light, as when the bright shining of a lamp gives you light" (Luke 11:36 NKJV).

And when The Home Depot says, "More saving. More doing," it's expressing the grand purpose of God, which is "**to save much people alive**" (Genesis 50:20).

By now, it's evident that no matter what TV channel you're watching or what radio station you're listening to, the message of God is saturating the airwaves at God speed, even if most people are oblivious to it.

But wait. There's more....

5TH GEAR:

Movies: I Was Blind, Now I See *the* Projection

NOW THAT your ears have been warmed up to how God operates, sprinkling His divine message in popular songs and commercials, it's now time to see and hear even more. So let's get really visual. You're about to have an eye-opening experience that can change the way you see everything and help rev you up to God speed. Because songs, children's stories, and ads are just the beginning. You're now going to see how God projects His message through your favorite movies. And, during this experience, you're going to learn a lot more about God's secret plan than you've ever been told in church or read about on the internet. You'll learn about who you really are and your intended destiny.

Most folks simply don't realize they never even have to open a Bible to become exposed to God and His Master Plan. His message is thoroughly embedded into everything that's been created. Scripture even says as much:

> "For his invisible attributes, that is, his eternal power and divine nature, have been clearly seen since the creation of the world, being understood through what he has made. As a result, people are without excuse" (Romans 1:20 CSB).

So, just in case you're one of those people who thinks you can't be held responsible for disturbing thoughts and actions because you never heard the message of God, you have no excuse. Because, as we're seeing, the message is everywhere and in everything, and even films are jam-packed with His good news. So let's raise the curtain to reveal what you've never seen.

BACK TO THE FUTURE

The *Back to the Future* trilogy is a blockbuster series of films from the 1980s whose premise is that people's own existence, their very lives, are in jeopardy to the point of extinction when their intended destiny is tampered with.

This is shown brilliantly and comically through the use of time traveler Marty McFly (Michael J. Fox), whose life—along with the lives of his family members—is being "erased from existence" when he veers off the natural path of time, courtesy of a time machine made out of a stainless steel DeLorean. He needs to get back to the future to set things right, to put events on their proper course.

The second part of the trilogy shows how dramatically dark and unnerving the world becomes when an evil, rich, and powerful ogre is in charge of events. This takes place when the deceptive Biff Tannen (Thomas F. Wilson) steals a sports almanac and uses his purloined knowledge of the past and future for harmful purposes, becoming fabulously wealthy through deceit, controlling a city, bribing police, and even murdering Marty's father.

Now, how can this possibly be related to the Bible?

Let's start with the obvious. The evil Biff (whose name means "whack") represents the devil, the one always whacking us, who is a liar and murderer (John 8:44).

He corrupts a pleasant place to live, turning it into a dark and disturbing city filled with violence. As Scripture says, "the land is full of bloody crimes, and the city is full of violence" (Ezekiel 7:23).

Meanwhile, Marty is a child of the future, whose own existence is the result of love between his parents, a man and his bride. As we've seen many times already, the story of the Bible is the story of a Man representing God who is marrying His bride, humanity. The result of the love the two have for each other is the birth of eternally alive children, the ubiquitous "children of God."

"Here I am with the children God gave me" (Hebrews 2:13 CSB).

The constant theme throughout *Back to the Future* is that since events have become skewed, as in going off the correct path and continually veering toward evil, everyone's life is in peril. The movie depicts this by having Marty and his siblings fade out of existence on a photograph.

Doesn't this killer threat sound like the situation the world is in today? Because humanity as a whole has veered off God's path and is drowning in sin and all kinds of evil actions, then there is nothing left for us except death, completely erasing us from existence. As Scripture says, "The wages of sin is death" (Romans 6:23).

Thus, when scientist Doc Brown (Christopher Lloyd) tells Marty, "We're sending you back to the future!" he's telling the boy, at God speed, that he's sending him back to his intended destiny of life, so that he can remain alive forever. This is our future that we all need to get back to. The future is an eternity of glory.

There are some interesting side notes from this fantastic production.

The license plate on the car that travels through time reads: OUTATIME.

This could be a double- or triple-entendre. First, it may refer to the vehicle itself being "out of time," as in not bound by the restraints of time, since it can travel through all time periods: past, present, and future. Remember, "Jesus Christ is the same yesterday, today, and forever" (Hebrews 13:8 NKJV).

Second, it could also be a veiled prophecy, telling all of us living in our modern age that we're all "out of time," as in "time's up" for us:

"The end of all things is at hand" (1 Peter 4:7).

"Our end is near, our days are fulfilled; for our end is come" (Lamentations 4:18).

Third, it could be implying that we're living out of our proper timing, as in being out of sync with God, and therefore will not reap our reward at "the proper time."

"Let us not get tired of doing good, for we will reap at the proper time if we don't give up" (Galatians 6:9 CSB).

"Humble yourselves, therefore, under the mighty hand of God, so that he may exalt you at the proper time" (1 Peter 5:6 CSB).

One funny moment in the trilogy's first film occurs early when Marty initially travels thirty years back in time, from 1985 to 1955, to see his mother's family in their younger years. One of his relatives there is his Uncle Joey, who in 1985 missed out on a welcome-home cake made for him because he failed to get sprung from prison. But when Marty sees him in 1955, Uncle Joey is just a baby boy, who, in a foreshadow of his future behind bars, is wearing a shirt with black-and-white prison stripes, spending time surrounded by wooden bars in the mini-jail of his crib.

That's when Michael J. Fox utters his hilarious line: "Better get used to these bars, kid."

I surmise the writers of the film had little idea how biblical they were getting with that comment. Because people need to realize that our spirit is in jail right now, behind bars in our physical bodies because of our disobedience, having broken God's law. But God intends to free us prisoners. Scripture says so in many different ways:

> "I was **imprisoned** in the earth, whose **gates lock shut** forever" (Jonah 2:6 NLT).

> "In order to open blind eyes, to **bring out prisoners** from the dungeon, and those sitting in darkness from the **prison house**" (Isaiah 42:7 CSB).

> "I will say to the **prisoners**, 'Come out in freedom,' and to those in darkness, 'Come into the light' (Isaiah 49:9 NLT).

> "You will know the truth, and the truth will **set you free**" (John 8:32 CSB).

Now, with this greater understanding, you can better understand the significance of Michael J. Fox's quip in *Back to the Future*. When Marty tells the baby (who is actually his prison-bound uncle Joey who would never be released from prison), "Better get used to these bars, kid," it's actually God who is making the joke. God is telling the kid (all of us kids, in fact) that we better get used to living in captivity. We will continue to dwell in prison behind bars and gates, existing only in our human bones and flesh if we keep rebelling against Him, if we keep fighting the Law (which is God)—because, as we learned in the classic song earlier, when you fight the law, the law wins.

Finally, when Marty McFly goes "back in time" and returns to his correct future, his time-traveling vehicle speeds into a former movie theater that has since become the "Assembly of Christ." Signs on the front of the church say, "Salvation is free" and "Jesus is calling you the young!"

In other words, when we get back in time, when we get back in sync with God, and go back to our intended future, we human beings race into the assembly of Christ where salvation is free and Jesus calls us young forever!

DIE HARD

In the classic action movie *Die Hard*, Bruce Willis plays a tough but kind-hearted lawman who flies in from a faraway place to try to save his relationship with his estranged wife. He gets caught up in a hostage event and spills lots of his blood in the process of putting to death the ruthless lawbreakers. He eventually frees the prisoners and unites with his wife at the end.

Yes, folks, this is the plot of the Bible. Jesus is a tough but kindhearted Lawman who comes from a faraway place (the higher dimension of heaven) to try to make things right with His estranged wife (humanity) while He spills His blood and puts unrepentant lawbreakers to death, known as "the second death" (Revelation 21:8).

And just as Bruce Willis frees the captives, "The LORD sets prisoners free" (Psalm 146:7 NIV) and he unites with his wife at the end, as "the marriage of the Lamb has come, and His wife has made herself ready" (Revelation 19:7 NKJV).

One extremely profound line of dialogue spoken by Willis sums up what Jesus is telling humanity: "Come on. You wanna stay alive? You stay with me."

And, of course, the title *Die Hard* is an allusion to everlasting life, since people who are diehards just keep going and going and going, like the famous car batteries of the same name or the Energizer Bunny.

I AM LEGEND

I Am Legend stars Will Smith as Dr. Robert Neville, a high-ranking virologist in the United States Army who tries to convince people infected with a horrible mutation-causing disease that he can heal them from their deathlike zombie state and, despite their ferocious resistance, he ultimately sacrifices his own life and saves them. The doctor explains the cure is in the blood, and he begs the darkness-loving, infected people: "You are sick, and I can help. I can fix this. I can save everybody!… Let me save you!" But they reject his offer and seek to kill him. In the end, blood provides the rescue for everyone, while the monstrous people who sought to kill the healer suffer a fiery end to their existence.

The story closely follows the plot of the Bible, as Jesus, who is a high-ranking military officer known as the LORD of Armies (Psalm 24:10 CSB) and the captain of our salvation (Hebrews 2:10) tries to convince people He can heal them from their deathlike existence known as mortal life.

Despite stiff-necked resistance and rebellion against Him, as most refuse to be rescued, He ultimately sacrifices His own life and saves everyone by using blood, "for the blood is the life" (Deuteronomy 12:23). Of course, those who fight against Him have a fiery end in what the Bible calls "the furnace of fire" (Matthew 13:42).

Will Smith's character, Dr. Robert Neville, also represents Jesus in each one of his names and job descriptions. The name Robert Neville actually means "a new place to live that's bright with glory."

At the movie's start, we see him on the cover of *Time* magazine, with the headline: "Savior, Soldier, Scientist." Jesus, of course, is all of these:

> "Entry into the eternal kingdom of our Lord and **SAVIOR** Jesus Christ will be richly provided for you" (2 Peter 1:11 CSB).

> "The LORD advances like a warrior; he stirs up his zeal like a **SOLDIER**" (Isaiah 42:13 CSB).

And He is a scientist, a doctor whose main goal is to heal people, as He said: "It is not those who are healthy who need a doctor, but those who are sick" (Luke 5:31 CSB).

The movie shows the doctor airing his message on all frequencies to all people. "I am broadcasting on all AM frequencies," Neville says. God, too, is broadcasting His message everywhere at all times:

> "The heavens declare the glory of God, and the expanse proclaims the work of his hands. Day after day they pour out speech; night after night they communicate knowledge.... Their message has gone out to the whole earth, and their words to the ends of the world" (Psalm 19:1–4 CSB).

The message on the airwaves in the film says: "If you are out there, if anyone is out there, I can provide **food**, I can provide **shelter**, I can provide **security**. If there's anybody out there, anybody, please, you are not alone."

This resembles the message God is broadcasting:

"My flesh is true **food**" (John 6:55 CSB).

"You are my **shelter**" (Psalm 119:114 CSB).

"I will heal my people and will let them enjoy abundant peace and **security**" (Jeremiah 33:6 NIV).

The monsters in the film, known as Darkseekers because of their severe aversion to light, represent all of us regular people, fallen humanity, who have become grotesque monsters because we have rebelled against the light that is God and are now living in darkness, with no desire to come to the light. "God's light came into the world, but people **loved the darkness** more than the light, for their actions were evil" (John 3:19 NLT). Will Smith's character notes: "Social de-evolution appears complete. Typical human behavior is now entirely absent."

The film explains, "a deadly virus burned through our civilization, pushing humankind to the edge of extinction." That deadly virus we're all infected with and is pushing us toward extinction is called mortality. We're all spiritually dead—the walking dead, so to speak, because we're intended to be living forever.

It is only through the use of blood that the "army doctor" known as Jesus saves us from our mortality so we can inherit immortality. Scripture makes a very big deal about the transformation of our bodies when we make the jump from mortal to immortal beings: "When this corruptible body is clothed with incorruptibility, and this mortal body is clothed with immortality, then the saying that is written will take place: Death has been swallowed up in victory" (1 Corinthians 15:54 CSB).

The final moments of the film note that the doctor dedicated his life to the "cure and the restoration of humanity." The Bible speaks of the time of this final cure and "the final **restoration** of all things" (Acts 3:21 NLT) when God says He "will **restore** health to you And heal you of your wounds" (Jeremiah 30:17 NKJV).

The very last words spoken in the movie are "Light up the darkness," and the Bible says: "The LORD, my God, lights up my darkness" (Psalm 18:28 NLT).

Even when we look at the title of *I Am Legend*, the name and purpose of God are being declared.

"'I AM'" is the personal name of God" (Exodus 3:14).

And the word *legend* can mean more than one thing, including a story coming down from the past, and an explanatory list of the symbols on a map or chart. Jesus is both of these, as He is the greatest story coming down to us personally from our past. And, as we're seeing in this book, He Himself represents all the symbols on the map to eternal life, also known as the Bible.

EVERY VAMPIRE MOVIE EVER MADE

From the legendary *Dracula* with Bela Lugosi to the popular *Twilight* series to Wesley Snipes starring in *Blade*, there is no shortage of vampire films produced by Hollywood. While each movie has its own unique elements, here are some popular, recurring themes:

- Vampires are evil, undead creatures, who thrive in darkness and have a serious aversion to light.

- They are sustained by feeding off human beings, drinking their blood, often using sharp fangs to bite people.

- They are sometimes repelled by seeing a cross, a visible symbol of Jesus Christ's death penalty.

- In some tales such as the *Blade* series, vampires are instantly transformed into ashes and dust when killed.

Here's the Bible inspiration for all this.

Vampires are creatures of darkness because darkness represents evil. They are rebellious beasts of people who creep around opposing God, who is represented by light.

> "You make darkness, and it is night, In which all the beasts of the forest creep about" (Psalm 104:20 NKJV).

As noted before in *I Am Legend*, "people loved the darkness more than the light, for their actions were evil" (John 3:19 NLT).

Interestingly, Scripture uses vampire-sounding language to describe how evil individuals treat other people, actually using razor-sharp fangs to devour innocent folks:

> "Will those who do evil never learn? They **eat up my people** like bread" (Psalm 14:4 NLT).

> "There is a generation whose **teeth are swords**, whose **fangs are knives, devouring the oppressed** from the land and the needy from among mankind" (Proverbs 30:14 CSB).

The Dracula character obviously can be viewed as a representation of Satan the devil, the enemy of Christ, as Scripture says he's looking to devour people:

> "Stay alert! Watch out for your great enemy, the devil. He prowls around like a roaring lion, looking for someone to devour" (1 Peter 5:8 NLT).

And what do vampires specifically devour? Blood, of course. "For the life of a creature is in the blood" (Leviticus 17:11 NIV). So when vampires suck the blood out of someone, they are sucking the life from that person. Spiritually speaking, they are taking away the person's eternal life, and the victim usually becomes undead, the walking dead, infected just like other vampires.

Dracula's aversion to Jesus's cross is alluded to in the New Testament:

> "There are many whose conduct shows they are really enemies of the cross of Christ" (Philippians 3:18 NLT).

And, as depicted in the *Blade* series, the end of the story for the wicked is their transformation into dust and ashes, as Scripture notes, "the wicked; for they shall be ashes" (Malachi 4:3).

NATIONAL TREASURE

National Treasure is the story of a man played by Nicolas Cage who is seeking a priceless treasure, one worth more than any other possession on Earth. He has to decipher numerous, cryptic clues and endure fierce opposition from a master thief who is trying to hinder his path and steal the treasure for himself. In the end, the good man overcomes all opposition and is able to solve the mystery, locate the incalculable treasure, and share it with the world.

This is a main plot line of the Bible, based on mankind's point of view in the quest for true treasure. It's a theme repeated in countless stories about the hunt for buried treasure on land or sunken treasure beneath the sea. We human beings are the ones seeking the priceless national treasure, which is nothing short of divine glory, everlasting life with God. The Bible calls it "an inexhaustible **treasure**" (Luke 12:33 CSB).

In this current age in which we live, we're even instructed on how to acquire the never-ending treasure of everlasting life in the coming age:

> "Tell them to use their money to do good. They should be rich in good works and generous to those in need, always being ready to share with others. By doing this they will be **storing up their treasure** as a good foundation for the future so that they may experience **true life**" (1 Timothy 6:18–19 NLT).

And, as we've seen before, God has purposely hidden His message, and He is urging us to decipher it, just as Nicolas Cage has to decode the clues in the movie:

> "It is the glory of God to conceal a matter and the glory of kings to investigate a matter" (Proverbs 25:2 CSB).

The clever thief who opposes Cage is played by Sean Bean, and he represents the ultimate thief, the devil: "A thief comes only to steal and kill and destroy" (John 10:10 CSB).

As the conclusion of the movie so fittingly reveals, the end of the story for those who follow God's words is to receive and share an immeasurable treasure. The end of our story, at least for obedient believers, is far more than physical wealth. It's inheriting *all things*, becoming a member of God's own family, and sitting down with Him on His throne and ruling alongside Him:

> "To him who overcomes I will grant to sit with Me on My throne" (Revelation 3:21 NKJV).

> "He who overcomes shall inherit all things, and I will be his God and he shall be My son" (Revelation 21:7 NKJV).

That, my friends, is the epitome of a national treasure.
Want more movies? You got it.

A CHRISTMAS STORY

One of America's most beloved seasonal films is *A Christmas Story*. And among its memorable scenes is one featuring a man celebrating his winning of "a major award." That fantastic prize turns out to be a lampstand shaped like the leg of an attractive woman. When originally delivered, this leg lamp was deeply and securely hidden in a box marked "Fragile," comically mispronounced as "Fra-jee-lay." Called "indescribably beautiful," it was prominently displayed in the house for everyone to see, and the man (Darren McGavin), who was victorious in receiving the lampstand, gloried in his victory that he attributed to "mind power." He danced and sang, "I won! I won! I won!"

I realize this is a very silly scene, but if we take a closer look, it may surprise you to learn it contains the message of the Bible. Here's the translation at God speed: The leg lamp is what the Bible calls a lampstand, which is merely a stand that holds lamps to share their light. Lamps and lampstands are mentioned often in Scripture, including this remark from Jesus:

> "No one lights a lamp and puts it in the cellar or under a basket, but on a lampstand, so that those who come in may see its light" (Luke 11:33 CSB).

This quote directly relates to the movie, as the lamp in the film was initially hidden away in a crate marked "Fragile." What it's saying is that we human people in the flesh are the fragile boxes who carry the hidden lamp (the light, or presence, of God) inside of our bodies.

> "You, LORD, are my lamp; the LORD turns my darkness into light" (2 Samuel 22:29 NIV).

And that "indescribably beautiful" light of God is intended to be taken out of its shipping container (our physical body) and placed on a stand for all others to see its glorious light when this time in our flesh is completed. It's a metaphor for being raised from the dead and taken out of our box. We then stand with God with our brilliant light blazing at full strength. Like the man in the film, we'll rejoice when we finally win the major award, the biggest prize ever. We should all remember that we're instructed to "run in such a way to **win the prize**" (1 Corinthians 9:24 CSB). Thus, upon being raised out of our personal crates to glory, there will be jubilant celebration as each of us shouts, "I won! I won! I won!"

Of course, in the movie, the leg lamp gets destroyed and ends up being thrown out. This, too, is reminiscent of what's in Scripture:

> "The light of the righteous shines brightly, but the lamp of the wicked is put out" (Proverbs 13:9 CSB).

> "For the evil have no future; the lamp of the wicked will be put out" (Proverbs 24:20 CSB)

Therefore, we should make every effort to run our race well, fight the good fight, and win the prize, the greatest "major award" we can imagine.

ELYSIUM

Elysium is a space-age tale starring Matt Damon and Jodie Foster about dying residents on a diseased and polluted Earth desperately looking to become citizens of a paradise in the heavens so they can be healed.

Conspiring forces of darkness try to stage a coup against the paradise government in the sky, but after many battles and the bloody self-sacrifice of the savior of mankind, played by Damon, who was told he could "save everyone," the evildoers are destroyed, and everyone on Earth is rescued and healed.

The name Elysium actually means paradise, heaven, the New Jerusalem and the abode of the blessed after death. If we apply the Syro-Chaldaic language in use at the time of Christ to this word, it can be translated as "the dwelling place of my God." In the film, those who dwell there never get sick and never age.

Here's the Bible translation of the plot at God speed. We human beings, the residents of Planet Earth who are actually made up of the dust of the earth, are all in the process of dying. We're mortal and have no way to be saved and healed of our mortality except to reach the healing paradise, the dwelling place of our God where we never get sick and never age.

The dark forces in the film represent evil ones, the devil and his angels, who tried to stage a coup against God to usurp His sovereignty and become the highest rulers. Scripture calls it "war in heaven" (Revelation 12:7), with the devil saying in his heart, "I will ascend above the heights of the clouds; I will be like the most High" (Isaiah 14:14).

The Bible is filled with stories of our individual battles against evil to gain life everlasting, perhaps best summed up with: "Fight the good fight of faith, lay hold on eternal life" (1 Timothy 6:12).

And, of course, it is through the bloody self-sacrifice of the Savior of mankind, Jesus, that our sins are forgiven, so we can be rescued and healed to reach the paradise.

> "Jesus gave his life for our sins, just as God our Father planned, in order to rescue us from this evil world in which we live" (Galatians 1:4 NLT).

> "According to the law almost everything is purified with blood, and without the shedding of blood there is no forgiveness" (Hebrews 9:22 CSB).

In the end, the saved people become citizens of God's paradise. Jesus says "the victorious...will be citizens in the city of my God—the new Jerusalem that comes down from heaven from my God" (Revelation 3:12 NLT). We indeed make it to Elysium, the dwelling place of my God.

EDGE OF TOMORROW AND GROUNDHOG DAY

Two films that on the surface appear very different from each other are actually quite similar when it comes to their underlying theme. They are the science-fiction thriller *Edge of Tomorrow* starring Tom Cruise and the folksy romantic comedy *Groundhog Day* with Bill Murray.

What both movies have in common is an important message the Bible is conveying: Every day we're alive needs to be replayed over and over until our personal conduct is perfected and evil is purged and destroyed.

Edge of Tomorrow stresses this notion of repeating the day with its catchy tagline of "Live. Die. Repeat." The subtitle for *Groundhog Day* is similar: "He's having the day of his life...over and over again."

The evil in Tom Cruise's movie is a powerful, dark force looking to take over the world and kill all of mankind. It's up to Cruise to be killed every single day and relive that same day over and over, being trained in the proper way, improving his decisions and perfecting his actions so he can overcome the evil.

In *Groundhog Day*, Bill Murray is initially a dark-mannered weatherman forced to relive the same day thousands of times until he, too, is properly trained, learning to do good and stop being the consummate jerk, completely purging the evil from himself.

This common plotline between the films can easily be seen when applying biblical verses such as these:

"Learn to do good" (Isaiah 1:17 NKJV).

"Train yourself to be godly" (1 Timothy 4:7 NIV).

"You must purge the evil from you" (Deuteronomy 13:5 CSB).

"Be perfect, therefore, as your heavenly Father is perfect"
(Matthew 5:48 CSB).

Regarding *Edge of Tomorrow* and its slogan of "Live. Die. Repeat," these phrases allude to everyone's resurrection from the dead in our next day of existence, our "tomorrow." We currently live *today*, in the present, but we're all mortal. We temporarily exist today on the verge, or edge, of *tomorrow*, which is the afterlife, and that's when we'll be raised from the dead. Much of Scripture is focused on bringing back people from the grave *tomorrow*. Even in the Old Testament, there are hidden prophecies alluding to this wonderful event, such as: "Then Joshua told the people, 'Purify yourselves, for **tomorrow** the LORD will do great wonders among you'" (Joshua 3:5 NLT).

There are actually two separate and distinct resurrections, the First and Second Resurrection to which Jesus referred: "those who have done good to the resurrection of life, and those who have done evil to the resurrection of judgment" (John 5:29 ESV). So no matter who we are, we all experience the movie's tagline. We **live**. We **die**. Then we **repeat**.

RAIDERS OF THE LOST ARK

Finally, one of the most popular films of all time is *Raiders of the Lost Ark*, starring Harrison Ford as Dr. Indiana Jones, the strapping college professor and archaeologist who hunts for the ark of the covenant spoken of in the Bible, eventually unearthing it and bringing it out of Egypt. Right on its face, the movie is telling a story about a high-profile, real-life object mentioned in the Bible. But there's so much more to learn if we probe this Hollywood parable at God speed, because, as Dr. Jones poignantly declares in the film, "They're digging in the wrong place."

The plot centers on locating the lost ark, the container representing the very presence of God, digging it out from its hiding place beneath the earth, and removing it completely out of Egypt. This, dear friends, is one of the main themes of the Bible concerning the story of you and me. So let's dig in the right place to understand what the movie is truly projecting.

As should be obvious by now, the earth where the ark is hidden symbolizes people, since we're made up of the earth. The ark, representing God's own presence, has been "lost," hidden inside the earth in the land of Egypt.

Now this is where it gets very interesting. When we unlock the meaning of the word *Egypt*, the true significance of removing something out of Egypt will explode into an astonishing brightness of clear understanding. There are actually two meanings for the word itself, both of which hold true. The ancient Egyptian meaning for *Egypt* simply means "black land" or "dark place." Meanwhile, the Bible word translated as *Egypt* is *Mizraim*, and it means what it sounds like in English: *MISERY* or "double distress." Thus, *Egypt* denotes a dark place of misery.

There's one other fact about Egypt that makes the meaning of the word even more clear. It is likened to a prison, a place of captivity or, as the Bible so often declares, a "house of bondage."

"I am the LORD your God, who brought you out of the land of Egypt, out of the house of bondage" (Exodus 20:2 NKJV).

When we put all this together, the word *Egypt* is another way of describing where all human beings dwell in our fleshly, earthen vessels. It's our physical bodies and physical world. We all live in a captive place made of earth. It's a dark prison, a place from which we cannot escape, where we deal with plenty of misery. (The United States even used a "misery index" in the 1970s to quantify how miserable life can be.) In our own personal Egypt, we experience darkness that is both spiritual and physical.

The spiritual darkness is simple to grasp. It merely refers to evil, as Jesus famously explained that "men loved **darkness** rather than light, because their deeds were **evil**" (John 3:19).

The physical darkness is also easy to understand when we make the jump to God speed and let Scripture unlock the meaning. It is simply the fact that all of our human bodies in the flesh are considered darkness when compared to the brilliant, dazzling white light that God as a Spirit being is.

Remember, "God is light, and in him is no darkness at all" (1 John 1:5).

And Jesus in his glorified spirit form is the brightest light we can possibly imagine.

"His face was like the sun shining in all its brilliance" (Revelation 1:16 NIV).

Physical people, on the other hand, are not made up solely of light as God is but are composed of the earth and are literally covered with its darkness:

"See, darkness covers the earth and thick darkness is over the peoples" (Isaiah 60:2 NIV).

All human beings in the flesh, irrespective of skin tone, are dark when compared with the brilliant light beaming from God in spirit form.

There are many Bible verses discussing darkness, blackness, night, and living in the shadow of death, and they're all broadcasting the same message. They refer to our existence in our darkened state, life in our mortal, physical flesh.

Here are some examples:

"Though I walk through the valley of the shadow of death" (Psalm 23:4).

"To give light to them that sit in darkness and in the shadow of death" (Luke 1:79).

"He brought them out of darkness and the shadow of death, and brake their bands in sunder" (Psalm 107:14).

"The people that walked in darkness have seen a great light: they that dwell in the land of the shadow of death, upon them hath the light shined" (Isaiah 9:2).

"You make darkness, and it is night, In which all the beasts of the forest creep about" (Psalm 104:20 NKJV).

"The night is nearly over, and the day is near; so let us discard the deeds of darkness and put on the armor of light" (Romans 13:12 CSB).

In these passages, "darkness," "night," and "the shadow of death" mean the same thing, referring to our physical, mortal, human flesh. We're currently sitting in our human bodies made of flesh and bones. That's the higher meaning of darkness at God speed. Darkness represents the flesh. At every moment, we display on our skin the shadow of death, which is mortality, as we're all in the process of wearing out. But we are meant to possess something much better and brighter, the armor of the light of God, which is eternal life, bringing us out of the darkness, out of these mortal bodies of flesh. Here's another famous verse:

> "Then said the king to the servants, Bind him hand and foot, and take him away, and cast him into **outer darkness**; there shall be weeping and gnashing of teeth" (Matthew 22:13).

Here's the translation: Anyone who disobeys the King, God, is taken away from the Light and bound in a prison of human flesh, which is "outer darkness." We all need to understand that our personal outer covering, our skin, is, in fact, our own "outer darkness." If the outer part of our body is not clothed in Light, the Spirit of God, then we are clothed in outer darkness. And, during the time we're dwelling in these human bodies of flesh, we all understand there is plenty of weeping and gnashing of teeth, because life in our current, physical form is full of pain and misery, which, once again, is what the word *Egypt* means in the Bible's original language.

When Exodus 10:21 says "There may be darkness over the land of Egypt, even darkness which may be felt," it's talking at God speed about the darkness of our human flesh. That's precisely why it says it's a **darkness which may be felt**! Because we can feel our own darkness when we feel our own skin! Go ahead, take your hand and touch any part of your body right this second. You're now feeling the darkness that may be felt! Astonishing, isn't it?

This plague of darkness on ancient Egypt was not solely for the people of antiquity. All of us, in our personal prison of our physical body, are experiencing the same plague at this moment. This condition of darkness, or the night, simply refers to the state of dwelling in the human flesh, as opposed to living in the Day, the Light of God. At the beginning, we've been told:

> "And God called the light Day, and the darkness he called Night" (Genesis 1:5).

This is not merely referring to the physical creation of a typical day and night ages ago. On the spirit level, God is calling the Light (Himself) by the name of "Day." And the darkness—which is the earth, the flesh, all human beings—is known by another name, and that term is "Night." God's Spirit is represented by daylight, and physical human beings are represented by darkness and night.

If you have never heard this part of the story, while the plague of darkness affected those in Egypt for three days, Scripture notes that God's people living in Goshen "had light in their dwellings." (Exodus 10:23) The word *Goshen* is not just a place. It literally means "drawing near." So, on the spirit level, what God is saying is that if we remain far away from God through disobedience, we live in darkness, we live in the flesh. But when we draw near to God and obey His instructions, it is then we start the process of becoming children of God, "children of light and children of the day." (1 Thessalonians 5:5) It is then that we have Light, possessing God inside our dwelling, inside our very own bodies. It's the same story repeated using different words.

On a related matter concerning Egypt, many have wondered why the book of Revelation says Jesus was crucified in Egypt, while the gospels indicate he was executed at Jerusalem. The Bible explains the place "which spiritually is called Sodom and **Egypt**, where also our Lord was crucified" (Revelation 11:8).

The key to understanding this is the phrase "which spiritually is called." That's telling us to make the jump to God speed, because it indicates that although Jesus may have been physically slain in Jerusalem, the spiritual meaning at God speed is that He was in the spiritual place called Sodom and Egypt. The word *Sodom* means "burning" or "flaming" and *Egypt* is the "dark place of misery." This fleshly world in which we live is a place of darkness and distress where we're being refined in a flaming furnace. Hence, spiritually speaking, Jesus was killed in this flaming place that is dark and miserable.

This is why the Bible makes such a big deal out of leaving Egypt, whether it was ancient Israelites during the famous Exodus or even Jesus as a child being called out of Egypt. Because we're all dwelling in spiritual Egypt, this dark place of misery. In fact, Scripture uses the exact phrase "out of Egypt" more than seventy times, and "out of the land of Egypt" more than eighty times.

"Out of Egypt have I called my son" (Matthew 2:15).

> "And by a prophet the LORD brought Israel **out of Egypt**, and by a proph-
> et was he preserved" (Hosea 12:13).

The Egypt out of which we're all being called is, when understood at
God speed, this physical human body and mindset of the flesh. We're not
meant to be held prisoner in this body and mindset forever. We're meant
to abandon the lusts and works of the flesh and even this body itself once
we die and are resurrected and **preserved** in an everlasting body, as we just
read in Hosea 12:13.

Knowing what we now know about connecting the dots at God speed,
Raiders of the Lost Ark is broadcasting the spiritual story of the Bible. The
ark of the covenant, representing God's dwelling place, was buried in the
land of Egypt, hidden in darkness under the earth, in a place of bondage or
captivity, which is inside physical people. But it's not meant to stay there.

The entire Bible is the instruction on how to make our personal Exodus out of this dark prison, to be freed from this place of misery so we can
join God in the light, as the Creator declares:

> "I will say to the prisoners, 'Come out in freedom,' and to those in dark-
> ness, 'Come into the light'" (Isaiah 49:9 NLT).

We human beings have become lost, wandering away by rebelling
against God, but Jesus came "to seek and to save that which was lost"
(Luke 19:10).

If we now read the entire verse from Isaiah 60:2 about darkness covering the people, it also tells us the amazing rest of the story, that we're not
meant to stay in the dark:

> "For look, darkness will cover the earth, and total darkness the peoples;
> but the LORD will **shine over you**, and **his glory will appear over
> you**" (Isaiah 60:2 CSB).

Yes, once we get in line with the divine Master Plan, the bright presence of God will make our darkness disappear, and, in the end, we'll be
shining brilliantly with the glorious light of God!

6TH GEAR:

The News: *The* Good, *the* Bad, *and the* Ugly

EVEN IF you don't listen to songs, tell children's stories, or watch TV commercials and movies, you're still being inundated with the message of God on yet another frequency. And that's through the news and historical events that take place every single day. That's right, folks, the words you hear in the news, even when they're "bad news," are all part of the Good News.

If you never thought about it this way, Jesus was and is a newscaster, informing people of very good news of how they can never die. The Bible many times even uses the phrase "good news," including:

> "The time is fulfilled, and the kingdom of God has come near. Repent and believe the good news!" (Mark 1:15 CSB).

When a newspaper splashes a headline such as "Runaway Child Rescued from Blazing Inferno," it's actually broadcasting the good news at God speed—if you have your eyes and ears open—because the report is picturing much more than a physical rescue. On the spirit level, all of us are the runaway children. We all have departed from God, and our end would be death in a blazing inferno, except for our rescue provided by the One who saves us, God.

When the local news on TV or radio announces a wandering toddler has been reunited with his family, it is broadcasting the happy end to all of our stories, since we are all the toddlers who have wandered away from our true Parent, and we'll be reunited with the divine Family when we stop our rebellion and return to God.

If we examine news through history, there's a reason the Renaissance, meaning rebirth, followed the Dark Ages. Because the Dark Ages represent our entire time dwelling in the flesh. What follows is our own renaissance, our rebirth into the light-filled spirit existence in the kingdom of God.

Since much of the news that gets aired these days is bad news, reporting ugly events filled with pain and sorrow, you may not realize you're still being bombarded with the Good News. What do I mean? Let's start with some of the biggest and deadliest news stories to help explain.

In 2020, a novel coronavirus called COVID-19 emerged and rapidly spread across the globe, reportedly killing more than three million worldwide as of this writing. The pandemic forced countless businesses and parks to close, devastating a roaring American economy and creating a palpable sense of fear and anxiety among millions living in lockdown mode.

In September 2019, Hurricane Dorian, a catastrophic Category 5 storm with winds of 185 mph, devastated the Bahamas, leaving more than seventy people confirmed dead and more than two hundred others missing. Those missing may never be found. Over the course of two days, the Bahamas, which is made up of more than seven hundred islands in what was considered by many to be a tropical paradise, was pummeled beyond recognition. The headline on the Drudge Report and other news sources shouted: "Paradise Lost."

On December 26, 2004, a 9.1-magnitude "megathrust" earthquake rocked Aceh on the northern tip of Sumatra island in Indonesia, causing a massive tsunami that raced across the Indian Ocean. More than 220,000 people (that's nearly a quarter of a million people) were killed by the giant wave in Indonesia and other countries, making it one of the worst natural disasters in history.

On March 11, 2011, a severe 9.0-magnitude quake shook Japan, creating a towering tsunami that leveled communities along Japan's northeastern coast. Some nineteen thousand people were left dead or missing as the wall of water traveling at the speed of a jet plane devoured everything in its path. The waves flooded the Fukushima Daiichi Nuclear Power Plant, creating reactor meltdowns in the worst atomic accident since the meltdown at the Chernobyl nuclear power plant in the former Soviet Union in 1986.

On April 15, 1912, more than 1,500 people sailing from England to the United States lost their lives when the RMS Titanic struck an iceberg in the North Atlantic and sank to the ocean floor, making it one of the deadliest peacetime marine disasters in history.

On September 11, 2001, infamously known as "9/11," nearly 3,000 people were killed in the United States during an onslaught of terrorist attacks devastating New York City, the Pentagon, and rural Pennsylvania. The attacks comprised the deadliest terrorist act in world history, and the most devastating foreign attack on American soil since Japan attacked Pearl Harbor on December 7, 1941, which left more than 2,400 dead.

OK, you get the idea. That's a lot of people perishing during catastrophes which have made screaming headlines across the world. But how is it possible that all this bad news can be part of the Good News? The answer is at God speed and lies in the fact that God is not merely about sunshine and happiness all the time.

What I'm about to tell you may blow your mind, because I know there are some folks who may not be able to handle it, even many God-fearing Bible-believers. What I'm going to show you is a decent number of Bible verses which explain exactly who is really responsible for the catastrophes, regardless of the mayhem being perpetrated by human beings or what people would term "natural causes." The passages will also clearly reveal **the reason** many disasters are taking place.

The simple truth right out of Holy Scripture is that God Himself is causing the disasters. Read it for yourself in your own Bible:

"I am about to bring disaster on everyone" (Jeremiah 45:5 CSB).

"Therefore, the LORD says: "I am planning disaster against this people, from which you cannot save yourselves. You will no longer walk proudly, for it will be a time of calamity" (Micah 2:3 NIV).

"If a disaster occurs in a city, hasn't the LORD done it?" (Amos 3:6 CSB).

"And the LORD said, I will destroy man whom I have created from the face of the earth" (Genesis 6:7).

"This is what the LORD says: 'I am about to bring disaster on you and will eradicate your descendants" (1 Kings 21:21 CSB).

"I will send famine and dangerous animals against you. They will leave you childless. Plague and bloodshed will sweep through you, and I will bring a sword against you. I, the LORD, have spoken" (Ezekiel 5:17 CSB).

> "This is what the LORD God of Israel says: 'I am about to bring such disaster on Jerusalem and Judah that everyone who hears about it will shudder'" (2 Kings 21:12 CSB).

> "Therefore, this is what the LORD says: I am about to bring on them disaster that they cannot escape. They will cry out to me, but I will not hear them" (Jeremiah 11:11 CSB).

> "The LORD has prepared everything for his purpose—even the wicked for the day of disaster" (Proverbs 16:4 CSB).

> "I make peace and create calamity; I, the LORD, do all these things" (Isaiah 45:7 NKJV).

Yes, I know it's a difficult pill for many people to swallow, but God is the Creator of *all* things, and disasters are among those things, albeit not pleasant ones. It's abundantly clear by these and many other verses in Scripture that God takes full responsibility for calamities.

This, of course, brings up the question of why. Why, if God is a loving Being, is He creating all this horrific mayhem? God actually spells out the reason quite plainly:

> "And they will know that I am the LORD; I did not threaten to bring this disaster on them without a reason" (Ezekiel 6:10 CSB).

> "Disaster will come to you in the future, because you will do what is evil in the LORD's sight" (Deuteronomy 31:29 CSB).

> "This disaster happened because the people of Israel sinned against the LORD their God" (2 Kings 17:7 CSB).

> "All this disaster has come on us, yet we have not sought the favor of the LORD our God by turning from our iniquities and paying attention to your truth. So the LORD kept the disaster in mind and brought it on us, for the LORD our God is righteous in all he has done. But we have not obeyed him" (Daniel 9:13–14 CSB).

> "This is what the Lord GOD says: Look, one disaster after another is coming!...I will not look on you with pity or spare you. I will punish you for your ways and for your detestable practices within you. Then you will know that it is I, the LORD, who strikes" (Ezekiel 7:5–9).

> "Listen, earth! I am about to bring disaster on these people, the fruit of their own plotting, for they have paid no attention to my words. They have rejected my instruction" (Jeremiah 6:19 CSB).

God makes it more than obvious. He causes catastrophes of all kinds—famines, plagues, wars, and more—because people aren't paying attention to His instructions. They have disobeyed the divine law, refusing to obey Him and instead choosing to engage in evil, detestable practices.

One infamous disaster in recent times is the 9/11 terror attacks mentioned moments ago. The onslaught of death from that single day in 2001 will echo far into the future. But what millions of people don't realize is that terror itself is a direct promise from God. He says it's the result of disobeying His rules:

> "But if you do not obey Me, and do not observe all these commandments...I also will do this to you: I will even appoint **terror** over you" (Leviticus 26:14–16 NKJV).

It could not be clearer. Irrespective of the thoughts and motivations in the minds of the perpetrators, terrorism is a result of breaking the divine code, the instructions of our Maker.

The collapse of New York City's Twin Towers on 9/11 is a perfect example of how God broadcasts His message in the news, because similar disasters are mentioned in the New Testament. Here's a brief, but relevant, passage as Jesus was discussing catastrophes, one of which was a tower collapse:

> "At that time, some people came and reported to him about the Galileans whose blood Pilate had mixed with their sacrifices. And he responded to them, 'Do you think that these Galileans were more sinful than all the other Galileans because they suffered these things?'"
>
> "No, I tell you; but unless you repent, you will all perish as well."
>
> "Or those eighteen that the tower in Siloam fell on and killed—do you think they were more sinful than all the other people who live in Jerusalem?"
>
> "No, I tell you; but unless you repent, you will all perish as well" (Luke 13:1–5 CSB).

So here we have Jesus, God in the flesh, giving an important lesson about disasters in the news, and He even mentions one involving a large tower that fell and killed many people. He asks if the people who died in those disasters were more sinful than any other typical citizen. And His answer is *no*! The fatal victims, whether it was in Jesus's day or on September 11, 2001, were not more sinful than other people. The problem is that **every human being** is sinful, and God caused the disaster to happen as a lesson. And what is the lesson? "Unless you repent, you will all perish as well." The message is for all of humanity in all time periods—past, present, and future.

In other words, we're all dead in God's sight already because of our sins and will be dead forever unless and until we repent, which means to turn around and stop our rebellious behavior toward God and get with His glorious program of eternal life! It's simple: Rebel and perish, or repent and live forever.

That's the news broadcast at God speed on 9/11 and those other catastrophic dates. And that's the glorious hope provided amid all these horrible calamities in the news. God has even inked it in Scripture that if people stop their ridiculous rebellion against Him, He'll stop disasters from occurring:

> "However, if that nation about which I have made the announcement turns from its evil, I will relent concerning the disaster I had planned to do to it" (Jeremiah 18:8 CSB).

> "Perhaps when the people of Judah hear about every disaster I plan to inflict on them, they will each turn from their wicked ways; then I will forgive their wickedness and their sin" (Jeremiah 36:3 NIV).

> "If I shut up heaven that there be no rain, or if I command the locusts to devour the land, or if I send pestilence among my people; If my people, which are called by my name, shall humble themselves, and pray, and seek my face, and turn from their wicked ways; then will I hear from heaven, and will forgive their sin, and will heal their land" (2 Chronicles 7:13–14).

Thus, the bad news taking place in our world is not just some random, haphazard mayhem. The catastrophes, calamities, and disasters of all stripes are attention-getters, reminding people that we're all going to perish, to be dead forever, unless we get our act together and get with the program.

If we connect the dots with what we've learned already, news headlines from today's newspapers will make much more sense, when they're understood at God speed. The bottom line is that bad news can be likened to an attention-getting spanking that a parent gives his or her child. But God does not like spanking His kids.

> "Why do you want more beatings? Why do you keep on rebelling?"
> (Isaiah 1:5 CSB).

He creates the bad news with an intention: to prompt us all to do some inward reflection and make drastic changes to how we think and act, to put an end to our ludicrous, wicked ways and get on the path of everlasting life. And painless life without end is truly Good News. So when you see and hear all kinds of fatal events in the news headlines today, remember that God is merely broadcasting the same message He has been airing since the beginning: "Unless you repent, you will all perish as well."

> "I don't want you to die, says the Sovereign LORD. Turn back and live!"
> (Ezekiel 18:32 NLT).

7TH GEAR:

Just Sayin'...

ONE OF the most intriguing ways to comprehend things at God speed is to examine famous sayings and idioms, as many are clearly broadcasting the messages of the Creator through simple words and phrases. Remember, "the Word was God" (John 1:1), so it makes perfect sense that God would be using words to embed divine messages in common phrases.

One just needs to have a good working knowledge of the Bible, along with synonyms, words that mean the same as other words. Plus, to make things interesting, we have to remember that sometimes words have two meanings.

I'm going to present a list here of some very well-known sayings, proverbs, catchphrases, whatever you wish to call them, and then provide you a possible or even likely definition when it comes to divine messaging. Sometimes, the message will be straightforward without much explanation needed. In other cases, there may be a little "splainin' to do," as Ricky Ricardo used to say on *I Love Lucy*.

Let's start with some easy ones you should have no trouble understanding by now, based on what you've already learned here.

LIVE HAPPILY EVER AFTER

To "live happily ever after" means to live happily for the rest of one's life and is most often used in storybooks and fairy tales, indicating that people, usually a couple, dwell together in a perpetual, joyful state.

As I already mentioned in the section about children's stories, this phrase is actually telling the end of the Bible story, as people who get right with God will live happily ever after, as in being alive forever in a very happy state of mind.

> "You will live in joy and peace" (Isaiah 55:12 NLT).

"Live happily ever after" is related to some other popular expressions, including "get a life," "happy ending," and "let's live here," which is one of the final lines spoken by Bill Murray in his *Groundhog Day* film. Obviously, the keyword is *live*, as in being alive forever, which should make anyone happy.

RISE AND SHINE!

"Rise and shine" is an instruction telling someone to wake up from sleep and get moving with the day.

Interestingly, almost this exact phrase is breathed by God: "**Arise, shine**, for your light has come, and the glory of the LORD shines over you" (Isaiah 60:1 CSB).

It's stated another way in the New Testament:

> "Wake up, sleeper, rise from the dead, and Christ will shine on you" (Ephesians 5:14 NIV).

This totally agrees with what was noted before in discussing Madonna feeling shiny and new in her "Like a Virgin" song. When we're awakened from our sleep of death when we rise from the grave, we will be shining:

> "Then the righteous will **shine** like the sun" (Matthew 13:43 CSB).

Thus, at the moment we're brought back to life by God, we will "rise and shine!"

CUT FROM THE SAME CLOTH

To be "cut from the same cloth" simply means to be very similar to each other.

Biblically speaking, we have been cut from the same cloth as God, as we're very similar to Him, since we're His children. Scripture uses words such as "rock" and "quarry" instead of cloth to convey the exact same idea:

> "Look to the rock from which you were cut, and to the quarry from which you were dug" (Isaiah 51:1).

LIKE FATHER, LIKE SON

"Like father, like son" is said when a son resembles his father, and shows similarities to his dad in mannerisms, interests, behavior, and the like.

Scripture says the precise thing about God the Father and His Son, Jesus:

> The Son is the radiance of God's glory and the exact representation of his being, sustaining all things by his powerful word. (Hebrews 1:3 NIV)

And not only is Jesus like His Father, we will be like God too!

> "Dear friends, we are already God's children, but he has not yet shown us what we will be like when Christ appears. But we do know that we will be **like him**..." (1 John 3:2 NLT).

STAND CORRECTED

Most people already understand that to "stand corrected" is to admit when we're incorrect or when we've been proven wrong. This is something hugely important we all need to learn in life—to admit when we're wrong. But there is a higher spirit meaning to "stand corrected," and it has to do with receiving eternal life when we're corrected by God.

> "But consider the joy of those **corrected** by God!" (Job 5:17 NLT).

> "The wicked are overthrown and perish, but the house of the righteous will **stand**" (Proverbs 12:7 CSB).

In other words, when we're corrected by God, we will live forever. We will "stand corrected." And it all starts by admitting that our own way, when it's opposing God, is the wrong way.

CLEANUP NEEDED IN PRODUCE

I heard this phrase on the loudspeaker while shopping at a supermarket, as someone had apparently made a big mess of something in the produce section, and it needed to be cleaned up. And then it hit me.

"Cleanup needed in produce" summarizes our current state of affairs in our personal lives and in our world in general. We human beings are the produce, "the offspring of God" (Acts 17:29).

We've made a big mess of ourselves and our world, and we need to be cleaned up. This desire for clean thoughts and a pure heart is expressed numerous times in Scripture, including:

> "Create in me a **clean** heart, O God; and renew a right spirit within me" (Psalm 51:10).

> "If you keep yourself **pure**, you will be a special utensil for honorable use. Your life will be **clean**, and you will be ready for the Master to use you for every good work" (2 Timothy 2:21 NLT).

And, in keeping with the supermarket analogy, people in the Bible are actually referred to as produce, with a variety of agricultural terms like crops, harvest, trees, fruit, and so on.

> "As soon as the crop is ready, he sends for the sickle, because the harvest has come" (Mark 4:29 CSB).

> "A good tree can't produce bad fruit; neither can a bad tree produce good fruit" (Matthew 7:18 CSB).

So the next time you're at the supermarket and you hear "cleanup needed in produce," realize you're hearing a divine message from God for all of his produce, which is us, to clean up our act.

RUNAWAY BRIDE

"Runaway bride" is a descriptive and somewhat comical phrase for any woman who sprints away from her spouse-to-be. She simply does not want to marry, or unite, with her man. The concept was made into a popular, romantic-comedy film in 1999 starring Richard Gere and Julia Roberts as the *Runaway Bride*. One classic line expressed by Ms. Roberts in the film explained her own mindset: "I'm profoundly and irreversibly screwed up."

Here's the spirit template behind this well-known phrase.

Like the song "Runaway Train" mentioned earlier, the runaway bride represents humanity as a whole that is going the wrong direction on a one-way track, running *away* from God instead of toward Him. We are the bride of God collectively dashing away from His presence and love, as most of us are unwilling to follow His instructions. That's precisely what makes us profoundly screwed up, not wanting to be united with our Divine Spouse.

We've seen these verses before, but they can't be stressed enough because God's "bride" is a reference to all of us human beings:

> "I am married unto you" (Jeremiah 3:14).

> "Let us be glad, rejoice, and give him glory, because the marriage of the Lamb has come, and his bride has prepared herself" (Revelation 19:7 CSB).

And since the Garden of Eden when the first human bride was tricked by the devil and initiated the rebellion against her Ultimate Man, our running away from God has never stopped, despite constant pleas from God for His beloved, all humanity, to come back: "Return to Me, and I will return to you" (Malachi 3:7 NKJV).

Eventually, there will come a time when people's hearts will be touched by God so they'll desire Him again and no longer run away.

> "Then I will give them a heart to know Me, that I am the LORD; and they shall be My people, and I will be their God, for they shall return to Me with their whole heart" (Jeremiah 24:7 NKJV).

BABY ON BOARD

This cute little sign declaring "baby on board" is a reminder that a vehicle is carrying a precious cargo of a young child or children. It's not only found on cars, but also some pregnant women sport that message on T-shirts. It's similar to the fun phrase "a bun in the oven."

When thinking at God speed, the analogy refers to God and human beings. God is the ultimate vehicle, and He is carrying and transporting His beloved cargo, us babies, the children of God. We're the babies on board with Him.

Meanwhile, each individual believer's body is also a vehicle, and the precious cargo we're carrying inside is the presence of God, the unborn child of God who, when ready for birth, will come out of darkness, out of the flesh, and be "born again" into the spirit world. When we're on board with God, we are all the babies on board.

NOW HIRING SERVERS

I recently saw the phrase "now hiring servers" on a restaurant billboard, and it can be found in the Help Wanted section of countless newspapers.

It made me realize that at the present time, God Himself is now hiring servers, who, in Scripture, are called servants or workers.

> "Hallelujah! Give praise, servants of the LORD" (Psalm 113:1 CSB).

> "For the kingdom of heaven is like a landowner who went out early in the morning to hire workers" (Matthew 20:1 CSB).

And as far as the phrase "Help Wanted" is concerned, that sentiment is expressed many times in Scripture, as people are openly requesting and wanting God's help:

> "Help me, O LORD my God" (Psalm 109:26).

> "Come quickly to me, O God. You are my help and my deliverer" (Psalm 70:5 NIV).

The "help wanted" theme is found right at the beginning, as the second human being created is called "a helper":

> "And the LORD God said, 'It is not good that man should be alone; I will make him a helper comparable to him'" (Genesis 2:18 NKJV).

LESS IS MORE

The expression "less is more" is the popular notion that simplicity and clarity are better than overblowing something, thus leading to good design.

On the spirit level, it is promoting the message about being less in one's own sight, as opposed to being proud and arrogant. In other words, to be small, humble, and meek is "more." It's a greatly preferred trait over being full of oneself.

This is demonstrated often in Scripture, using phrases synonymous to "less is more."

> "Blessed are the **meek**: for they shall inherit the earth" (Matthew 5:5).

When Jesus explained the kingdom of God, He said, "It is like a grain of mustard seed, which, when it is sown in the earth, is **less** than all the seeds that be in the earth: But when it is sown, it groweth up, and becometh **greater** than all herbs, and shooteth out **great** branches" (Mark 4:31–32).

> "All of you clothe yourselves with humility toward one another, because God resists the proud but gives grace to the humble. Humble yourselves, therefore, under the mighty hand of God, so that he may exalt you at the proper time" (1 Peter 5:5–6 CSB).

DON'T SOIL YOURSELF

When most people hear the phrase "don't soil yourself" these days, they probably understand it as something to the effect of "don't worry" or "don't poop your pants."

But there is a more straightforward meaning, and that's simply instructing us not to get soiled, as in dirty, messy, or filthy. This, of course, is a main theme of the Bible, to keep ourselves clean spiritually, and not to soil ourselves with the filth of evil.

> "Yet there are some in the church...who have not **soiled** their clothes with evil. They will walk with me in white, for they are worthy" (Revelation 3:4 NLT).

> "But now, put away all the following: anger, wrath, malice, slander, and **filthy** language from your mouth" (Colossians 3:8 CSB).

WASH YOUR HANDS, WASH YOUR FEET, WASH YOUR CLOTHES

How many times do we wash our hands or wash our feet in life? How many times do we do laundry and wash our clothes? Probably too many to keep an accurate count. And there's good reason for keeping everything clean, both on the physical level and the spirit level as well.

In the physical world, keeping one's hands, feet, and clothing clean, free of grime, germs, and foul odor is important in keeping our bodies healthy. But there's so much on the spirit level in these phrases and practices, that it's worth a close look.

Let's start with the word *wash*. It's a simple term that everyone understands, meaning to cleanse, usually with water, the universal solvent. On the spirit level, the filth we're removing from ourselves is sin, our iniquity, our evil actions breaking God's instructions.

> "**Wash** me thoroughly from my **iniquity**, And **cleanse** me from my **sin**"
> (Psalm 51:2 NKJV).

> "Wash and make yourselves clean. Take your evil deeds out of my sight;
> stop doing wrong" (Isaiah 1:16 NIV).

A person's hands are the instruments by which he or she does things, whether they be good or bad. Thus, the people who are granted eternal life in God's kingdoms are the ones who have "clean hands":

> "Who may ascend the mountain of the LORD? Who may stand in his
> holy place? The one who has **clean hands** and a pure heart, who
> has not appealed to what is false, and who has not sworn deceitfully"
> (Psalm 24:3–4 CSB).

A person's feet are the instruments that have us either walking toward God or away from Him. For most people, it's usually away:

> "Their feet run to evil" (Isaiah 59:7).

People are instructed, though, to walk the straight, godly path with their feet:

> "Keep your feet away from evil" (Proverbs 4:27 CSB).

And there are those who have done so:

> "I have kept my feet from every evil path so that I might obey your word"
> (Psalm 119:101 NIV).

The phrase "wash your feet" is not just intended for our own benefit, it's for others as well. In a famous part of the New Testament, Jesus personally washed the feet of His own disciples, even over the initial objection of the apostle Peter. But when He was finished washing their feet, He said:

> "If I then, your Lord and Teacher, have washed your feet, you also ought
> to wash one another's feet. For I have given you an example, that you
> should do as I have done to you" (John 13:14–15 NKJV).

Now, here's where it gets interesting as we connect the dots and think at God speed. We've already seen that our feet are what takes us to evil, walking the wrong, sinful, ungodly path. So when Jesus tells us to wash one another's feet, He is instructing His followers to help keep everyone else clean, spiritually speaking. In other words, part of the divine instruction in serving others is to "wash their feet," that is, keep them clean from whatever sin there is in this world that makes them filthy in God's sight. Just as Jesus washed His disciples' feet, He said it was an example for us to wash others. Thus, more people will be made and kept clean and granted eternal life!

Along the same lines as washing our hands and feet is washing our clothes, garments, and robes. On the spirit level, it represents keeping God's commandments and purifying ourselves by accepting the death penalty that Jesus took on Himself in our place.

> "These are they which came out of great tribulation, and have **washed their robes**, and made them white in the blood of the Lamb" (Revelation 7:14).

> "Blessed are those who **wash their robes**, so that they may have the right to the tree of life and may enter the city by the gates" (Revelation 22:14 CSB).

CHANGE YOUR CLOTHES

Related to washing clothes is something you probably do quite often, and that is change your clothes. And, no surprise, the concept is stressed in the Bible, not focusing on a physical change of garments on your body but changing your sinful way of life and becoming obedient to God for a change, putting on a new outfit of obedience:

> "Get rid of the foreign gods that are among you. Purify yourselves and **change your clothes**" (Genesis 35:2 CSB).

> "See, I have taken away your sins, and now I am giving you these **fine new clothes**" (Zechariah 3:4 NLT).

By now, it should be clear. Washing our hands, feet, and clothing as well as changing our clothing is not just about removing the physical dirt and grime from our bodies and garments. When we hear such phrases with our ears open to listen to the divine message at God speed, we're actually being told to clean up our act, to stop our filthy rebellion against our Maker, and be cleansed of all wickedness so we can emerge from the ground from whence we came and rise to an everlasting life of impeccably clean thoughts and actions. Our final change of clothing will be to remove of our garment of flesh and be clothed with spirit as God's immortal children.

CHANGE OR DIE

In a similar vein, we often hear the phrase "change or die" in the business world, as companies continuously need to change, as in adapt or reinvent themselves, in order to survive. One 2020 news story in *Variety* magazine used the exact phrase "change or die" in its headline to describe the media industry, saying "many industry execs believe they need to change the ways they've done business—or see their companies perish."

Once again, this broadcasts the message of Scripture, which tells us countless times to repent, to change our ways for the better, and amend our doings, all of which mean the same thing. And if we don't? We're dead.

> "Repent, repent of your evil ways! Why will you die...?"
> (Ezekiel 33:11 CSB).

> "Unless you repent, you too will all perish" (Luke 13:3 NIV).

I GIVE YOU MY WORD

When people hear the phrase "I give you my word," they understand that someone is telling them the truth in the most personal way. This, of course, has all sorts of spirit meaning behind it.

First, as mentioned before, God is personally represented by the Word:

> "In the beginning was the Word, and the Word was with God, and the Word was God" (John 1:1).

> "His name is called The Word of God" (Revelation 19:13).

And Jesus, known as the Word, says He is the truth: "I am the way, the truth, and the life" (John 14:6).

Thus, the phrase "I give you my word" can be understood in more than one way:

1. I give you God

2. I give you Jesus

3. I give you the Truth

With our spirit ears open, these are all saying the same thing.

YOU ARE WHAT YOU EAT

From our earliest ages, we're all taught "you are what you eat," as people understand that our bodies are actually composed of and sustained by the nutrients in the food we consume. This needs no further explanation on the physical level. But now let's turn on our spirit ears, or in this case, our spirit taste buds, to understand what this popular phrase means.

First, what is it that we eat? Of course, the answer is food, bread, meat, and the like, and Scripture uses all these words to describe what we toss down that giant hole in our face. And on the spirit level, what is the real food? Jesus said:

> "For my flesh is real food and my blood is real drink" (John 6:55 NIV).

In case you never made the connection, the main course at the Passover meal is lamb, and Jesus is called "the Lamb of God, who takes away the sin of the world!" (John 1:29 CSB).

In the same vein, during the Feast of Unleavened Bread, people ingest bread that is not puffed up, because conceited people are usually puffed up with pride. In other words, during that festival, we consume the humble Jesus, who says: "I am the bread of life!" (John 6:48 NLT).

So hopefully you understand that the real nourishment we're intended to consume on the spirit level is God Himself, and everything for which He stands. God even comments about people purchasing what they think is food but really has no eternal benefit.

> "Why do you spend silver on what is not food, and your wages on what does not satisfy? Listen carefully to me, and eat what is good, and you will enjoy the choicest of foods" (Isaiah 55:2 CSB).

So the phrase "you are what you eat" has an astonishingly glorious message. It is saying that we are, or at least we will become, all that God is, because we are eating (consuming and digesting) God on the highest level, the spirit level, as we accept His teachings into our mind.

When we accept God's promises and become obedient people, human beings are to "be filled with all the fullness of God" (Ephesians 3:19 NKJV).

This is why God says: "I am the LORD your God...Open your mouth wide, and I will fill it" (Psalm 81:10 CSB).

I CAN BUY THAT

Among the most popular sayings in the English language are "I can buy that" and its opposite, "I don't buy it," and ironically, neither has anything to do with an actual purchase of something.

It has to do with going along with an idea, to agree with it. But if you don't buy it, you obviously don't think it's true.

This notion of "buying" an idea comes directly from Scripture:

> "Buy the truth, and sell it not; also wisdom, and instruction, and understanding" (Proverbs 23:23).

In other words, believe the truth, and don't get rid of it, as in selling it, once you have it. Now, I can buy that.

MY FEET ARE KILLING ME

Millions of people worldwide use the phrase "my feet are killing me," to describe the aches and pains in their feet, especially after a long time standing, walking, running, or working. There's even a new TV show on TLC that debuted in 2020 called *My Feet Are Killing Me*.

But now that you're learning to see the invisible messages broadcast at God speed, there's an important communication from God being aired that could save you from the "killing" and grant you eternal life.

The word to focus on is *feet*. We all know what feet are and how they help us stand, give us balance, and allow us to walk or even run at great speeds.

But on the spirit level when it comes to our character and actions we take, we're either walking uprightly and balanced toward God, or walking or running away from Him, as in being disobedient to His instructions:

> "My son, do not go along with them, do not set foot on their paths; for their feet rush into evil, they are swift to shed blood" (Proverbs 1:15–16 NIV).

The result of our feet walking in the wrong direction is misery and destruction:

> "Their feet run to do evil, and they rush to commit murder. They think only about sinning. Misery and destruction always follow them" (Isaiah 59:7 NLT).

Many times in Scripture, God urges us to use our feet properly, to "walk worthy of God who calls you into His own kingdom and glory" (1 Thessalonians 2:12 NKJV) so that we never again have to say, "My feet are killing me." We can live forever.

PLENTY OF FISH IN THE SEA

The phrase "there are plenty of fish in the sea" is often used to comfort people who just broke up with their loved one and are heartbroken. It's an adage letting everyone know there are plenty of other people out there in the world with whom we can have a relationship. There's even a website called Plenty of Fish designed to help people find true love.

But why is the word *fish* used to represent people? And why does the term *sea* represent the world? Because that's how Scripture uses those terms, with God equating human beings living in our world with fish swimming in the sea. Fish represent people, and the sea is the place where the fish dwell. It's that simple. Here's how the Bible puts it:

> "You have made mankind like the fish of the sea" (Habakkuk 1:14 CSB).

> "'Come, follow me,'" Jesus said, 'and I will send you out to fish for people'" (Matthew 4:19 NIV).

> "The Lord said…I will bring my people again from the depths of the sea" (Psalm 68:22).

Knowing this concept of fish representing people can help us understand the beginning and end of our story, as we have been given dominion, which is godly rulership, over other people:

> "And God said, Let us make man in our image, after our likeness: and let them have dominion over the fish of the sea" (Genesis 1:26).

When most people read this verse, they often think only on a physical level, about human beings having sovereignty over literal marine creatures swimming in rivers, lakes, or the ocean. But once again, with our spirit eyes and ears open at God speed, the Maker is saying He created mankind to be like Him, to have benevolent rulership over other individuals.

If we read the entire verse, we can see the Bible uses every kind of beast, not just fish, to refer to all of mankind.

> "They will rule the fish of the sea, the birds of the sky, the livestock, the whole earth, and the creatures that crawl on the earth" (Genesis 1:26 CSB).

SLEEP WITH THE FISHES

On the subject of fish, there's a famous saying popularized by *The Godfather* film, and that is when someone "sleeps with the fishes." In the movie, the line refers to a mobster getting whacked, as in killed, with his body dumped in some large body of water where fish dwell.

At God speed, this is an exact metaphor for the spiritual state of most human beings at this very moment. As we just learned with "plenty of fish in the sea," fish represent people, and the sea is the place where the fish dwell. Sleep, as we've seen, symbolizes death in Scripture, as it talks of sleeping "the sleep of death" (Psalm 13:3).

Thus, when we connect the dots, the phrase "sleeping with the fishes" simply means "being dead among the people" in both *The Godfather* and the Bible. Anyone who is not awake, who is not alive spiritually, is sleeping with the fishes, dead among everyone else in this giant sea where we all swim in our daily lives.

Related sayings such as "asleep at the wheel," "asleep at the switch," and "napping on the job" all convey a similar message. We're meant to be alive and awake, staying alert and paying attention, not sleeping the sleep of death. As we've read before: "Wake up, sleeper, rise from the dead, and Christ will shine on you" (Ephesians 5:14 NIV).

STOP NEEDLING ME

Everyone at some point in life has experienced some sort of teasing or torment at the hands of others, and they understand the phrase "stop needling me." It's similar to "don't poke the bear" and "death by a thousand pricks," as people get easily annoyed by all sorts of tiny jabs and irritants. Even in the comedy world, people use terms such as barbs, jabs, poking fun, nailing, and skewering.

But did you know the roots of such sayings are found in the Bible? The concept is simple and has to do with what needles and pricks have in common. They are sharp, piercing objects causing discomfort and sometimes severe pain. In case you never thought about it, here are some typical examples of needles, thorns, and prickers we experience in everyday life:

* A less-than-courteous driver cutting you off on the highway

* A car mechanic overcharging you

* Your boss firing or laying you off from your job

* Someone giving you a personal insult

* An annoying friend, relative, or co-worker

* A romantic interest rejecting you

* Someone lying about you

* A nonlethal crime committed against you

* Anyone pressing your buttons to irritate, harass, or make fun of you

While none of these are life threatening, they all needle you, poke at your peace of mind, test your patience, and disturb your sense of calm, causing anxiety, stress, and worries. They are human thorns, thistles, splinters, barbs, briers, and prickers. They're the penetrating stingers on human bees, wasps, hornets, and scorpions. They are sharp blades on human knives, spears, swords, axes, and arrows.

This is all reflected in Scripture in a variety of ways that will help you hear the song God is singing on the spirit level:

"But the godless are like **thorns** to be thrown away, for they tear the hand that touches them" (2 Samuel 23:6 NLT).

"They surrounded me like **bees**; they were extinguished like a fire among **thorns**; in the name of the LORD I destroyed them. They pushed me hard to make me fall" (Psalm 118:12–13 CSB).

"Telling lies about others is as harmful as hitting them with an **ax**, wounding them with a **sword**, or shooting them with a **sharp arrow**" (Proverbs 25:18 NLT).

"But if you don't drive out the inhabitants of the land before you, those you allow to remain will become **barbs** for your eyes and **thorns** for your sides; they will harass you..." (Numbers 33:55 CSB).

"For the ground that drinks the rain that often falls on it and that produces vegetation useful to those for whom it is cultivated receives a blessing from God. But if it produces **thorns** and **thistles**, it is worthless and about to be cursed, and at the end will be burned" (Hebrews 6:7–8 CSB).

"The seed that fell among **thorns** stands for those who hear, but as they go on their way they are choked by life's worries, riches, and pleasures, and they do not mature" (Luke 8:14 NIV).

"Faithful people have vanished from the land; there is no one upright among the people. All of them wait in ambush to shed blood; they hunt each other with a net. Both hands are good at accomplishing evil: the official and the judge demand a bribe; when the powerful man communicates his evil desire, they plot it together. The best of them is like a **brier**; the most upright is worse than a **hedge of thorns**" (Micah 7:2–4).

By now, it should be more than obvious. All these sharp splinters, thorns, and stingers in nature stand for all those inflicting emotional and physical pain as they oppose God's way of peace. They are the needles that prick us and cause us to bleed. With this in mind, we can now fully understand one of the most famous, yet enigmatic, sayings in all history, which happens to come from the Bible itself:

> "It is easier for a camel to go through the eye of a **needle** than for a rich man to enter into the kingdom of God" (Mark 10:25).

On a physical level, this saying is incomprehensible to millions of readers, as they wonder how the giant beast that is a camel could pass through the eye, or hole, of a needle. The physical animal simply cannot accomplish such a feat. But when we think about this at God speed on the spirit level, the meaning becomes clear.

Camels represent faithful and obedient believers. We're the servant animals, the beasts of burden who do God's will. And when we're confronted by a needle of any kind, any of the sharp, human cutters and prickers listed above, we can defeat them, figuratively "pass through" them, by employing our supernatural shield of faith:

> "In every situation take up the **shield of faith** with which you can **extinguish all the flaming arrows** of the evil one" (Ephesians 6:16 CSB).

It's our faith and trust in God that allows us to do the so-called impossible and pass through the eye of the needle. Jesus confirms this as he answers the question of "Who then can be saved?" in the same parable about the camel passing through the eye of the needle:

> "With men it is impossible, but not with God: for with God all things are possible" (Mark 10:27).

MAN UP!

This is a command for people to grow some intestinal fortitude, stop being such complete and utter wimps, and rise to the occasion. At God speed, it's telling us to be courageous and strong, not to be cowards, and in the end we will rise up, as in be elevated to the next level where the Divine Man in the spirit story dwells, the coming kingdom of God. There are countless commands in the Bible to be courageous and not to fear, including:

> "Be of good courage, and let us behave ourselves valiantly for our people"
> (1 Chronicles 19:13).

> "Fear not, little flock; for it is your Father's good pleasure to give you the
> kingdom" (Luke 12:32).

TOMORROW IS ANOTHER DAY, LIVE TO SEE ANOTHER DAY, SEE YOU TOMORROW, COME BACK TOMORROW

Well-known phrases dealing with tomorrow and another day may seem to most people inconsequential or trivial. But they actually deal with our future. Because that other day, the next day that is tomorrow, is our future. It's what Fleetwood Mac refers to in the song, "Don't Stop," when the band tells us not to stop thinking about tomorrow.

We all know there is the past, the present, and the future. It's common in our language to refer to the past as if it were one day, "yesterday." We often call the present "today." And we all refer to the indefinite future as "tomorrow." So all of time is actually encompassed within three days: yesterday, today, and tomorrow.

Even with something as simple as checking your flight status on any airline, the carriers will ask for your specific flight for yesterday (the past), today (the present), and tomorrow (the future).

This counting of time exists because it's the way God accounts for all time, and it's mentioned throughout Scripture, in both the Old and New Testaments, as the phrase "three days" occurs dozens of times.

Jesus Himself is mentioned as being the same in all three time periods: past, present, and future.

> "Jesus Christ is the same yesterday, today, and forever"
> (Hebrews 13:8 NKJV).

THE NEW YOU

The phrase "the new you" is most often used today to describe a major change in someone, be it character, attitude, or even something about one's physical appearance, such as a dazzling new hairstyle or dropping unwanted weight and getting in shape.

This notion has a related meaning in the Bible, as God urges people to put off the old self, and put on the new you:

> "Do not lie to one another, since you have put off the old self with its practices and have put on the **new self**. You are being renewed in knowledge according to the image of your Creator" (Colossians 3:9 CSB).

> "Put on the **new self**, the one created according to God's likeness in righteousness and purity of the truth" (Ephesians 4:24 CSB).

In other words, "the new you" is referring to our new life in God:

> "This means that anyone who belongs to Christ has become a **new person**. The old life is gone; a new life has begun!" (2 Corinthians 5:17 NLT).

This should not be a surprise, as Jesus said at the end of the story: "Look, I am making everything **new**" (Revelation 21:5 CSB).

DESTINED FOR GREATNESS

"Destined for greatness" is a very uplifting saying, as it gives people hope for the future, letting them know their awesome destiny in advance.

Most people, however, don't realize they've been destined for incredible greatness all along, if they get with God's program of obedience:

> "Then the sovereignty, power, and **greatness** of all the kingdoms under heaven will be given to the holy people of the Most High" (Daniel 7:27 NLT).

It's simpler than we think. Human beings who are obedient to God have their destiny already set, as they are destined to be glorified as the actual sons of God:

> "We declare God's wisdom, a mystery that has been hidden and that God destined for our glory before time began" (1 Corinthians 2:7 NIV).

> "He predestined us to be adopted as sons through Jesus Christ for himself, according to the good pleasure of his will" (Ephesians 1:5 CSB).

Another Bible version of that last verse makes it even clearer, how we've been destined for greatness:

"God decided in advance to adopt us into his own family by bringing us to himself through Jesus Christ. This is what he wanted to do, and it gave him great pleasure" (Ephesians 1:5 NLT).

Make no mistake about it. If you make the effort to be on God's team, you're destined for greatness.

8TH GEAR:

It's Only Natural

AMONG THE most clear-cut ways to understand God speed is to study nature, as everything that has been made in the natural world is, in one way or another, broadcasting the message of the Creator. The Bible makes no secret of this:

> "For his invisible attributes, that is, his eternal power and divine nature, have been clearly seen since the creation of the world, being **understood through what he has made**. As a result, people are without excuse" (Romans 1:20 CSB).

> "The heavens declare the glory of God, and the expanse proclaims **the work of his hands**. Day after day they pour out speech; night after night they **communicate knowledge**.... Their **message** has gone out to the whole earth, and their **words** to the ends of the world" (Psalm 19:1–4 CSB).

With this in mind, let's take a look now at some very evident things in the natural world that shed light on what God is saying at the spirit level.

THE SMELL TEST

Virtually everyone is familiar with "the smell test." If something smells sweet or emits a pleasant fragrance, it's associated with goodness or truth. But if something doesn't pass the smell test, it does not smell good. It stinks, it reeks, and its rottenness suggests there's something dreadfully wrong. Using our sense of smell properly in our natural world is one of the easiest ways to understand God speed.

Here are some Bible verses that transmit the big difference between good and bad scents:

> "The **fragrance of your perfume** is intoxicating; your name is **perfume** poured out. No wonder young women adore you" (Song of Songs 1:3 CSB).

> "May your breasts be like clusters of grapes, and the **fragrance** of your breath like apricots" (Song of Songs 7:8 CSB).

> "And it shall come to pass, that instead of **sweet smell** there shall be **stink**" (Isaiah 3:24).

> "These people are a **stench** in my nostrils, an **acrid smell** that never goes away" (Isaiah 65:5 NLT).

> "The LORD is angry with all the nations, furious with all their armies. He will set them apart for destruction, giving them over to slaughter. Their slain will be thrown out, and the **stench of their corpses** will rise" (Isaiah 34:2–3 CSB).

> "'The **stench of death** filled the air! But still you would not return to me,' says the LORD" (Amos 4:10 NLT).

Obviously, delicious aromas such as perfume or sweet fruit represent good things in the mind of God. But when He mentions a stink, stench, or acrid smell, He's broadcasting the message of anything that is foul, rotten, or wrong, often referring to rebellious people or their putrid actions.

Here in our physical world, the worst smell we can encounter is the horrific stench of death. Whether it's a dead animal decaying in your attic or a dead human being decomposing at a crime scene, there is nothing more rank than a dead creature. There's an important reason for this at God speed. It's because there is nothing worse than the eternal death of any person. The worst thing that can happen to us is death, and, therefore, the worst smell is the foul odor of death.

Death is the absence of life, and through our physical sense of smell, God is letting everyone know the opposite ends of our existence. We can have very pleasant, everlasting life that we can sense through things that smell good. Or we can have death, the essence of which is aired through rancid odors. Spiritually speaking, good thoughts and actions smell good to God, while wicked thoughts and actions smell bad to Him. It's as simple as that.

God has even declared that people who truly follow Him are a life-giving perfume, the actual sweet fragrance of Jesus Christ. On the other hand, rebels who remain attached to this mortal world are of the opinion that believers stink:

> "For to God we are the **fragrance of Christ** among those who are being saved and among those who are perishing" (2 Corinthians 2:15 CSB).

> "To those who are perishing, we are a **dreadful smell of death and doom**. But to those who are being saved, we are a **life-giving perfume**" (2 Corinthians 2:16 NLT).

Thus, if you have a nose for news, the good news of life everlasting, you can follow your nose by using the smell test to help discern that which is good versus that which is evil. We should always exercise all of our senses, as we don't wish to end up like lifeless idols condemned by God:

> "They have ears, but they do not hear; **Noses** they have, but **they do not smell**" (Psalm 115:6 NKJV).

THE CENTER OF IT ALL

When we look at our solar system, we see a magnificent, inspiring ball of fire called the sun at the center, and planets of different size held together in orbits as they revolve around this life-giving sun. The solar system exists this way because it's an analogy for God, who is the center of all things, holding everything together in orbit around Him.

> "He is before all things, and by him all things hold together" (Colossians 1:17 CSB).

What's surprising to some is that in Scripture, God is actually represented by the sun:

> "For the LORD God is a sun" (Psalm 84:11).

> "I am...the bright and morning star" (Revelation 22:16).

It's also interesting how God is known as the "Son," a word that sounds exactly like "sun."

And God's personal dwelling, whether it's called His "sanctuary," "Jerusalem," or "the Lamb," is located at the center of everything, with all other things moving around the center.

> "The sanctuary of the LORD shall be in the **center**" (Ezekiel 48:10 NKJV).

> "This is what the Lord GOD says: I have set this Jerusalem in the **center** of the **nations**, with countries all around her" (Ezekiel 5:5 CSB).

> "For the Lamb who is at the **center** of the throne will shepherd them" (Revelation 7:17 CSB).

Everything (including us) revolves around God, who is the center of all things yesterday, today, and tomorrow. So when we say something as basic as the earth revolves around the sun, at God speed it's another way of saying we human beings (who are made up of the earth) revolve around God. Yeah, it's "heavier" than gravity, man.

This model can be seen not only looking outward into our vast solar system, but also inward at the tiniest building blocks in our physical universe, down to the atomic level.

As we all learned in science class, every atom has a center called a nucleus. This nucleus has a positive charge. And just like the sun in our solar system, the nucleus has objects orbiting around it that are never able to escape its pull. Those objects swirling around the middle of an atom are called electrons and always carry a negative charge.

Hopefully, at this point, the higher spirit meaning should be getting clear. The nucleus, the center of everything, represents God. The positive charge of the nucleus reflects God's positive character, and its exceedingly small size depicts the fact that God is exceptionally meek and humble.

Just as the nucleus at the atom's center is surrounded by negatively charged electrons whose orbit cannot escape its pull, so God is surrounded by negative people who can't escape the presence of God:

> "The wicked surround the righteous" (Habakkuk 1:4 NKJV).

> "I can never escape from your Spirit! I can never get away from your presence!" (Psalm 139:7 NLT).

It's interesting to note that electrons move in shells outside the nucleus, with lots of empty space in between, and atoms always keep trying to fill their shells. In other words, they naturally don't like being alone and empty. They're looking to bond. This is how and why they join with other atoms, uniting to form a molecule of any substance, such as water.

This is significant because the structure and movement of atoms fit the Bible template of what the earth and people are. They are shells of empty space looking to be filled, seeking to be inhabited, and to bond with others. When we remember that people are the earth, since we consist of earth, we can see clearly that all of creation, including people, are intended to be filled:

> "He is God; he who fashioned and made the earth, he founded it; he did not create it to be empty, but formed it to be inhabited" (Isaiah 45:18 NIV).

> "But as truly as I live, all the earth shall be filled with the glory of the LORD" (Numbers 14:21).

> "Christ, who fills all things everywhere with himself" (Ephesians 1:23 NLT).

Unfortunately, most people have corrupted God's intentions, and have, at least for now, filled themselves with violence and evil instead of God's own presence.

> "Now the earth was corrupt in God's sight, and the earth was filled with wickedness" (Genesis 6:11 CSB).

And regarding the bonding, people are given this urgent instruction from the apostle Paul: "Above all, put on love, which is the perfect bond of unity" (Colossians 3:14 CSB).

It's also intriguing and somewhat cute that this basic building block in our physical world, the atom, sounds the same to our ears as the name of the basic building blocks of humanity, as men and women both share the name "Adam."

> "In the day that God created man, in the likeness of God... Male and female created he them; and blessed them, and **called their name Adam**" (Genesis 5:1–2).

Yes, both men and women, the very foundation blocks of our human society, are both named Adam. The natural order of mankind (Adam) is to bond with other people, just as atoms are designed to unite with other atoms and build into something greater than itself. And just as atoms are not meant to be alone, God said, "It is not good that the man [Adam] should be alone" (Genesis 2:18).

And here's an astonishing bonus. The original Hebrew word for "being alone" is…drumroll please…"bad." I kid you not. B-A-D. Feel free to look it up in your own Bibles and lexicons. When God says it's not good for man to be alone, the original word He used for being alone is "bad," spelled and pronounced the exact same way we read and say this word in English. Is it possible there might be a hidden or blatantly obvious message there? I strongly suspect so. Perhaps something to the effect of: "It's bad to be alone." But even if there's not, the sentence can be playfully read as: "It's not good for man to be bad."

In summary, it's unmistakable that even the smallest building block in our physical universe, the atom, is operating at God speed. Its nucleus represents God as the most humble and positive center of everything, the entity holding all things together. All the negative objects are orbiting Him, never able to get away. Atoms are looking to be filled, to be completed, just as we are intended to be filled and completed with God's own presence. The natural order of things is to bond with others, just as men and women unite in marriage, people bond with other people in friendship, and everyone joins with God in spirit. The entire universe, both seen and unseen, is blaring the consistent and everlasting message that being united with God and other people is good, while being disconnected and alone is not good, or as the Bible fittingly declares in Hebrew, bad.

SUNRISE

One of the most beautiful things we can witness in life is seeing the sun rise, and, thankfully, sunrise happens every single day.

Whether we're standing at the beach or in our backyards, sunrise features a brilliant light appearing to emerge from the earth and rising in the sky. That's what takes place on the physical level at human speed. Now let's make the jump to God speed to explain what the Creator is broadcasting on the spirit level with the dawn of each new day.

Let's start with some basic facts. The sun, as we all know, is a very large, burning star providing nonstop light and warmth to our small earth from the morning to the evening. It is a source of life and all living things need the energy from the sun to grow. Without it, life would eventually die. All the same things can be said about God. We've already seen how God is called a sun and the bright morning star, but there's more:

> "But unto you that fear my name shall the Sun of righteousness arise with healing" (Malachi 4:2).

> "God is light" (1 John 1:5).

> "Jesus spoke to them again: 'I am the light of the world'" (John 8:12 CSB).

> "I am...life" (John 11:25).

Thus, while the sun is not God, it is actually a representation of God on many levels. Scripture declares God is a sun—the Sun of righteousness as a matter of fact—the bright morning star, who is the light of the world and life itself. Without this light of God, there is only darkness and certain death.

And we must not forget that God has promised to transform believers from their dark flesh into the bright morning star, just as He Himself is the morning star:

> "To the one who is victorious and does my will to the end...I will also give that one the morning star" (Revelation 2:26–28 NIV).

Hence, at God speed, every sunrise is actually a picture of our glorious future, our resurrection from the dead. Just as Jesus was raised from the dead, the brilliant light emerging from the dark earth to become the bright morning star, faithful believers shall also be transformed into light, emerging out of the dark earth, exiting the flesh, and rising in the sky, the heavens, providing light to others. From the beginning of the daylight cycle, God is declaring our end result. The darkness of night, this state of flesh we're in, disappears and we rise to our new, immortal life of shining light.

Again, the word "sun" sounds to the ear exactly like "son," so sunrise can be heard as son-rise, the rising of the son, as in a son of God, which is what men and women are all intended to become when we emerge from this earth, no longer made up of earth, but consisting of the brilliant light of spirit.

For sunrise to occur, the earth is actually turning toward the sun for us to witness the rising of the sun. The earth represents people, and we, the people, must turn toward the Son (Sun) in order for the resurrection, the rising of the sons of God to take place, to get out of this darkness, this flesh, in which we currently dwell.

A BLACK HOLE

We've all heard the term "black hole," and it has three meanings: 1) an extremely dark place in space, possibly the result of a collapsed star; 2) a void or empty space; and 3) an underground prison cell.

All three of these definitions match the Bible. Let's examine them in reverse order.

3. An underground prison cell: We human beings are living in the jail cell of our underground prison, our own personal black hole. Our hearts and minds are situated beneath the ground, since our physical bodies are made up of "the dust of the ground" (Genesis 2:7).

2. A void or empty space: "I looked at the earth, and it was formless and empty" (Jeremiah 4:23 CSB). People in their human forms are black holes because without the presence of God filling us up, we are formless and void, merely a dark, empty space. Science actually demonstrates this, as it's well known that all matter in our physical universe is mostly comprised of empty space, from the atomic level all the way up to the expansive blackness of outer space. We dwell amid vast nothingness: "All the nations are as **nothing** before him; they are considered by him as **empty nothingness**" (Isaiah 40:17 CSB).

1. A dark place in space, possibly the result of a collapsed star: "I looked to the heavens, and their light was gone" (Jeremiah 4:23 CSB). Why does this same Bible verse mentioned a moment ago talk about the earth being formless and empty, as well as the heavens having their light gone? Because it's talking about what happens when God's creation rebels against Him. The earth being formless and void is the result of human rebellion. We're a giant void without God. And the heavens having their light gone is what happens when angels go to war with God, becoming "fallen"

angels, or **collapsed stars**. Remember, there was "war in heaven" (Revelation 12:7) and angels are referred to as stars in Scripture. "The seven **stars** are the **angels** of the seven churches" (Revelation 1:20).

So here's the simple translation of black holes when our eyes and ears are operating at God speed. Both human beings and angels who rebel against God are, in effect, black holes. We are empty spaces or voids not completely filled with the spirit of God, existing temporarily in a dark prison. We're filled with a bunch of nothingness. The dark places in the heavens called black holes may be the physical result of collapsed stars, but on the spirit level, they can represent angels that fell, angels who rebelled against God and collapsed on themselves.

WEED, THE PEOPLE

Anyone who has ever grown any kind of plant is familiar with a common problem, and that is weeds. Weeds are vigorous growths that often look like other plants but actually inflict harm on them, overtaking and choking the life out of their fellow occupants in a garden or field. But if we really dig deep into the subject, there are some surprising bits of information we can farm.

In case you never understood it, both beneficial plants and harmful weeds are broadcasting the message of the Bible, as they both represent people, good and bad, respectively. The dictionary even defines a weed as a person, saying it is "an obnoxious growth, thing, or person."

Healthy plants such as wheat represent good, obedient people filled with truth. And weeds represent the harmful, disobedient people, who are choking the life out of the good people.

Jesus Himself used this example to describe the two different kinds of people in the world, and what will happen to both. Here it is:

> "He presented another parable to them: 'The kingdom of heaven may be compared to a man who sowed good seed in his field.

> "But while people were sleeping, his enemy came, sowed weeds among the wheat, and left.

> "When the plants sprouted and produced grain, then the weeds also appeared.

"The landowner's servants came to him and said, "Master, didn't you sow good seed in your field? Then where did the weeds come from?"

"'An enemy did this,' he told them.

"'So, do you want us to go and pull them up?' the servants asked him.

"'No,' he said. 'When you pull up the weeds, you might also uproot the wheat with them.'

"'Let both grow together until the harvest. At harvest time I'll tell the reapers: Gather the weeds first and tie them in bundles to burn them, but collect the wheat in my barn'"(Matthew 13:24–30 CSB).

As usual, the disciples of Jesus did not understand what He was talking about, so they asked Him for a detailed explanation, and they got one:

"His disciples approached him and said, 'Explain to us the parable of the weeds in the field.'

"He replied: 'The one who sows the good seed is the Son of Man; the field is the world; and the good seed—these are the children of the kingdom. The **weeds are the children of the evil one**, and the enemy who sowed them is the devil. The harvest is the end of the age, and the harvesters are angels.

"'Therefore, just as the weeds are gathered and burned in the fire, so it will be at the end of the age.

"'The Son of Man will send out his angels, and they will gather from his kingdom all who cause sin and those guilty of lawlessness. They will throw them into the blazing furnace where there will be weeping and gnashing of teeth. Then the righteous will shine like the sun in their Father's kingdom. Let anyone who has ears listen'" (Matthew 13:36–43 CSB).

I don't think I can improve on the explanation by Jesus because He made it so simple. The weeds represent the devil's children, those who follow the drumbeat of rebellion against God. They are guilty of lawlessness themselves, and they cause other people to sin. Their end is to be lit on fire and burned in a blazing furnace.

Now, here's where it gets surprising and kind of fun. The word *weed* in modern English has more than one connotation, as we all know. It's often used as a synonym for marijuana or pot. Some people talk about smoking weed, getting "high," "wasted," "lit," and "burned out." In fact, smokers of weed are often referred to as "burnouts."

And, lo and behold, the Bible itself uses all these terms. As we've just read, the weeds at the end of this age are gathered up, **lit on fire** and **burned**. They are literally **burned out** of God's kingdom. So, lawless people who choke others by causing them to sin are weeds. And, spiritually speaking, people who smoke weed, that is, breathe in the harmful essence of other evil people (weeds), become burnouts. They're headed for destruction by being burned out of God's presence.

Note that the sensation people say they experience when smoking weed is called getting "high." The word "high" in Scripture is often associated with being exalted, in both a positive and negative sense. When someone exalts himself to a high place, that's considered arrogance, and he or she is destined to be brought down from being high and become humbled. Here's an example: "Exalt him that is low, and abase him that is **high**" (Ezekiel 21:26).

So even the sensation that people say they experience from weed, becoming high, is tied to a sense of self-induced arrogance, a highness that God opposes.

And what about "wasted"? Yes, the Bible ties in weeds with being wasted, because people who don't follow God are living in "a place overgrown with **weeds**...and a perpetual **wasteland**" (Zephaniah 2:9 CSB).

If you recall that famous song "Baba O'Riley" (also known as "Teenage Wasteland") by the British rock group The Who, the band sings about rebellious people, saying that all of them are "wasted."

This is exactly the message of the Bible, that millions upon billions of people over the years have become wasted, ruined, and destroyed. They're not usable for God's purposes. Thus, they're laid waste and will perish:

> **"For the nation and kingdom that will not serve thee shall perish; yea, those nations shall be utterly wasted"** (Isaiah 60:12).

In a similar vein, people often say they're "stoned" after smoking weed, and it's well known that the penalty for violating God's laws was actually being stoned to death:

> "They are to be **stoned**; their death is their own fault" (Leviticus 20:27 CSB).

It's just mind-blowing that even in the culture of weed-smoking as people get high, lit, wasted, stoned, and burned out, the end has been declared from the beginning.

SINK YOUR TEETH INTO THIS

Why is it there are so many creatures on Earth that have the ability to pierce, puncture, poison and shred human beings, causing agonizing pain and even death? There's an astounding yet very simple reason.

We all know about the fangs on lions and tigers and bears (oh, my!) as well as those on wolves and many snakes. Barracudas, piranhas, and sharks all have razor-sharp teeth. Think of the classic shark movie *Jaws*. And there are plenty of small, puncturing creatures that can do serious damage to the point of death, including scorpions, bees, hornets, wasps, bullet ants, ticks, and deadly mosquitoes. Believe it or not, it's all part of the spirit song that God has been singing for thousands of years.

Simply put, animals represent people, both good and bad. You probably know this to some extent already, as people who love and obey God are called lambs or sheep many times in Scripture and are collectively the peaceful flock of God's pasture.

> "You are My flock, the flock of My pasture; you are men, and I am your God" (Ezekiel 34:31 NKJV).

Jesus famously told Peter, "Feed my lambs" (John 21:15). He wasn't talking about a group of sheep that are animals penned up in His backyard. We realize He was referring to people represented by the woolly beasts, so everyone already understands a little bit of God speed.

He also told His disciples, "I send you forth as lambs among wolves" (Luke 10:3).

And also: "Watch out for false prophets. They come to you in sheep's clothing, but inwardly they are ferocious wolves" (Matthew 7:15 NIV).

The obvious translation is that lambs represent good people, and wolves are the bad, because wolves with their daggerlike fangs and their crafty character represent people who are the opposite of innocent lambs. They are cunning, lying, thieving individuals who can tear peaceful folks to shreds in all respects: physically, emotionally, and spiritually. And it's not just wolves. A quick look at other biting and stinging creatures will open your eyes as to why they do what they do.

GETTING BUGGED

Mosquitoes can be more than just an itchy nuisance. They can kill you.

As PBS reported in 2016, the deadliest animal in the world is the mosquito, killing hundreds of thousands of people every year. The most vulnerable are most at risk, specifically children and pregnant women. "No other bite kills more humans or makes more sick," the network explained in its *Deep Look* program. A mosquito actually stabs people's flesh with six needles at once, sucks out our blood, and often leaves us with "a parting gift in her saliva, a virus or parasite than can sicken or kill us."

What does this all mean on the higher, spirit level of God speed? When mosquitoes drill into you with their needles and suck out your blood, the metaphor is clear. They represent evil people who pierce your mind, and are sucking out your life, "for the blood is the life" (Deuteronomy 12:23). They are bleeding you of your eternal life. With their tiny piercings, they withdraw your lifeblood and leave you with, at the very least, an irritation, and at most, complete death, both physically and eternally.

SNAKES

Another famous stabber in our natural world is the serpent. Many varieties of snakes have fangs that latch onto their victims and inject deadly poison that paralyzes and/or kills the prey. Not only do these killers pump lethal venom with every bite, they also can use their sharp teeth to pull their victims down into their body, completely devouring them.

Like mosquitoes and other beasts of the field, fang-faced snakes represent people—evil people, to be specific. And the Bible is filled with Scriptures repeating this.

> "There is a generation whose teeth are swords, whose fangs are knives, devouring the oppressed from the land and the needy from among mankind" (Proverbs 30:14 CSB).

> "I will unleash on them wild beasts with fangs, as well as venomous
> snakes that slither in the dust" (Deuteronomy 32:24 CSB).

Keep in mind, the word *dust* refers to people, since mankind is formed out of "the dust of the ground" (Genesis 2:7). So when God says He's unleashing wild beasts with fangs and venomous snakes that slither in the dust, He's not only talking about physical animals, He's also singing the spirit song about wicked people. He's simply saying He will have you confronted by evil deceivers who slither among you with their toxic ideas, piercing your mind and injecting your intellect with poison, effectively killing you eternally.

Of course, the most famous serpent in all of Scripture is not even a physical animal. It's "the ancient serpent, who is called the devil and Satan, the one who deceives the whole world" (Revelation 12:9 CSB).

Right at the beginning, God makes sure we know that "the serpent was more cunning than any beast of the field which the LORD God had made" (Genesis 3:1 NKJV). In other words, the devil is the most deceptive, sly, crafty, lying person in history.

Serpents are well known for crawling on their belly. This run-on-the-tummy movement of theirs is saying something on the spirit level. It indicates a snake (an evil person) is motivated by its belly, its appetite, which is another way of expressing a lust or personal desire to commit evil.

> "You will move on your belly and eat dust all the days of your life"
> (Genesis 3:14 CSB).

> "They feed on the sin of my people; they have an **appetite** for their iniq-
> uity" (Hosea 4:8 CSB).

And what does it mean to "eat dust?" Simply put, it's to spiritually devour people through intimidation and other means, consuming and controlling their minds in fearful captivity, overcoming their spirit. It's depicted in nature by the way snakes swallow other creatures whole.

> "Will those who do **evil** never learn? They **eat up my people** like bread
> and wouldn't think of praying to the LORD" (Psalm 14:4 NLT).

If a businessman says in a menacing tone to someone, "I'm gonna eat you alive," it's a serious threat he's making, looking to dominate, overwhelm, and eventually defeat or destroy that person. He's not actually placing someone inside his mouth and gnawing on that person's body; unless, of course, his business is cannibalism.

SCORPIONS

Another example of a highly dangerous animal is the scorpion. Just looking at this bizarre creature or saying its name can send shivers down one's spine. It sports a prominent stinger on its tail, and getting stung by that barb can be excruciatingly painful and fatal in some cases.

You may be starting to sense the pattern here. Whether they be fangs, needles, or stingers, the weapons on these beasts are designed to **pierce** their victims. They puncture to inflict their harm, leaving a poison inside victims.

The reason is a spiritual one. The harmful creatures are in a spiritual war with us, looking to pierce the defenses of our mind and poison us with their toxin of deception, shred us apart, and/or devour the life right out of us. To put it more bluntly, they want us dead. Not just physically dead but spiritually dead so that we won't have eternal life.

Now that you know this, your eyes will be open to more Scriptures.

> "They had tails with stingers like scorpions, so that with their tails they had the power to harm people" (Revelation 9:10 CSB).

Again, on the spirit level, scorpions are evil people. But what do their tails represent? The Bible has the answer:

> "The tail is the prophet, the one teaching lies" (Isaiah 9:15 CSB).

Yes, folks, lies are the ancient weapons that kill people very effectively and eternally, since they prevent people from coming to the truth. And the prophets who voice those lies are known as the tails of scorpions when we simply connect the dots in Scripture. It's also ironic and interesting that a tail sounds exactly the same as tale, which, of course, is another word for a lie.

The good news is we possess the antidote for all these deadly stingers and biters. We've been given the way of escape, to have complete power over the enemy, which is what *Satan* means, and all of the enemy's human replicants. God Himself has indicated this:

> "Do not be afraid of them and do not be afraid of their words, even though **briers** and **thorns** are beside you and you live among **scorpions**. Don't be afraid of their words or discouraged by the look on their faces, for they are a **rebellious** house" (Ezekiel 2:6 CSB).

> "Look, I have given you authority over all the power of the **enemy**, and you can walk among **snakes** and **scorpions** and crush them. Nothing will injure you" (Luke 10:19 NLT).

Once again, we should not think only about the natural, physical world of animals when reading this. The Bible is speaking on the higher, supernatural level of God speed and is talking about evil people who look and act in the enemy's image, the likeness of Satan the devil. God is labeling these people thorns, serpents, and scorpions, just like someone might call a lying, cheating spouse a snake. But as true believers, we can walk among these evildoers fearlessly, completely crushing them without harm to us if we remain obedient to God. The ultimate sting, according to Scripture, is the sting of death, also called the sting of "Sheol," referring to the place of the dead. But that fatal sting will be removed, as God says:

> "I will ransom them from the power of Sheol. I will redeem them from death. Death, where are your **barbs**? Sheol, where is your **sting**?" (Hosea 13:14 CSB).

> "When this corruptible body is clothed with incorruptibility, and this mortal body is clothed with immortality, then the saying that is written will take place: Death has been swallowed up in victory. Where, death, is your victory? Where, death, is your **sting**?" (1 Corinthians 15:54–55 CSB)

Now before we unclench our teeth from this business about scorpions and snakes, there are a couple of interesting Bible stories dealing with biting snakes that few ever talk about.

One has to do with a viper latching onto the apostle Paul's hand when he was shipwrecked on the island of Malta.

The locals thought he was a murderer when they saw the snake fastened to his hand. But they changed their mind when "he shook off the beast into the fire, and felt no harm" (Acts 28:5).

Once again, there's an unseen or unheard story being broadcast at God speed. The beast is attaching itself to Paul's hand. Our hands symbolize our actions, they're the tools we use to make or do something. In other words, the biter (the devil) is trying kill this champion for God by affecting his actions, trying to make him sin. And what's the antidote? The proper course of action? The remedy is to merely shake off the suggestion of disobedience. When this resistance against rebellion takes place, the evil one ends up getting shaken off and burned in an unquenchable fire, while the faithful believer is not harmed in any way. In other words, the righteous person keeps on living forever.

The other famous story is one quoted by Jesus, right before the most famous line of the Bible, which is John 3:16. After being freed from slavery in Egypt, God's people in the wilderness were fiercely complaining against Him. And that's when this happened:

> "Then the LORD sent poisonous snakes among the people, and they bit them so that many Israelites died" (Numbers 21:6 CSB).

By now, you should recognize what this is saying on the higher level. God plagues the bitter malcontents with all kinds of evil opposition that can lead to the eternal death penalty.

But once the complainers admitted their sin, God provided the only way out of their death penalty:

> "Then the LORD said to Moses, 'Make a snake image and mount it on a pole. When anyone who is bitten looks at it, he will recover.' So Moses made a bronze snake and mounted it on a pole. Whenever someone was bitten, and he looked at the bronze snake, he recovered" (Numbers 21:8–9 CSB).

Think about this at God speed now. The image of the snake mounted on a pole is nothing less than a picture of Jesus, a foreshadowing of His death and resurrection. Remember, Christ was nailed to a wooden stake when He was executed, literally "pierced because of our rebellion" (Isaiah 53:5 CSB). He personally took on the image of the deadly snake, placing the sins of the entire world on Himself so we, His creation, can escape our certain death penalty.

Thus, when the people of ancient Israel in the wilderness looked at the image of the snake on the pole, they got physically healed and lived, as in saved. But it's painting the picture for all of us on how to be rescued eternally. And that is exactly what Jesus meant when He recounted this spectacular teaching moment in the New Testament:

"Just as Moses lifted up the snake in the wilderness, so the Son of Man must be lifted up, so that everyone who believes in him may have eternal life. For God loved the world in this way: He gave his one and only Son, so that everyone who believes in him will not perish but have eternal life" (John 3:14–16 CSB).

If we believe in and follow the instructions of our Creator named Jesus, we possess the key to everlasting life, the way to escape our death penalty, our mortality. This is how we rocket to our divine velocity, reaching God speed.

9TH GEAR:
Life Activities

THUS FAR, we've learned how the ancient Scriptures are the template for everything from songs, stories, advertising, movies, sayings, nature, and the news. Now it's time to get up close and personal and demonstrate how what's written in the Bible is running your life. It's truly stunning to see how our everyday activities in life are broadcasting the divine message at God speed on every frequency.

WHO ARE YOU? I AM...

One of the most basic things in life is knowing your own name. After all, how can you understand who you are if you don't even know your name? And what I'm about to tell you might just blow your mind about your own identity, because every time you answer the question of "Who are you?" you're actually saying something incredibly significant about not just your current state, but your origin and ultimate destiny as well. Allow me to explain.

Let's say someone asks a question such as "Who are you?" or "What's your name?"

I'd respond: "I am Joe." You, of course, would answer with: "I am [insert your own name]."

It's a straightforward, no-nonsense response, and you probably wouldn't think twice about it. But that's about to change. Right now.

When I say, "I am Joe," I'm actually saying God's name first followed by my own personal name of Joe. What do I mean? We have to remember that God's specific name that He said He'd be using for all eternity is "I AM."

> **"I AM WHO I AM**. This is what you are to say to the Israelites: **I AM** has
> sent me to you.... This is my name forever; this is how I am to be remem-
> bered in every generation" (Exodus 3:14–15 CSB).

Not only is God's personal name "I AM," but also that name itself is
a memorial in all generations. It's not only how we remember Him, it's the
way to keep remembering Him through our own identity.

The Creator of everything has shaped our language so that even when
we identify ourselves in answering the question of "Who are you?" or
"What's your name?" we are attached to God's very own name! We remember God when we identify ourselves because we all ultimately come from
God. He is our origin, as He likes to remind us of this fact:

> **"Is this how you repay the LORD, you foolish and senseless people? Isn't
> he your Father and Creator? Didn't he make you and sustain you?"**
> (Deuteronomy 32:6 CSB).

As we see, Scripture says God is our Father, so just as a child bears the
name of his or her father in today's world, we carry the name of God every
time we say "I am" followed by our own name.

Not only is God the Creator of everything and everyone, He's also our
destiny. He's what we all have to look forward to as overcomers of evil. It is
then that we'll have His glorious name permanently attached to us for all
eternity as the very offspring of God:

> **"The one who is victorious...I will write on them the name of my God..."**
> (Revelation 3:12 NIV).

> **"Then I saw the Lamb standing on Mount Zion, and with him were 144,000
> who had HIS NAME and HIS FATHER'S NAME written on their fore-
> heads"** (Revelation 14:1 NLT).

Are you understanding this? We're going to have the eternal name of
God, "I AM," attached to us permanently if we overcome evil, because we'll
be a part of God's very own family! And we all declare the end right now,
every time we say "I am...." Which brings me to a related topic.

MARRIAGE AND THE NAME CHANGE

Why do most women change their original family name to the name of
their husband's family when they get married? Irrespective of tradition or

how the practice developed in society, there's a completely spirit-based reason for this, as God once again is declaring the end from the beginning.

The answer is actually quite simple when we realize the Bible is one giant wedding story. God is actually marrying His bride, humanity as a whole, to whom He is offering eternal life as members of His own family.

We've seen these verses before, but they cannot be stressed enough, as God Himself says to us:

> "I am your husband" (Jeremiah 3:14 NIV).

> "Let us be glad, rejoice, and give him glory, because the marriage of the Lamb has come, and his bride has prepared herself" (Revelation 19:7 CSB).

So, why is it that the bride changes her name to that of her husband? Because that's the end of the story, which also happens to be the beginning of the couple's life together. When our marriage with God is consummated when He returns in the future, believers actually take on the name of God! Yes, folks, this is plastered all over your Bible, but many people don't like to admit it because they're a bit uncomfortable with you knowing your divine destiny. We've just read a couple of the glorious verses outright declaring that we'll be receiving the very name of God in Revelation 3:12 and 14:1. But there's more:

> "Our desire is for your name" (Isaiah 26:8 CSB).

> "They shall see His face, and His name shall be on their foreheads" (Revelation 22:4 NKJV).

> "To them I will give...a name better than sons and daughters; I will give them an everlasting name that will endure forever" (Isaiah 56:5 NIV).

Additionally, many times in Scripture we find the phrase "for your name's sake" or "for His name's sake," but most people don't completely grasp the obvious truth of what that means. God does what He does for His name's sake. In other words, He takes action for the sake of us human beings being permanently given His own name at the end of the story, when He unites with us in marriage.

Even in the famous Psalm 23, beloved by millions of Christians, we're told:

> "He renews my life; he leads me along the right paths for **his name's sake**" (Psalm 23:3 CSB).

In other words, God is renewing our lives (as in bringing us back from the dead) so we can take His name forever. He's doing it for the sake of us holding onto His name. This phrase concerning God's "name's sake" is everywhere in the Bible. Here are a few more:

> "For You are my rock and my fortress; Therefore, for Your name's sake, Lead me and guide me" (Psalm 31:3 NKJV).

> "Revive me, O LORD, for Your name's sake!" (Psalm 143:11 NKJV).

> "Help us, O God of our salvation, For the glory of Your name; And deliver us, and provide atonement for our sins, For Your name's sake!" (Psalm 79:9 NKJV).

Just think of the phrase: "Blessed is he who comes in the name of the LORD!" (Psalm 118:26 NKJV). This blessing applies to all believers, because we are going to permanently have the name of the Lord.

Yes, as incredible as it sounds, the Bible is declaring the glorious end to our personal story, right from the beginning. From the beginning of any marriage, the bride takes the name of the husband, because they are joined together as one unit. This is true not only here in our physical world but also in the spirit world as we become one with God, receiving the glory of God's name, written on our foreheads, "the everlasting name that will endure forever."

It gives an entirely new significance to one of the Ten Commandments:

> "You shall not take the name of the LORD your God in vain" (Exodus 20:7 NKJV).

While most people understand that on the physical level, the commandment tells people not to misuse God's name, there's the higher, spirit meaning at God speed. And it's a promise that when we take the name of God, as in permanently receiving the name of God when we're spiritually married to our Creator, we shall not be taking it in vain, as in taking it without success. It will be for our everlasting glory. Now you know who you really are.

MAKING LOVE, ACTUALLY

We've touched on marriage, so isn't it about time for a little hubba-hubba?

Now that I have your attention, here's an important lesson on sexuality you probably never got from your parents or friends—and definitely not from your biology teacher in school. This is where I come in, because it's time that everyone should understand what making love actually is all about. It's quite simple to learn, especially with eyes and ears open. I realize some folks are not always comfortable discussing anything sexual, but we're all adults here, and I'll keep this clean so as not to offend sensitive eyes or ears.

Let's start with the physical basics before making the jump to God speed.

As you likely know already, in a healthy sexual relationship, the man wants to be close to his woman, and she wants to be close with him. He wants to be so close to her, in fact, that he seeks to put himself inside the woman, and the woman gladly welcomes him inside her. They often commence their actions with tender kisses and caresses. Then things build to a higher level.

As the man gets excited, blood surges so he can firmly and confidently enter and remain inside his loved one. The woman, too, experiences a similar surge, as she becomes prepared to facilitate the man's arrival.

After a time of what might appear to be the man and woman playfully and lovingly wrestling or struggling with each other, both reach a point of climax, experiencing phenomenal pleasure, as the man releases part of his own body, his seed, inside the woman. That seed from the man, when it unites with an egg from the woman's body, can subsequently develop inside the womb, being nourished in the woman's matrix until it's ready for life on the outside, crowning as it emerges as a newly born child of both the man and woman.

Now here's the spectacular meaning of all of this. As should be obvious by now, the man represents God and the woman represents His bride, which is all of humanity, both male and female. God loves His bride and wants to be united with her intimately; and people who love God, seeking to obey Him, want to join their Divine Spouse as well. As the Bible puts it, "the two are united into one" (Genesis 2:24 NLT).

When the loving starts, there's often sweet kissing. And what does a kiss on the lips represent?

"An honest answer is like a kiss on the lips" (Proverbs 24:26 NIV).

Thus, telling the truth to everyone at all times is important in the start of a loving relationship with God. Scripture even shows God's bride to be enthralled with the kissing:

> "Let him kiss me with the kisses of his mouth—for your love is more delightful than wine" (Song of Songs 1:2 NIV).

The blood surge experienced by both parties is the engorging excitement of life as two people get thrilled to merge into one, making them complete, because, once again, "the blood is the life" (Deuteronomy 12:23).

The surge causes a certain firmness in the body parts of both the man and woman, alluding to standing firm in the faith, which Scripture urges us to do.

> "Be alert, stand firm in the faith, be courageous, be strong" (1 Corinthians 16:13 CSB).

The woman's body gets prepared to welcome the man inside her, and this is akin to our own preparation, making ourselves ready throughout our lives to have God dwell inside us:

> "**Prepare** the way of the LORD; Make His paths straight" (Matthew 3:3 NKJV).

> "To **make ready** a people **prepared** for the Lord" (Luke 1:17).

> "The marriage of the Lamb has come, and his **bride** has **prepared herself**" (Revelation 19:7 CSB).

> "**Prepared** as a **bride** adorned for her husband" (Revelation 21:2).

The wrestling or struggling that the man and woman are engaged in points to our lifelong struggle, overcoming all resistance and prevailing at the end. This is what the famous name *Israel* means, "because you have **struggled** with God and with humans and have overcome" (Genesis 32:28 NIV).

The glorious sensation both parties feel at the conclusion of lovemaking is a fantastic preview of the euphoric glory we'll experience at the end of this age when we're crowned with glory and filled with exceeding joy.

> "You will have the **wonderful joy** seeing his glory when it is revealed to all the world"(1 Peter 4:13 NLT).

> "And when the Great Shepherd appears, you will receive a crown of **never-ending glory** and **honor**" (1 Peter 5:4 NLT).

The end of the act of lovemaking is just the beginning, as God is both "the beginning and the end" (Revelation 22:13).

It marks a new beginning because the Man in the spirit story, who is God, has left His presence, His very own seed, inside the woman, inside His believers. The "seed" is the presence of God in anyone willing to receive it, and the Bible says that explicitly:

"This is the meaning of the parable: The seed is the word of God" (Luke 8:11). We need to remember that "the word of God" is another name for Jesus. "His name is called The Word of God" (Revelation 19:13).

As this holy seed of God unites with the body of the woman (the believers), new and additional divine life starts to be formed, creating the children of God: "For his Spirit joins with our spirit to affirm that we are God's children" (Romans 8:16 NLT).

The unborn child is then fed in a womb of darkness for a time, until it has been perfected enough to be born into a much brighter world. The same holds true on the spirit level.

The Seed (the presence of God) unites with the woman (an obedient human being). A new spirit life commences in the dark womb, this physical world of darkness in which we currently dwell:

> "Before I was born the LORD called me; from my mother's **womb** he has spoken my name" (Isaiah 49:1 NIV).

Inside this spiritual matrix, or mothering place, the new person "must grow in the grace and knowledge of our Lord and Savior Jesus Christ" (2 Peter 3:18 NLT).

Once nourished to the point of perfection, the new person can be "born again" into God's kingdom, as we're told: "unless one is born again, he cannot see the kingdom of God" (John 3:3 NKJV).

And just as a baby is crowning when first emerging from the womb, so those born again into the spirit world will be "crowned" with "glory and honor" (Psalm 8:5 NLT).

The ultimate result of loving God is the birth of God's children, when we humans become transformed into immortal beings, just like Jesus is immortal, since "we shall be like him; for we shall see him as he is" (1 John 3:2).

> "Then, when our dying bodies have been transformed into bodies that will never die, this Scripture will be fulfilled: 'Death is swallowed up in victory'" (1 Corinthians 15:54 NLT).

Yes, folks, God is reproducing Himself through human beings. He's having and raising children of God! As a bonus, once we've been born of God, we won't even be able to disobey God, because that original Seed, the presence of God Himself, remains in us forever:

> "Whoever has been born of God does not sin, for His **seed** remains in him; and he cannot sin, because he has been born of God" (1 John 3:9 NKJV).

Now you know why lovemaking and the resulting birth of children are so sublime. They're more glorious than you likely ever imagined. A man making love to a woman is a real-life, pleasure-packed picture of the entire Master Plan of God, from the initial desire to be intimately close with someone to the conception, development, and ultimate birth of God's own children of glory, the very "offspring of God" (Acts 17:29).

SLEEPING AND WAKING UP

Surely everyone on Planet Earth is familiar with the cycle of sleeping and waking up. It's among the most basic things that people do on a daily basis, going to sleep and then waking up to live another day.

But *why* do we sleep? Believe it or not, "scientists simply don't know for sure," as BBC News reported.

However, there is an answer, and it's among the clearest examples of God's plan for us. That's because the terms "sleep" and "waking up" mean more than what most people think, especially when we focus on the higher, spirit meaning at God speed.

Let's start with sleep. To put it simply, the word *sleep* in Scripture doesn't just mean snoozing away in our physical bodies. It's often associated with death. For instance: "I sleep the sleep of death" (Psalm 13:3).

Perhaps the best illustration is Jesus awakening his friend Lazarus out of sleep, which wasn't your typical, natural, naptime sleep, but actually death:

"'Our friend Lazarus has fallen asleep, but I'm on my way to wake him up.'

"Then the disciples said to him, 'Lord, if he has fallen asleep, he will get well.'

"Jesus, however, was speaking about his death, but they thought he was speaking about natural sleep.

"So Jesus then told them plainly, 'Lazarus has died'" (John 11:11–14 CSB).

Hence, the term *sleep* plainly refers to death in the spiritual story that the Bible is. It's a daily reminder to us all that we are mortal, and we are going to die at some point. In other words, because we're not awake all the time, we're not immortal. We go to sleep because we're going to die. If we don't have God running our lives right now, we're actually already dead, spiritually speaking. Without God, we are spiritually sleepwalking. Just as a person who walks in their sleep may be moving around and even talking at times, he or she is not really awake. And in our daily lives, even though we may be walking, talking, and even conducting business, we're still spiritually dead without God, thus making us sleepwalkers.

Incidentally, Scripture tells us that God never sleeps: "Indeed, he who watches over Israel never slumbers or sleeps" (Psalm 121:4 NLT). And that's because God is not dead. He is life, and He remains alive forever.

Moreover, we all know that going to sleep is not the end of our story in the daily cycle of us mortals. There's more to come. And that's the good news. It's called waking up the next day. As the prophet Daniel notes:

"And many of them that sleep in the dust of the earth shall awake" (Daniel 12:2).

Waking up from a solid sleep is one of the best feelings a physical human being can have. It's when we're totally refreshed, bursting with energy to live the brand-new day of tomorrow that has suddenly become today. That's because every single time we wake up, we're being told the end of the story: that we'll be awakened by God to live in the next day, tomorrow, which is the day of eternal life for the obedient servants of God. We're instantly refreshed to begin life again.

Here are some very simple verses about our awakening from the sleep of death:

> "Wake up, sleeper, rise from the dead, and Christ will shine on you" (Ephesians 5:14 NIV).

> "I lie down and sleep; I wake again because the LORD sustains me" (Psalm 3:5 CSB).

> "As for me, I will see Your face in righteousness; I shall be satisfied when I awake in Your likeness" (Psalm 17:15 NKJV).

> "Wake up, wake up; put on your strength, Zion! Put on your beautiful garments, Jerusalem, the Holy City!" (Isaiah 52:1 CSB).

> "But your dead will live, LORD; their bodies will rise—let those who dwell in the dust wake up and shout for joy...the earth will give birth to her dead" (Isaiah 26:19 NIV).

Thus, it's plain to see the daily cycle of being awake, going to sleep, and then awakening again the following day is another way God is telling us that we live, then we die, and then we are awakened to another day of life. At God speed, sleeping equals death, and being awake equals being alive.

On a related matter, have you ever wondered why, generally speaking, people get about eight hours of sleep every day?

Yes, we're all unconscious and paralyzed for somewhere around eight hours a day, which means a third of our lives is spent in slumberland.

But could there be a spiritual answer as to why a third of our lives is associated with death? I'm going to suggest the answer is yes, if we merely connect a few more dots from the Bible.

The answer is located near the very end of Scripture, where the numerical figure of one-third plays a prominent role.

> "There was a great fiery red dragon.... Its tail swept away a third of the stars in heaven and hurled them to the earth" (Revelation 12:3–4 CSB).

The fiery red dragon is Satan the devil, and the third of the stars in heaven refers to a third of the angels in heaven who fought on the devil's side in a war against God:

> "Then war broke out in heaven: Michael and his angels fought against the dragon. The dragon and his angels also fought, but he could not prevail, and there was no place for them in heaven any longer. So the great dragon was thrown out—the ancient serpent, who is called the devil and Satan, the one who deceives the whole world. He was thrown to earth, and his angels with him" (Revelation 12:7–9 CSB).

As we see, a third of the angels became "dead" to God, so to speak, because of their rebellion against their own Creator. They lost their ability to be alive in God's sight by fighting against Him. They became spiritually dead. They "fell," which is the possible origin of the phrase "fall asleep," because these angels "fell" from heaven and were thrown to the earth, to the place where the dead (sleeping) people are.

Is it possible that God is reminding human beings through the approximate time we spend asleep about the rebellion by His own angels? Since a third of the angels became dead to Him, we may spend a third of our time sleeping, as in appearing to be dead. I'm just bringing it up because there's a spiritual reason for everything, and it's high time that we wake up and pay attention, in addition to smelling the coffee.

TRAVELING ANYWHERE

Millions of us travel each day to get to our destination, whether it be for work, school, vacation, or just to hang out somewhere. But do we realize that by doing this routine activity, we're broadcasting the plan of God? It's so simple, yet so profound at the same time. Here's the explanation.

Let's say you're planning to go on vacation to Walt Disney World in Florida, a place where you hope to enjoy plenty of happiness. If you're not a fan of Disney, feel free to substitute any place to your liking. To reach this destination, you need to drive on a road or fly on a plane (or both) to get there. The point is, you need to take the correct way, the correct path to reach the proper destination. You need the right directions and then stay on the path to get there. Otherwise, if you just take a road at random and don't know how to get there, you'll likely never reach the place you're trying to get to.

But starting out on the proper route is no guarantee you'll actually get there. Many things can go wrong along the way. For instance, if you're not paying attention or you get distracted, you could drive off the highway and possibly crash and die. The same result could happen if you fall asleep at the wheel. You have to remain alert at all times. If you break all sorts of traffic laws, such as speeding or reckless driving, you're risking your own life and the lives of others who are trying to get to their destination as well. But if you know where you're going, how to get there, and obey the rules of the road, chances are excellent you'll get to where you wish to go.

Here's how this is an analogy at God speed for the Master Plan. The happy destination we need to get to is God and where He lives. We can call it the kingdom of God, heaven, eternal life, and paradise, since the Bible uses all these terms interchangeably.

To get there, we need to know the right way. And what is the right way? Jesus answers this question, famously saying, "I am the way." His full statement is "I am the way, the truth, and the life. No one comes to the Father except through Me" (John 14:6 NKJV). Thus, if we don't start with Jesus as our guide, we'll never get to our destination of immortality.

And what's the direction to get there? Here's the divine answer: "If you want to receive eternal life, keep the commandments" (Matthew 19:17 NLT).

Thus, by definition, following the directions of God, also known as the commandments, is the correct direction to reach the destination of life everlasting.

Now, what about all those things that can go wrong that can prevent us from getting to the destination? If we break the law, that's a certain way to end the journey. And Scripture says sinning is, in fact, breaking the law:

> **"Everyone who sins breaks the law; in fact, sin is lawlessness"**
> **(1 John 3:4 NIV).**

And what's our reward for breaking God's law and sinning? It's the end of life, the dreaded D-word: "The wages of sin is **death**" (Romans 6:23). Simply put, we crash and burn when we break the instructions of God.

In addition to obeying the rules of the road, we need to seriously pay attention while driving to avoid any accidents to ensure our safe arrival. As we mentioned before in discussing "Stairway to Heaven," the Bible talks incessantly about listening very hard and paying attention: "Pay attention, you stupid people! Fools, when will you be wise?" (Psalm 94:8 CSB).

We all need to watch the road, be alert and avoid falling asleep during our journey, and the Bible stresses this with very similar language. Here's just one example:

> "Watch! Be alert! For you don't know when the time is coming. It is like a man on a journey, who left his house, gave authority to his servants, gave each one his work, and commanded the doorkeeper to be alert. Therefore be alert, since you don't know when the master of the house is coming—whether in the evening or at midnight or at the crowing of the rooster or early in the morning. Otherwise, when he comes suddenly he might find you sleeping. And what I say to you, I say to everyone: Be alert!" (Mark 13:33–37 CSB).

Simply put, to get to our intended destination, we need to stay on God's path. And the Bible uses those exact words: "Stay on the path that the LORD your God has commanded you to follow. Then you will live long and prosperous lives in the land you are about to enter and occupy" (Deuteronomy 5:33 NLT).

TEACH YOUR CHILDREN WELL

Whether you love school or hate it, most everyone realizes that education is important. After all, we need to know how to do certain things in order to live. From our earliest moments as young children, we're taught about everything: how to speak intelligently, how to listen, how to behave properly, how to treat others, even how to play games and sports. As we get older, the teaching gets more advanced as we learn additional skills for a trade or to engage in commerce. We're simply not born with much knowledge, and we all need to be taught how to do pretty much everything in order to grow and succeed in life. The learning never really stops.

Why is this the paradigm? Because the Bible itself is the template for learning, as God has provided the instruction book not only for this life here on Earth but also how to be granted eternal life. We teach our children to do well because God, who is our Parent, is teaching His own children, namely us, how to do well. It's the message in the famous song, "Teach Your Children" by Crosby, Stills, Nash & Young.

Learning is growing, and that's especially true when we learn about God: "You will grow as you learn to know God better and better" (Colossians 1:10 NLT).

Scripture is filled with instructions about teaching and learning.

> "And these words which I command you today shall be in your heart. You shall teach them diligently to your children, and shall talk of them when

you sit in your house, when you walk by the way, when you lie down, and when you rise up" (Deuteronomy 6:6–7 NKJV).

"Come, my children, listen to me; I will teach you the fear of the LORD" (Psalm 34:11 NIV).

"Learn to do what is good" (Isaiah 1:17 CSB).

Unfortunately, as many people don't pay attention to their parents and teachers in life, many also don't pay attention to their divine Parent, and that leads to a very bad result, namely destruction for themselves and their own kids. God says so Himself:

"My people are destroyed for lack of knowledge. Because you have rejected knowledge, I also will reject you.... Because you have forgotten the law of your God, I also will forget your children" (Hosea 4:6 NKJV).

EVERY BREATH YOU TAKE

We often take breathing for granted, but the inhalation of fresh air into our lungs is what keeps us alive from moment to moment. If our breathing completely stops, we die in a short matter of time. So breathing is a natural form of life support.

Why is this? Because breath itself comes from God (it's actually a representation of God), and He's loaning it to us on a temporary basis in our current bodies made of dust. Let's go back to the beginning to be reminded of our ancient past:

"And the LORD God formed man of the dust of the ground, and **breathed** into his nostrils the **breath** of **life**; and man became a **living** being" (Genesis 2:7 NKJV).

"The Spirit of God has made me, and the **breath** of the Almighty gives me **life**" (Job 33:4 CSB).

Right off the bat, we can see the act of breathing comes from God, and we're actually inhaling life, the breath of life, which is equated with the Spirit of God in every breath we take, even at this moment. Again, if we stop breathing completely, if we stop taking in the breath of life, which is the Spirit of God, we're dead.

And here's something you likely never thought of concerning that verse in Genesis about God breathing the breath of life into us. It's not just talking about our past. It's talking about our present and eternal future as well. Not only were we created long ago from the dust of the ground, it's happening right now and will again when we're brought back out of the ground and given eternal life.

When I say it's happening now, we again have to realize that God has formed each and every one of us "out of the ground," because that's what we're made up of: the earth, the dust, the clay, the mud, the ground— however you wish to say it. We in the flesh consist of the same chemicals that are in the ground, and God is giving us every breath we breathe right now in our earthen bodies. We're breathing right now without even thinking about it because God is causing it to happen. Even when we sleep and have no control over our breath, God is still sustaining us with His life-support system because He's giving us the breath of life so we can wake up the next morning.

And regarding our future, we all know that we're mortal and are going to die. Our breathing will stop. But Genesis 2:7 is telling us our personal future as well. Because there's a resurrection coming. When we listen at God speed, it says our Creator is going to form us out of the ground (the dust of the earth where everyone's remains are) a second time and breathe the breath of life back into us, raising us to life again to become a *living being*! The end of our story, which is eternal life for mankind, was declared from the beginning.

IN SICKNESS AND IN HEALTH

No one likes getting sick, no matter what the ailment. It's painful and it leaves us feeling miserable and sometimes in excruciating pain.

But what is the true source of disease, whether it's high fever or the well-known inflammation common in arthritis and many other physical problems? The answer may surprise you, because the Maker of all things, God Himself, is responsible for it all:

> "The LORD will strike you with wasting disease, with fever and inflamma-
> tion, with scorching heat and drought, with blight and mildew, which will
> plague you until you perish" (Deuteronomy 28:22 NIV).

Now why would a loving God strike His own people with inflammation, fever, and all sorts of sicknesses? He provides the clear reason just seven verses earlier. He is broadcasting His message by means of sickness, explaining it's the result of disobeying His instructions:

> **"But if you refuse to listen to the LORD your God and do not obey all the commands and decrees I am giving you today, all these curses will come and overwhelm you" (Deuteronomy 28:15 NLT).**

God is using every tool He has in the box to get our attention to stop our ways that lead to being dead forever. And, yes, He slaps us with pain and diseases to wake us up out of our idiotic rebellion, literally beating some sense into our sick selves:

> **"Why do you want more beatings? Why do you keep on rebelling? The whole head is hurt, and the whole heart is sick" (Isaiah 1:5 CSB).**

Now, lest you think that God is all about whacking people with sickness and health problems all the time, He's about healing as well, which is the ultimate goal. The inflammation and fevers we suffer with temporarily are intended to get us back on the path to God, the path to everlasting life. Scripture tells us that God is both the Inflictor of wounds as well as the Healer:

> **"I am the one who wounds and heals" (Deuteronomy 32:39 NLT).**

> **"He forgives all your iniquity; he heals all your diseases" (Psalm 103:3 CSB).**

Interestingly, the Spirit of God is not keeping to Himself His divine power to heal. He's actually giving us human beings "the gifts of healing by the same Spirit" (1 Corinthians 12:9).

> **"Summoning his twelve disciples, he gave them authority over unclean spirits, to drive them out and to heal every disease and sickness" (Matthew 10:1 CSB).**

And the healing ability was not just for times in the ancient past. It will continue far into the future, as God will give His believers the power to heal other people:

"The tree of life was on each side of the river, bearing twelve kinds of fruit, producing its fruit every month. The leaves of the tree are for **healing** the nations" (Revelation 22:2 CSB).

Now we can finally make sense of this cryptic prophecy from Revelation. God, the ultimate tree of life, will provide His followers, who are the offshoots of God and the leaves sprouting from that tree of life, the divine power to heal and save other nations, other peoples who have not known or lived by the truth. They will finally be taught and healed by "the leaves," the people firmly attached to the tree of life!

10TH GEAR:

God's Word *at* God Speed

NOW THAT your mind has been revved up to see God's ubiquitous presence in our everyday, physical world, it's time to shift into super-high gear and make the jump to God speed more complete. We're going to look at the Word of God itself in more detail but without focusing on its physical meaning. We'll use the same technique we've used through this entire book, letting the Word of God be the quickening force to bring to life the higher, Spirit-filled meaning of some of the most famous events in the Bible as well as some obscure ones.

What will become clear is that what has been inked on the pages of Scripture for centuries is not merely an accurate, historical account of events from ancient times. You will see these events in a brand-new light, awakening you to astonishing concepts that may never have crossed your mind before. Or, if they did cross your mind, perhaps you didn't wish to believe them because they sounded too glorious for you to handle. You'll realize that much more is being broadcast in Bible passages than meets the naked eye. You'll understand how God is, in fact, continually explaining the end of the story, the conclusion of all things, right from the start, "declaring the end from the beginning" (Isaiah 46:10). So let's hit the accelerator and bring you up to God speed.

THE BIRTH OF GOD

Perhaps the most famous story in the Bible is the birth of Jesus, God in the flesh who was born in Bethlehem, laid in a manger, had visits from shepherds who announced the good news, and had to escape into and be brought out of Egypt. The details can be found in the second chapter of the gospels of Luke and Matthew, but millions of people who know the historical event well are not aware of what is being aired on the spirit level. That changes now.

Let's start with some very basics. Jesus, whose name in Hebrew is Yeshua, meaning "God saves" or "God will save," was born in Bethlehem, called the city of David. The word *Bethlehem* means "house of bread" or "house of food" and the word *David* means "beloved." The meanings of the words are important because they help paint the picture of the spiritual story at God speed.

Scripture makes a very big deal about the Son of God being laid in a manger. It mentions it three times in the same chapter.

> "And she brought forth her firstborn son, and wrapped him in swaddling clothes, and laid him in a **manger**; because there was no room for them in the inn" (Luke 2:7).

> "And this shall be a sign unto you; Ye shall find the babe wrapped in swaddling clothes, lying in a **manger**" (Luke 2:12).

> "And they came with haste, and found Mary, and Joseph, and the babe lying in a **manger**" (Luke 2:16).

And just what is a manger? It's not a stable, a barn, or a cave as some people mistakenly think. A manger is simply a feeding box for animals. It's where the food is. Even in basic French class, one of the first verbs we all learn is "manger," which means "to eat."

And why is this significant? Because when we connect the dots from other parts of Scripture, we realize that this child lying in a feeding box in the "house of bread" or "house of food" in the "city of the beloved" is more than just a typical baby. He is our true food. The Son of God explained all this in His adult life when He declared:

> "My Father gives you the true bread from heaven" (John 6:32 CSB).

> "For the bread of God is He who comes down from heaven and gives life to the world" (John 6:33 NKJV).

> "Truly I tell you, anyone who believes has eternal life. I am the bread of life" (John 6:47–48 CSB).

"My flesh is true food and my blood is true drink" (John 6:55 CSB).

In other words, just as we are temporarily nourished and sustained in this physical life by food and drink, so we are nourished and sustained for all eternity when we feed on Jesus spiritually. Jesus is our true food, the bread that gives us eternal life, and God the Father had Him placed in the feeding box (the manger) in the house of food (Bethlehem) to emphasize the point.

We've all heard the expression, "you are what you eat," because we know that whatever food we consume becomes part of us. The same holds true when we get Jesus inside our minds. He actually becomes part of us and will sustain us forever when we're raised from the dead and exist eternally with Him.

But wait. There's more. It's time to look at the shepherds in the story, who were given a glimpse into the unseen kingdom of God when an angel appeared to them and told them not to be afraid.

"I proclaim to you good news of great joy that will be for all the people:
'Today in the city of David a Savior was born for you, who is the Messiah,
the Lord'" (Luke 2:10–11 CSB).

Scripture outright declares that what the shepherds are hearing is "good news" for "all the people."

We're given a portion of the good news from the angel, as he said, "a Savior was born for you, who is the Messiah, the Lord."

But the rest of the story of the "good news" is revealed when Jesus began His ministry as an adult. And the good news Jesus was preaching focused on the future "kingdom of God":

"Afterward he was traveling from one town and village to another, preaching and telling the **good news** of the **kingdom of God**" (Luke 8:1 CSB).

"The time is fulfilled, and the **kingdom of God** has come near. Repent
and believe the **good news**!" (Mark 1:15 CSB).

That future kingdom had been foretold far long ago by the Old Testament prophet Isaiah who, in a single prophecy, mentioned both the beginning of Jesus's human life with His birth and the end of the story with His being the head over His kingdom, the everlasting government of God:

> "For a child will be born for us, a son will be given to us, and the govern-
> ment will be on his shoulders.
>
> "He will be named Wonderful Counselor, Mighty God, Eternal Father,
> Prince of Peace.
>
> "The dominion will be vast, and its prosperity will never end. He will
> reign on the throne of David and over his kingdom, to establish and
> sustain it with justice and righteousness from now on and forever"
> (Isaiah 9:6–7 CSB).

Now back to the shepherds, the people who keep and care for sheep. At God speed, a shepherd is one who cares for God's flock, the people who believe and follow their Maker.

Jesus is referred to as the "chief Shepherd" in 1 Peter 5:4, He calls Himself the "good shepherd" in John 10:11, and He famously told Peter, "Feed my sheep" in John 21:17.

So what happened with the shepherds at the manger scene?

> "They hurried off and found both Mary and Joseph, and the baby who was
> lying in the manger. After seeing them, they reported the message they
> were told about this child, and all who heard it were amazed at what the
> shepherds said to them" (Luke 2:16–18 CSB).

At first glance, this may not seem that important, but with our spiritual eyes and ears open at God speed, the message is staggering. The shepherds represent those who take care of God's flock of people. They followed divine instructions from a supernatural being (in this case, an angel) and saw the sign of a baby lying in a manger. And what did they do next?

> "They reported the message they were told about this child, and all
> who heard it were amazed at what the shepherds said to them"
> (Luke 2:17–18 CSB).

The shepherds, the caretakers of God's people, reported the message about the Savior, the true food from heaven who brings eternal life, and all who **heard** the message were amazed. This event clearly shows us not only the incredible events of that night but also what has been happening since then and will happen again in the future kingdom of God!

The shepherds, both then and now, are informing people of the divine message about the true food (Jesus), and those who have their ears open to hear the message are "amazed" at what the shepherds say. The people are amazed because they're hearing how they can be saved and receive everlasting life. Yes, it's very good news when you find out how you can avoid being dead forever! And there's still more.

Don't forget that God declares the end from the beginning, constantly focusing our attention on the end of the story, letting us know the conclusion of events right from the very start. So let's look at the final mention of the shepherds in the account of the birth of Jesus.

> "The shepherds returned, glorifying and praising God for all the things they had seen and heard, which were just as they had been told" (Luke 2:20 CSB).

The Bible text tells us "**the shepherds returned**."

This may rock your world, because not only is this explaining the events of that night in Bethlehem, but also it is a prophecy for the future when understood at God speed.

What I mean is that the shepherds (all leaders of God's people in this current time) are going to *return* in the future, to glorify and praise God for all the things they had seen and heard. This return will take place when they are resurrected from the dead and raised to immortal life to instruct people again on how to receive eternal life!

This has been forecast in Scripture, with prophecies from Jeremiah, as God Himself predicted the future time still ahead of us when He would "raise up" shepherds over His people to lead them in the divine way of life.

> "I will give you **shepherds** who are loyal to me, and they will shepherd you with knowledge and skill" (Jeremiah 3:15 CSB).

> "I will gather the remnant of my flock from all the lands where I have banished them, and I will return them to their grazing land. They will become fruitful and numerous. I will raise up **shepherds** over them who will tend them. They will no longer be afraid or discouraged, nor will any be missing. This is the LORD's declaration" (Jeremiah 23:3–4 CSB).

Just as Jesus is going to return in the future, so the shepherds will return as well, being literally "raised up" by God out of the ground and given eternal life to "shepherd the people with knowledge and skill."

This is a prophecy about what will be taking place in the kingdom of God, the kingdom which gets into full swing once Jesus returns to Earth.

It gives new meaning to Peter's instructions to the elders among the New Testament believers, as he gives them the task of shepherds over God's flock. Read it for yourself:

> "Shepherd God's flock among you, not overseeing out of compulsion but willingly, as God would have you; not out of greed for money but eagerly; not lording it over those entrusted to you, but being examples to the flock. And when the chief Shepherd appears, you will receive the unfading crown of glory" (1 Peter 5:2–4 CSB).

It's perfectly fitting that Peter mentions the unfading crown of glory for these leaders of God's people, because it was actually embedded in the manger story when the shepherds were listening to the angel of God.

As we read previously of the shepherds, "the glory of the Lord shone round about them" (Luke 2:9). They had a shining, brilliant light surrounding them.

This, too, when understood at God speed, is a prediction of how believers will actually have a bright radiance, a crown of light emanating from them in the coming kingdom when they become immortal and divine:

> "Then the righteous will **shine like the sun** in their Father's kingdom. Let anyone who has ears listen" (Matthew 13:43 CSB).

God is going to "raise up" His shepherds from the grave to rule and reign with Him.

> "Blessed and holy is the one who shares in the first resurrection! The second death has no power over them, but they will be priests of God and of Christ, and they will reign with him...." (Revelation 20:6 CSB).

> "And he who overcomes, and keeps My works until the end, to him I will give power over the nations—He shall rule them with a rod of iron" (Revelation 2:26–27 NKJV).

This is the glorious end to the message of Scripture. The result of everything that has taken place will be the followers of the chief Shepherd being raised up to eternal life, newly born children of God so they can rule and reign with God, instructing other people in a second resurrection that takes place a thousand years after Jesus's return to Earth.

> "The rest of the dead did not come to life until the thousand years were completed" (Revelation 20:5 CSB).

The good news given to the shepherds of the past is also the good news about the shepherds of the future. Those shepherds are anyone and everyone who believes the message of God, repents of their sin (the breaking of God's laws) and allows Jesus—the true food, the true bread from heaven found in the house of bread in the city of the beloved—to fill their own body and literally become part of them.

And we must not forget that every human birth, including that of Jesus, is a foreshadow of our second birth, when we're "born again" into the spirit kingdom of God. Remember what was discussed with the Happy Birthday song. Our ultimate, future birthday, our second birth when we're born again, will be a birth into our new bodies composed of spirit as children of God.

As Jesus said: "unless one is born again, he cannot see the kingdom of God" (John 3:3 NKJV). It is after our second birth that we'll no longer be incarcerated in Egypt, in our dark place of misery, which is our physical bodies of flesh. Once we come out of Egypt, we'll be eternally alive, born into the real, spirit world on the divine level.

This is why the story of the birth of God includes the theme of coming out of Egypt:

"Out of Egypt have I called my son" (Matthew 2:15).

The fact that Jesus as a baby went to Egypt and then was brought out of it is an illustration of what is happening with you and me. We are the sons and daughters who are temporarily living in this miserable, spiritual Egypt, and we have to come out of it once we are called by God.

Hopefully you're now grasping the astounding truths that have been buried in the story of the birth of God for centuries. Because the Scriptures are not just about the birth of Jesus. They are pictures of our own glorious future as we are born into the same divine family of God. If we eat the true food, the One who lay in the feeding box for animals, we can come out of our beastly bodies of flesh, out of Egypt, and become children of God ourselves, shepherding others into the fold.

The end of God's story is merely the beginning. It is the beginning of immortal life with our Creator who made us to be like Him, giving us the knowledge to teach others how to learn to live God's way so that they, too, can inherit everlasting life.

All these pieces of the Bible are scattered throughout Scripture like a jigsaw puzzle and have been waiting to be properly fit together. And once perfectly joined, we can finally understand at God speed how truly fantastic the good news really is.

THE WOMAN CAUGHT IN ADULTERY

Many movies have portrayed the account of a woman caught in the act of adultery who subsequently is forgiven by Jesus, but when we listen to it at God speed, it takes on an amazing, new meaning. Here's the Bible passage:

> "'Teacher,'" they said to Jesus, 'this woman was caught in the act of adultery. The law of Moses says to stone her. What do you say?'

> "They were trying to trap him into saying something they could use against him, but Jesus stooped down and wrote in the dust with his finger.

> "They kept demanding an answer, so he stood up again and said, 'All right, but let the one who has never sinned throw the first stone!'

> "Then he stooped down again and wrote in the dust.

> "When the accusers heard this, they slipped away one by one, beginning with the oldest, until only Jesus was left in the middle of the crowd with the woman.

> "Then Jesus stood up again and said to the woman, 'Where are your accusers? Didn't even one of them condemn you?'

> "'No, Lord,' she said.

> "And Jesus said, 'Neither do I. Go and sin no more'" (John 8:4–11 NLT).

On the physical level, we see God forgiving a promiscuous woman after he wrote something mysterious on the ground with his finger. But when we listen at God speed, it's easy to understand the entire story is an illustration of what's going to happen to all of us when God returns.

The woman, as should be obvious, represents all of humanity. We all are the adulterous woman whom God is looking to forgive and will forgive upon our repentance, so He can marry His bride.

But the story features this fascinating bit about Jesus writing something in the dust with His finger. Here's the translation at God speed. It simply means that He is writing something inside people, since people are dust, as we've seen many times already.

And what is He writing? The likely answers can be found elsewhere in the Bible where He also is shown writing with His own finger. The famous Ten Commandments, the very law of God, was "written with the finger of God" (Exodus 31:18).

And Jesus said that in the future, "I will put my **law** in their inward parts, and **write** it in their hearts" (Jeremiah 31:33).

Jesus also said that in the future, "I will **write on them the name of my God**.... And I will also **write** on them my new name" (Revelation 3:12 NLT).

So it's very possible Jesus is using this spectacular teaching moment to let us all know that He's going to be writing on people (the dust of the ground) His laws and instructions, etching them inside minds and hearts with the end result of people receiving the name of God written on them.

This is what the accusers couldn't handle back then, and what the modern accusers still can't handle today. Hence, they slip away "until *only Jesus was left in the middle* of the crowd *with the woman*."

This is a message for the ages that has not been understood for thousands of years. As the crowd of accusers vanishes, the only ones left standing in the middle are Jesus and the previously adulterous woman. It's the Man and His woman, the Man and His bride, God and His forgiven and repentant followers! It's a prophecy about our glorious future united with God. The Creator and His bride will be left alone together at the center of it all, ruling and reigning together.

The Bible also says when the accusers of the adulterous woman *heard*, as in finally hearing the message of God, being convicted and corrected in their hearts, they're no longer accusing anyone. It's not only describing the physical event from two thousand years ago. It's a prophecy for the future. Because once God writes His instructions on everyone's heart, there won't be anyone left to accuse others of wrongdoing. People will finally get with the divine program.

One final point on this story. Its conclusion has a directive from Jesus to the woman to "Go and sin no more."

At God speed, this is actually a veiled prophecy for the future (in addition to the obvious physical instruction to that specific woman to whom He was speaking).

It's a promise for the future. Its ultimate fulfillment will take place once the woman (humanity) has been raised to immortal life, because it is then that people in the divine form will no longer be able to sin.

> "Whoever has been born of God **does not sin**, for His seed remains in him; and **he cannot sin**, because he has been born of God" (1 John 3:9 NKJV).

Yes, friends, once we've made the jump out of our physical bodies of flesh and become born of God as the literal children of God, we won't be able to sin anymore because God's very own presence, His "seed" (as the Bible calls it), remains in us for all time.

WATER INTO WINE AT A WEDDING ON THE THIRD DAY

The very first public miracle by Jesus was turning water into wine at a wedding feast. Even people who are not familiar with the Bible have usually heard of this story. But just in case you haven't, here it is:

> "On the third day a wedding took place in Cana of Galilee. Jesus's mother was there, and Jesus and his disciples were invited to the wedding as well.

> "When the wine ran out, Jesus's mother told him, 'They don't have any wine.'

> "'What does that have to do with you and me, woman?' Jesus asked. 'My hour has not yet come.'

> "'Do whatever he tells you,' his mother told the servants.

> "Now six stone water jars had been set there for Jewish purification. Each contained twenty or thirty gallons.

> "'Fill the jars with water,' Jesus told them. So they filled them to the brim.

> "Then he said to them, 'Now draw some out and take it to the headwaiter.' And they did.

> "When the headwaiter tasted the water (after it had become wine), he did not know where it came from—though the servants who had drawn the water knew. He called the groom and told him, 'Everyone sets out the fine wine first, then, after people are drunk, the inferior. But you have kept the fine wine until now.'

> "Jesus did this, the first of his signs, in Cana of Galilee. He revealed his glory, and his disciples believed in him" (John 2:1–11 CSB).

Let's now translate this at God speed, as it declares the end from the beginning.

We'll start by asking: What is the most important wedding celebration mentioned in the Bible? And, of course, the answer is the wedding feast when God (the Groom) returns to Earth to marry His bride, repentant believers.

> "Let us be glad, rejoice, and give him glory, because the marriage of the Lamb has come, and his bride has prepared herself" (Revelation 19:7 CSB).

> "Blessed are they which are called unto the marriage supper of the Lamb" (Revelation 19:9).

So, the wedding celebration at Cana in Galilee is, at God speed, a preview of the end of this physical age, and the beginning of the new time period in which God's marriage to humanity is consummated. Notice also how Scripture says this wedding takes place "on the third day."

As mentioned earlier, three days cover the past, present, and future: yesterday, today, and tomorrow, just as the airlines give us flight status for any trip. Yesterday is the past. Today is the present. Tomorrow is the future. And "Jesus Christ is the same yesterday, today, and forever" (Hebrews 13:8 CSB).

Hence, the wedding taking place on the third day is a veiled prophecy for the marriage feast of the Lamb, which takes place tomorrow, in our still-to-come future. The end of today's age is merely the beginning of the next one, the eternal one, starting in the future of tomorrow.

At the wedding in Cana, water is poured into six stone jars, filling them to the brim with twenty to thirty gallons each. And what do these jars represent? When we connect the dots in Scripture, it's obvious they represent human beings.

> "Zion's precious **children**...they are regarded as clay **jars**, the work of a potter's hands!" (Lamentations 4:2 CSB).

> "Now **we** have this treasure in clay **jars**, so that this extraordinary power may be from God and not from us" (2 Corinthians 4:7 CSB).

Interestingly, the water was poured into six jars, and six is the number of man, who was created on the sixth day of the week (Genesis 1:31) and whose work was to be done in six days (Exodus 20:9). Furthermore, if we weigh twenty to thirty gallons of water, that translates to 160 to 249 pounds. According to the Centers for Disease Control, the average weight of a woman is 170.6 pounds, and the average man weighs 197.9 pounds. Both figures just happen to fall within the range of what Jesus had mentioned about the water weight in the jars. It's not a coincidence. It's God speed.

In the Bible, water is associated with the Spirit of God on many occasions, including: "When he said 'living water,' he was speaking of the Spirit" (John 7:39 NLT).

Thus, the jars being filled with water represent human beings who are being filled with the Holy Spirit, the very presence of God Himself. And then what happens? An astounding, instantaneous transformation. In the blink of an eye, the water gets transformed from one state to another, becoming a more delicious, flavorful, and perfected product called wine.

What event does this sound like in the Bible? How about the instant transformation of our human, mortal, physical bodies into our immortal, perfected, spirit bodies? Yes, this wonderful event eventually will happen but not until the end when Jesus returns. The apostle Paul describes the quickening change this way:

> "It will happen in a moment, in the blink of an eye, when the last trumpet is blown. For when the trumpet sounds, those who have died will be raised to live forever. And we who are living will also be transformed. For our dying bodies must be transformed into bodies that will never die; our mortal bodies must be transformed into immortal bodies" (1 Corinthians 15:52–53 NLT).

So, just as the ordinary water at the Cana wedding had its physical nature miraculously changed in an instant to become something quite different (and some would say much better), so our ordinary bodies will be miraculously changed "in the blink of an eye" into something far superior: bodies that never die. The fact that the wine saved for the end is called the "good," "best," or "fine" wine, depending on your Bible translation, is likely referring to the good nature of those being granted eternal life. In other words, they have repented of their sins and will have become perfected in God's sight, just as good wine gets better with age. And the transformation takes place at the end, just as our transformation into our immortal bodies takes place at the end of this age.

Here are some other fascinating points about this spectacular event.

Jesus wasn't the only one invited to the wedding at Cana. His disciples were invited, too. It will be the same scenario at the end-time wedding as well, as we've already read: "Blessed are those invited to the marriage feast of the Lamb!" (Revelation 19:9 CSB).

The story also tells us that turning water into wine was "the first of his signs." In other words, it was the first public miracle of Jesus. So from the very start of His ministry, He was declaring the end from the beginning, pointing to the future wedding feast at His return.

The account also mentions that it was at this wedding in Cana that "He revealed his glory." We should ask ourselves: "Won't Jesus be revealing His glory when He returns at the future wedding feast as King of kings and Lord of lords?" The answer is a definite yes, and believers actually will share in that glory: "When Christ, who is your life, appears, then you also will appear with him in glory" (Colossians 3:4 CSB).

And there is one final point from the Cana wedding that is very easy to miss, yet it's extremely important.

"'Do whatever he tells you,' his mother told the servants" (John 2:5 CSB).

Here we have the parent of Jesus telling the servants to do whatever Jesus tells them to do. It sounds very much like the famous voice from the cloud stating: "This is my Son, the Chosen One; listen to him!" (Luke 9:35 CSB).

Isn't this the entire message of the Bible? To listen to Jesus and do whatever He tells us to do? We all need to come to the conclusion that we are meant to obey God. It's as simple as that. It's expressed countless ways throughout Scripture, but here are two famous quotes from the Old and New Testaments to drive that point home:

> "Fear God, and keep his commandments: for this is the whole duty of man"
> (Ecclesiastes 12:13).

> "If you want to enter into life, keep the commandments"
> (Matthew 19:17 CSB).

Yes, just as Mary said, we should all do whatever Jesus tells us to do.

The reason we all exist is that God is enlarging His family. He is giving human beings the chance to learn the ways that lead to eternal life, doing precisely what He wants. If we refuse to keep His instructions, we will be dead forever:

> "For the wages of sin is death; but the gift of God is eternal life through
> Jesus Christ our Lord" (Romans 6:23).

The miracle of water being instantaneously changed into wine on the third day has an incredible message at God speed.

Just as the water was transformed in an instant to become the best wine at the wedding feast in Cana, so we will be changed in an instant to become the perfected bride of Christ at the future marriage feast of the Lamb, which takes place tomorrow, on the third day. God's glory will be revealed along with our glory, and that is when life everlasting begins. And it was all foretold through the very first miracle of Jesus. At a wedding. Our end has been declared from the beginning.

THE BLIND MAN HEALED BY WASHING OFF MUD FROM HIS EYES

One of the most inspiring miracles recorded in Scripture is the famous healing of a man who had been blind from birth. What's especially interesting is the recipe Jesus used to give the man his sight. It involves putting mud on his face, specifically, his eyes. Here's the Bible account before we make the jump to God speed to understand its higher meaning:

> "After he said these things he spit on the ground, made some mud from
> the saliva, and spread the mud on his eyes.

"'Go,' he told him, 'wash in the pool of Siloam' (which means "Sent"). So he left, washed, and came back seeing.

"His neighbors and those who had seen him before as a beggar said, 'Isn't this the one who used to sit begging?'

"Some said, 'He's the one.' Others were saying, 'No, but he looks like him.'

"He kept saying, 'I'm the one.'

"So they asked him, 'Then how were your eyes opened?'

"He answered, 'The man called Jesus made mud, spread it on my eyes, and told me, "Go to Siloam and wash." So when I went and washed I received my sight'" (John 9:6–11 CSB).

All right. On the physical level, a man blind from birth has his sight restored after God puts mud on the man's eyes and then tells him to wash it off. Now let's make the jump to God speed. You already know how to do this, so let's just connect the dots in Scripture to reveal the more profound meeting.

When the Bible talks about mud or clay being spread onto the man's eyes, it's simply referring to the flesh that covers our spirit inside of us. Remember, mankind was created from the dust of the ground, the land, the dirt, the clay, the mud. Our fleshly covering is made of clay. We've got mud on our face, and it's a big disgrace, as Queen sang in "We Will Rock You." Scripture notes:

"He has thrown me into the **mud**. I'm nothing more than **dust** and **ashes**" (Job 30:19 NLT).

"He lifted me out of the pit of despair, out of the **mud** and the **mire**" (Psalm 40:2 NLT).

Meanwhile, "eyes" in Scripture can refer to spirits, as in "seven **eyes**, which are the seven **spirits** of God" (Revelation 5:6).

So when Jesus put mud, or clay as some Bibles have it, over the man's eyes, the meaning at God speed is that our personal spirit can't see properly because we're covered by the flesh, both physically and spiritually. Yes, we have skin covering our bodies, but more disturbingly, we have the lusts and works of the flesh, our personal desires and wrongful actions, blinding us from the truth.

Here are some Bible examples of our lusts and works of the flesh:

> "Now the works of the flesh are obvious: sexual immorality, moral impurity, promiscuity, idolatry, sorcery, hatreds, strife, jealousy, outbursts of anger, selfish ambitions, dissensions, factions, envy, drunkenness, carousing, and anything similar. I am warning you about these things—as I warned you before—that those who practice such things will not inherit the kingdom of God" (Galatians 5:19–21 CSB).

> "For all that is in the world, the lust of the flesh, and the lust of the eyes, and the pride of life, is not of the Father, but is of the world" (1 John 2:16).

> "Those who live according to the flesh have their minds set on what the flesh desires; but those who live in accordance with the Spirit have their minds set on what the Spirit desires" (Romans 8:5 NIV).

> "We all once conducted ourselves in the lusts of our flesh, fulfilling the desires of the flesh and of the mind, and were by nature children of wrath, just as the others" (Ephesians 2:3 NKJV).

> "Whoever sows to please their flesh, from the flesh will reap destruction; whoever sows to please the Spirit, from the Spirit will reap eternal life" (Galatians 6:8 NIV).

Obviously, when we're driven by what our flesh wants, that does not lead to eternal life. We're soiled by our individual desires and actions that don't agree with the Spirit of God. We have to wash our personal spirits clean of the "mud," which symbolizes the flesh. That is the precise reason Jesus tells the man to wash the mud off his eyes. He is telling mankind to remove the desires of our flesh from our spirits, our minds, so we'll no longer be spiritually blind.

Please also notice that the man was not healed instantly while he still had the mud on his face. God instructed him to *do* something, to take action, which was to go to a pool with the name of "Sent." When he obeyed God's commandment, when he went where he was being "sent" by God, it was then that he was healed. In other words, mankind gets healed and can see properly when we follow God's commands, go to the place to which we're being sent, and wash the desires of the flesh from our minds. In the final end, as you know, we completely get rid of our mud, our physical flesh, and will be transformed into spirit only. That's when we have life without end and will see perfectly.

DOUBTING THOMAS

Most people know that Jesus had twelve apostles, but they would be hard-pressed to name every one of them. However, one apostle whose name everyone seems to remember is Thomas, as he has become infamous as "Doubting Thomas."

He got that nickname because he doubted that Christ had risen from the dead until he had visual proof Jesus was alive again. Here's the Bible account before we make the jump to God speed for more astonishing truth:

> "Now Thomas, called the Twin, one of the twelve, was not with them when Jesus came. The other disciples therefore said to him, 'We have seen the Lord.'

> "So he said to them, 'Unless I see in His hands the print of the nails, and put my finger into the print of the nails, and put my hand into His side, I will not believe.'

> "And after eight days His disciples were again inside, and Thomas with them. Jesus came, the doors being shut, and stood in the midst, and said, 'Peace to you!'

> "Then He said to Thomas, 'Reach your finger here, and look at My hands; and reach your hand here, and put it into My side. Do not be unbelieving, but believing.'

> "And Thomas answered and said to Him, 'My Lord and my God!'

> "Jesus said to him, 'Thomas, because you have seen Me, you have believed. Blessed are those who have not seen and yet have believed'" (John 20:24–29 NKJV).

The first key that helps us shift to God speed here is actually the name of this apostle: Thomas. For those who don't know what Thomas means, it simply means "twin." So every Tom, Thom, or Tommy you've ever known actually carries the name "twin."

The Bible goes out of its way to stress this point, as it explains that Thomas was actually called "Twin" by his fellow apostles. So the word *twin* is really appearing twice in this passage. Verse 24 could be translated: "But the Twin, who was called the Twin, one of the twelve...."

The Bible is making this repetition to grab our attention to the significance of being a twin, because in the spiritual story that's being told, we as human beings are really twins of God. We look like God and we're intended to be doing what God does, such as "reign with him" (Revelation 20:6).

Remember, the first human beings, Adam and Eve, were both made in the image and likeness of God:

> "Then God said, 'Let us make man in our image, according to our likeness. They will rule....' So God created man in his own image; he created him in the image of God; he created them male and female" (Genesis 1:26–27 CSB).

Spiritually speaking, Adam and Eve—and all of us, for that matter, since we descended from them—are the twins of God and twins of each other. In a sense, we all can be called Thomas, Tom, or Tommy. And most can and should be called Doubting Thomas, because most of humanity as a whole has been doubting God and His plan for thousands of years.

Here's another important point in the story of Thomas that many people may have never realized. It has to do with the timing of this event, and what Jesus told Thomas. Remember, during the first time Jesus appeared to His disciples behind locked doors, Thomas the unbeliever was not among them.

But a week later, and most Bibles use the phrase "after eight days," Jesus appeared again to His apostles, and Thomas was with them during this *second* gathering. And Jesus specifically told the Twin, "Do not be unbelieving, but believing."

Now open your ears to hear the spirit story being broadcast at God speed. Eight days after the first appearance by God to His people, God appears a second time to specifically address the doubting twin, representing most of humanity who has doubted the Creator. He says, in effect, to stop being an unbeliever. This entire event is a veiled prophecy of the Second Resurrection, the judgment that takes place in the *second* round of gathering God's people—specifically, the unbelievers, those who did not get with the program in the First Resurrection.

Remember, believers are raised to eternal life when Jesus comes back at the First Resurrection.

> "Blessed and holy is he who has part in the **first resurrection**" (Revelation 20:6 NKJV).

But a thousand years later when the rest of the dead (the unbelievers) are brought back to life, is when the Second Resurrection takes place.

> "But the rest of the dead did not live again until the thousand years were finished" (Revelation 20:5 NKJV).

The First Resurrection corresponds to Jesus's first appearance to His believing disciples, without Thomas the unbeliever present. Then, in the second round, Jesus is appearing to Thomas the unbeliever (representing all unbelievers) eight days later, telling him to stop being faithless and believe. This is exactly what will happen for the majority of humanity, the rebels, during the second round of saving.

The reason the Bible mentions "eight days" is because it's making a connection to other prophecies about the "eighth day." For instance, the act of circumcision was performed on the eighth day.

> "And he that is eight days old shall be circumcised among you" (Genesis 17:12).

Circumcision is the removing of the foreskin from the flesh. It's telling us, at God speed, that the covering of flesh is going to be removed on the eighth day. Because that's when everyone else, all the fleshly unbelievers like Thomas, will finally have the lusts of their flesh removed and have a clear understanding to become an immortal member of God's family!

And it's not just circumcision that paints this picture. Look at God's holy days. The Feast of Tabernacles, which is a harvest festival, mentions the "eighth day" as well.

> "On the eighth day you are to hold a sacred assembly" (Leviticus 23:36 CSB).

> "You are to celebrate the LORD's festival on the fifteenth day of the sev-
> enth month for seven days after you have gathered the produce of the
> land. There will be complete rest on the first day and complete rest on
> the eighth day" (Leviticus 23:39 CSB).

So let's connect these dots to awaken your mind. This festival takes place "after you have gathered the produce of the land." This, my friends, is talking about resurrection. We are the produce of the land that God is gathering. We are the harvest. And there's a sabbath rest on the first day, representing the First Resurrection, and another exactly one week later, on the eighth day, the Second Resurrection, the start of another weekly time cycle. It's simply astounding how the Bible has embedded this message numerous times in Scriptures to which millions of people don't give a second thought.

Remember, Thomas is the twin. He's Number Two. He's the second. As in Second Resurrection! Are you understanding how God keeps repeating the same hints in different ways?

We also must not forget that Thomas the Twin, this Number Two, is the one who demanded visual proof of the risen Christ before he'd believe. This is the clincher, folks. Because faithless unbelievers, the ones who didn't believe because they did not see God, will finally stand before their risen Creator at the Second Resurrection and finally understand that everything they've denied has actually been true. Because for them, seeing is believing, as the saying goes. This is why Jesus says: "Thomas, because you have seen Me, you have believed. Blessed are those who have not seen and yet have believed."

Translation at God speed: "All you Number Two people, you doubting folks in the Second Resurrection, you only believe in Me now because you have seen Me. But all those faithful people who did not actually see Me but still believed in Me are truly the blessed ones. That's why they were raised in the First Resurrection and have already become the immortal children of God!"

This whole account gives even more meaning to those 1969 songs mentioned earlier. It was Major Tom to whom David Bowie sang "Can you hear me," and The Who wondered the same of Tommy. The Creator inspired those lyrics because it's God who is actually asking us, the Doubting Thomases, the twins of God who are unbelievers, if we can hear Him.

THE SECOND PASSOVER

While we're on this "second" theme, are you aware that there is something known as the second Passover in the Bible? Millions of people are very familiar with Passover, one of God's holy days in the first month of the year illustrating how people can be spared the death penalty by slaying and consuming a lamb, along with some other customs. But many are not familiar at all with the command for a second Passover. The instruction initially appears in the fourth book of Moses:

> "If anyone of you or your posterity is unclean because of a corpse, or is far away on a journey, he may still keep the LORD's Passover. On the fourteenth day of the **second** month, at twilight, they may keep it. They shall eat it with unleavened bread and bitter herbs. They shall leave none of it until morning, nor break one of its bones. According to all the ordinances of the Passover they shall keep it" (Numbers 9:10–12 NKJV).

There you have it. If someone is unclean because of a corpse or is far away on a journey, he or she could keep the Passover with all the same customs but in the *second* month instead of the first.

Now let's make the jump to God speed so you can understand the reason for this. It's nothing more than what we've already learned here. It's referring to the time of the *Second* Resurrection.

The people who are considered "clean," those following God properly, are spared death and are raised in the First Resurrection, which was discussed a moment ago. But those who are "unclean" have to wait until "next time." They have to wait until the Second Resurrection, which occurs in the next time period, the "second month."

The explanation of who is unclean may make you giggle. This passage says people can be unclean "because of a corpse" or if they're "far away on a journey."

Let's start with this corpse business. At God speed, this is referring to most of humanity, since most people who ever existed are spiritually dead. They're the walking dead. They are walking corpses. As Jesus famously told a man, "Follow me; and let the dead bury their dead" (Matthew 8:22).

Hence, most human beings are unclean "because of a corpse," since we are the spiritual corpses! We're all spiritually dead until we are given true life by our heavenly Maker.

And the reference to being "far away on a journey" is saying something very similar. It refers to people who are "far away" from God spiritually. They're on a journey moving away from the Creator as they avoid His commandments. They're wandering away in the land of Nod, as *Nod* means "wandering." Scripture is filled with descriptions about being far from God, and here are two famous ones:

> "The LORD is far from the wicked" (Proverbs 15:29).

> "These people honor me with their lips, but their hearts are far from me" (Matthew 15:8 NIV).

The point is that people are unclean because we are not close to God, not following His instructions properly. Most are like zombies who are spiritually dead. It is these people, these corpses who didn't make it in the first round, who will get their second chance at eternal life in the Second Resurrection, pictured by the second Passover in the second month.

To drive this point home, Scripture records an actual celebration of a second Passover, and the language throughout makes it quite clear it's not merely recording the historical event of the distant past. It's also picturing the joyous time in our future when a whole lot of people will be given their second chance. It's found in chapter 30 of 2 Chronicles, and I'll give you some excerpts here so you can understand the higher meaning at God speed:

> "The king, his officials, and all the community of Jerusalem decided to celebrate Passover **a month later than usual**. They were unable to celebrate it at the prescribed time because not enough priests could be purified by then, and the **people had not yet assembled** at Jerusalem" (2 Chronicles 30:2–3 NLT).

> "Don't become obstinate now like your fathers did. Give your allegiance to the LORD, and **come to his sanctuary** that he has consecrated forever. Serve the LORD your God so that he may turn his burning anger away from you, for when you return to the LORD, your brothers and your sons **will receive mercy** in the presence of their captors and will return to this land. For the LORD your God is gracious and merciful; he will not turn his face away from you if you return to him" (2 Chronicles 30:8–9 CSB).

"And there **assembled at Jerusalem much people** to keep the feast of unleavened bread in the **second** month, a **very great congregation**" (2 Chronicles 30:13).

"For there were **many** in the congregation that were **not sanctified**...

"For a **multitude of the people...had not cleansed themselves**, yet did they eat the passover otherwise than it was written. But Hezekiah prayed for them, saying, The **good LORD pardon every one That prepareth his heart to seek God**, the LORD God of his fathers, though he be not cleansed according to the purification of the sanctuary.

"And the LORD hearkened to Hezekiah, and **healed the people**. And the children of Israel that were present at Jerusalem kept the feast of unleavened bread seven days with **great gladness**: and the Levites and the priests praised the LORD day by day, **singing** with loud instruments unto the LORD.

"And Hezekiah spake comfortably unto all the Levites **that taught the good knowledge** of the LORD: and they did eat throughout the feast seven days, offering peace offerings, and **making confession** to the LORD God of their fathers" (2 Chronicles 30:17–22).

"The **entire assembly** of Judah **rejoiced**, including the priests, the Levites, all who came from the land of Israel, the **foreigners** who came to the festival, and all those who lived in Judah. There was **great joy** in the city, for **Jerusalem had not seen a celebration like this one**...." (2 Chronicles 30:25–26 NLT).

As we can see by the highlighted text, the singular event from the time of Hezekiah is actually broadcasting at God speed the wonderful message for people who have not properly prepared themselves at this time for God's return. They had not cleansed themselves, but in the **second** round, God is ready and willing to pardon and heal them, giving them eternal life, as long as they turn from their rebellion and seek Him. The people, including foreigners, those who knew little or nothing about God, will admit their wrongdoing and participate in an incredibly joyful celebration, a party to top all parties. It is the future celebration of formerly rebellious people who will finally beam with the goodness of God.

> "They will come home and sing songs of joy on the heights of Je-
> rusalem. They will be radiant because of the LORD's good gifts....
> Their life will be like a watered garden, and all their sorrows will be
> gone. The young women will dance for joy, and the men—old and
> young—will join in the celebration. I will turn their mourning into
> joy. I will comfort them and exchange their sorrow for rejoicing"
> (Jeremiah 31:12–13 NLT).

By now, it should be more than clear that the second Passover is really about the future, when we listen at God speed. It is the second chance for all those who have not properly prepared their character during this first round to become immortal children of God. Thank God for that second chance to be saved!

NEVER-ENDING LIGHT

And now, friends, here's some very good news. There is a time coming when night will not exist anymore. There will be only light. It's described at the end of the story and also at the beginning. Darkness and every-thing associated with it—evil, the physical flesh and the lusts thereof, and death—will be a thing of the past.

Many Bible verses reveal this and, when the dots are connected, they take on a staggering, glorious meaning when understood at God speed. So let's walk through them and put an end to the darkness, illuminating your mind with the shining light of truth.

The end of night is discussed at the very end of the story, in the final chapters of the book of Revelation.

> "There will be **no more night**. They will not need the light of a lamp or
> the light of the sun, for the Lord God will give them light. And they will
> reign for ever and ever" (Revelation 22:5 NIV).

> "The city does not need the sun or the moon to shine on it, because
> the glory of God illuminates it, and its lamp is the Lamb. The nations
> will walk by its light, and the kings of the earth will bring their glo-
> ry into it. Its gates will never close by day because it will **never be
> night** there. They will bring the glory and honor of the nations into
> it. Nothing unclean will ever enter it, nor anyone who does what is
> detestable or false, but only those written in the Lamb's book of life"
> (Revelation 21:23–27 CSB).

Making the jump to God speed should come quite easily at this point, because we merely connect these Scriptures with others to reveal the meaning of what God is saying on the spirit level. And we've already read many having to do with night and its associated words: darkness, evil, death, misery, Egypt, tears, and others. They all equate to the things of the flesh. Remember what we learned when discussing *Raiders of the Lost Ark*.

> "God is light, and in him is no darkness at all" (1 John 1:5).

> "His face was like the sun shining in all its brilliance" (Revelation 1:16 NIV).

While God in His spirit form is brilliant light, we as physical human beings are the opposite of light, and that is darkness. We are the night, when talking at God speed.

> "See, darkness covers the earth and thick darkness is over the peoples"
> (Isaiah 60:2 NIV).

Remember, the earth represents people, since that's what we're physically made from, and the above verse equates the earth with the peoples. The darkness, or thick darkness that covers all the people is our flesh. Our skin is much darker than the bright light of the sun. This is the darkness, the shadow of death, that we all bear on our bodies from the moment we're born. No matter how healthy we seem to be, we're actually dwelling in what God calls the "body of death."

> "What a wretched man I am! Who will rescue me from this **body of death**?" (Romans 7:24 CSB).

Here's another verse that equates darkness and night with physical people.

> "You make darkness, and it is night, In which all the beasts of the forest creep about" (Psalm 104:20 NKJV).

At God speed, we are the beasts, the physical animals creeping about in our bodies of darkness. Again, we are the night. Night represents the flesh. It is the "outer darkness" famously spoken of in this passage:

> "Then said the king to the servants, Bind him hand and foot, and take him away, and cast him into **outer darkness**; there shall be weeping and gnashing of teeth" (Matthew 22:13).

I know we've read it before, but it cannot be stressed enough to learn what our loving Creator is saying at God speed. If we're not obedient, we end up in "outer darkness," a body of flesh in which there's weeping—in other words, sorrow and pain. It is the "darkness which may be felt" mentioned in Exodus 10:21, because we can all touch our skin and feel our own darkness.

We all "walk through the valley of the shadow of death" (Psalm 23:4) and "sit in darkness and in the shadow of death" (Luke 1:79).

All these verses are saying the same thing, using a variety of words. They all point to our human condition in the flesh, as opposed to the spirit level, the God plane, which is represented by light, with no darkness at all.

This is why some Scriptures that may seem unrelated at first glance are actually tightly connected. For example:

> "Weeping may last through the night, but joy comes with the morning" (Psalm 30:5 NLT).

> "The night is nearly over; the day is almost here. So let us put aside the deeds of darkness and put on the armor of light" (Romans 13:12 NIV).

Both of these verses are alluding to the same thing at God speed. The weeping refers to our time in our physical flesh, when there is plenty of pain, sorrow, and tears. It happens in the night because the night refers to our human bodies. But joy comes with the morning. In other words, our eternal life comes with the light, with God, which is represented by the morning, when light returns and we actually get rid of our darkness, our flesh, and become shining spirit beings on the divine level.

This is why it indicates the night is nearly over and the day is almost here. Because our time in our "night bodies," our physical bodies of flesh, is about to be finished. Our bodies are going to have a brand-new, blazing covering of God's own spirit. We're going to "put on the armor of light."

This is why "there will be no more night" and it will "never be night" in the future, because human beings who were once in darkness of the night will no longer be made of flesh. We will be transformed from the darkness of night into the brightness of day, into the spirit of God when we will finally enjoy immortality.

> "For the LORD your God will be **your everlasting light**, and your God will be **your glory**" (Isaiah 60:19 NLT).

> "For you are all **children of light** and **children of the day**. We do not belong to the night or the darkness" (1 Thessalonians 5:5 CSB).

Yes, the Bible foretells the future destiny for all those who get with the program. "No more night" means no more flesh and everything associated with the flesh, including death!

> "And God shall wipe away all tears from their eyes; and there shall be **no more death**, neither sorrow, nor crying, neither shall there be any more pain: for the former things are passed away" (Revelation 21:4).

Night will no longer exist, because death will no longer exist. God is equating death with night and the flesh. People eventually will be changed from their bodies of death, their bodies of flesh, their bodies of the spiritual night into bodies of immortal life, their bodies of spirit, their bodies of the light of day. This is what's being said when we connect the dots and listen at God speed!

If this isn't enough to amaze you, there's more. The end of the story when the night, flesh, and death no longer exist is merely the beginning. It's the start of our eternal life as spirit beings and, shockingly, it was put into ink at the very beginning of the Bible itself. That's correct. All this business about the end of darkness, the end of flesh and the end of death is embedded in the book of Genesis, and it's easy to see when we read it at God speed. Because God declares the end from the beginning. Allow me to explain.

By now, it's obvious that the end of the human story is that we are brought out of the ground, out of our earthly bodies, and given eternal life when God breathes into us His spirit of life so that we become living beings for eternity. In stunning fashion, this final destination for us is recorded right at the start of Scripture, in the second chapter of Genesis. Here it is:

> "And the LORD God formed man of the dust of the ground, and breathed into his nostrils the breath of life; and man became a living being" (Genesis 2:7 NKJV).

Are you seeing and hearing this at God speed? Because this is not merely referring to the creation of the physical man Adam thousands of years ago. Remember, God declares the end from the beginning, and He's telling us the end of our story right from the start of Scripture. He's saying that He will once again form man out of the ground, whether it be from our walking physical bodies of dust or from the dust resting in our buried graves. It is then that He'll breathe into us His breath of life, His own immortal spirit, and we formerly human beings of flesh will become "living" beings, people made of spirit who are living forever!

This is not the only place in Genesis where our amazing future transformation from darkness to light is secretly embedded. In fact, if we examine the very first lines of Scripture, we can now understand the incredible message broadcast at God speed.

> "In the beginning God created the heavens and the earth. The earth was
> without form, and void; and darkness was on the face of the deep"
> (Genesis 1:1–2 NKJV).

At this point, you may be able to sense what I'm about to say. And, yes, I'm going to go there. Because it's truth that will stun millions. Not only are these two initial Bible verses talking about the ancient past with the creation of the physical universe, but also it's a veiled prophecy for the very end, when we're made immortal.

When Scripture says the earth was without form and void, it is saying, at God speed, that people were created without their finished form, because they were void, empty of God's spirit. The darkness on the face of the deep is talking about the darkness, the flesh, on our human faces. We all have the face of the deep. Remember, we are the ones living in "the deep," the abyss, this level that is far below the heights of heaven. It's the Deep State, where we're "Rolling in the Deep," as Adele sings.

But as we all know, we human beings made up of earth were not intended by God to remain empty of His presence. We're actually meant to have God inhabit our personal space. God has said so:

> "He who fashioned and made the earth, he founded it; he did not create it
> to be empty, but formed it to be inhabited" (Isaiah 45:18 NIV).

And as we step forward in the book of Genesis, we can see that God will take divine action with people, moving upon the face of the waters, which is our faces, to turn us into children of God who are no longer made of darkness, but made of light, since we'll have made it to the divine level.

> "And the Spirit of God moved upon the face of the waters. And God said,
> Let there be light: and there was light. And God saw the light, that it
> was good" (Genesis 1:2–4).

At God speed, the start to the Bible is blaring the end game for all of us. When God's Holy Spirit moves into us, the darkness (flesh) becomes light (spirit)! And when God sees us as the new light, His "children of light," He notes that it's now "good." Why? Because we're no longer evil. We're no longer of the darkness, of the flesh, of the night.

> "For you are all **children of light** and **children of the day**. We do not belong to the night or the darkness" (1 Thessalonians 5:5 CSB).

> "Then **the righteous will shine like the sun** in their Father's kingdom. Let anyone who has ears listen" (Matthew 13:43 CSB).

The next verses in Genesis confirm the stark difference between divine people made of light and fleshly human beings made of darkness, as He separated them and gave different names to both:

> "God divided the light from the darkness. And God called the light **Day**, and the darkness he called **Night**" (Genesis 1:4–5).

Yes, folks, as you have been reading in this entire book, the Day and light represent spirit beings on the divine level, while Night and darkness represent flesh and human beings on the physical level. If we think about it, the day is when we're awake and alert, as in alive. The night is when we're tired and go to sleep, and sleep symbolizes death in Scripture. As we've seen, it's called the "sleep of death" (Psalm 13:3).

It's nothing short of life-changing when we realize the Bible is broadcasting more than a physical message about ancient history. It is airing the tremendous future for everyone when it's read at God speed. The story of God is circular. It's a cycle that leads to eternal glory for us. The end of the story is merely the beginning, and there will be no more night and a never-ending light when the darkness of fleshly human beings is transformed by the breath of God into a new state of brilliance. The bright light of God's own family. In the beginning that is still ahead of us.

THE BEAST

When many people hear about "the beast" in Scripture, they automatically tense up with angst. But now that we know how to listen to Scripture at God speed, there's absolutely no need to shrink back in fear. We're going to take an eye-opening look now at what the Bible means by the beast, and what it means for you and your future.

As you already know, a beast is a mortal creature created by God, whether it's a lamb, dog, wolf, or serpent. Take your pick of your favorite animal. All beasts are animals, all animals are beasts. And now that you've made it this far into the book, it should be no surprise to learn that the beast, when heard at God speed, is merely another word to represent mortal man, as in all of mankind, since man is also a mortal creature created by God.

We'll take a look at Scripture in a moment to confirm this, but it's already obvious that beasts are personified as people all the time in normal conversation. People are referred to as scaredy cats, filthy dogs, birdbrains, wise owls, peaceful doves, war hawks, silly rabbits, busy bees, gorgeous and sly foxes, smelly pigs, lazy sloths, curious monkeys, creepy worms, lying snakes, and the ever-popular dumb asses. Many sports teams are named for animals, and we even call our children "kids," which, as you know, are young goats, young beasts. It's no coincidence that God has developed our language to broadcast His higher message by equating animals with people.

In the Bible, many Scriptures outright declare that people are represented by a variety of beasts, including lambs, wolves, fish, worms, and snakes, for starters. We've read some of these before, but it's important to cement this man-beast concept into our little bird brains:

> "You have made **mankind** like the **fish** of the sea" (Habakkuk 1:14 CSB).

> "You are My **flock**, the flock of My pasture; **you are men**, and I am your God" (Ezekiel 34:31 NKJV).

> "Feed my **lambs**" (John 21:15).

> "I send you forth as **lambs** among **wolves**" (Luke 10:3).

> "Do not fear, you **worm** Jacob, you **men** of Israel" (Isaiah 41:14 CSB).

> "You make darkness, and it is night, In which all the **beasts** of the forest creep about" (Psalm 104:20 NKJV).

Just as animals are personified in everyday conversation, so they are personified in the Bible, because beasts represent all of humanity. There are even instances in Scripture when beasts speak with human voices: a serpent talking to Eve in Eden (Genesis 3:4) and a "dumb ass speaking with man's voice" (2 Peter 2:16) in the story of Balaam's talking donkey (Numbers 22:28).

In a variety of ways, Scripture itself tells us outright that a beast represents humanity. Here, cattle are equated with people:

> "For the law of Moses says, 'You must not muzzle an **ox** to keep it from eating as it treads out the grain.' Was God thinking only about **oxen** when he said this? Wasn't he **actually speaking to us**? Yes, it was **written for us**, so that the one who plows and the one who threshes the grain might both expect a share of the harvest" (1 Corinthians 9:9–10 NLT).

The Word of God even refers to Samson's wife as a young cow, specifically a "heifer" (Judges 14:18).

Another way is the famous "number of the beast." Regarding this, we're now going to connect some dots from Scripture, so be sure to have your eyes and ears tuned to God speed, as it will become more than obvious once you see the words on the page.

As we've read before, six is the number of man, who was created on the sixth day of the week (Genesis 1:31) and whose work was to be done in six days (Exodus 20:9). (It may also be the reason people are buried six feet under, and social distancing had people six feet apart during the coronavirus pandemic of 2020.)

Now let's connect the beginning of the Bible in Genesis to the end in Revelation, with three different Bible translations of the same verse mentioning the "number of the beast":

> "Here is wisdom. Let him who has understanding calculate the number of the **beast**, for it is the number of a **man**: His number *is* 666" (Revelation 13:18 NKJV).

> "This calls for wisdom: Let the one who has understanding calculate the number of the **beast**, because it is the number of a **person**. Its number is 666" (Revelation 13:18 CSB).

> "Wisdom is needed here. Let the one with understanding solve the meaning of the number of the **beast**, for it is the number of a **man**. His number is 666" (Revelation 13:18 NLT).

The New Living Translation has a footnote indicating the word "man" could be translated as "**humanity**." Thus, all of these Bibles are saying exactly what I'm saying. The number of the beast is simply the number of man, the number of any person, the number of all humanity. (It's kind of funny that this mention of 666 appears in verse 18, which is 6+6+6. This may actually be a bit of divine humor at God speed.)

The reason the number six is repeated three times is nothing more than what we've learned already. It is covering all time periods: past, present, and future. Yesterday, today and tomorrow. Remember, "Jesus Christ is the same yesterday, today, and forever" (Hebrews 13:8 CSB).

The reason God says wisdom is required to understand this is because He's telling us to connect the spiritual dots that are scattered "here a little, and there a little" (Isaiah 28:10) throughout the entire Bible and listen to this at God speed. Getting wisdom is another way of saying "reaching God speed."

When it says the number of the beast is the number of a man, person, or humanity, it's especially referring to rebellious mankind in opposition to God. Because it's people who are defiant and disobedient in the past, present, and future who remain stuck in the flesh and will not make the jump out of this natural, physical body to become immortal light, eternal spirits who resemble God in His own family. Scripture says:

> "There is a natural body, and there is a spiritual body" (1 Corinthians 15:44).

> "And just as we have borne the image of the man of dust, we will also bear the image of the man of heaven" (1 Corinthians 15:49 CSB).

Recall the song mentioned earlier, "We Gotta Get Out of This Place." This place that we gotta get out of is our natural body, the body of flesh, the body of death, the body of the beast, the body of man! It'll be then that we come to our better life, when we move into our new divine spirit body. Getting out of this place is the last thing we ever do in the flesh. And once again, the band that made this song famous is called The Animals. Yes, folks. The ones reminding us to get out of this place are a group whose very name is synonymous with the beast.

MARK OF THE BEAST

Now that we know the number of the beast refers to rebellious men and women in the past, present, and future, another cryptic phrase that has confused many people for thousands of years is "the mark of the beast." While there have been countless theories floated, the answer to its meaning will become apparent when we merely connect the dots of Scripture and listen on the spirit level at God speed.

With the beast referring to all of mankind in opposition to God, the phrase "the mark of the beast" can easily be read as "the mark of man," or more specifically, "the mark of man in defiance of God." It's no more complicated than that when we keep in mind the spiritual story broadcast from the beginning.

So, let's ask ourselves: what is a mark? The dictionary defines it as a sign, an indication, a distinguishing trait or quality, a characteristic. It's also a symbol used for identification or indication of ownership. All these hold true when it comes to what the Bible says about the mark of the beast. It's the sign of all mankind who opposes God. Anything in defiance of the Creator denotes the mark, the indicator or identifying sign, of the beast. It's talking about the thoughts and actions of men and women who rebel against God by refusing to keep His commandments.

Meanwhile, when we read the entirety of Scripture, we find there are marks, or signs, for people who obey God.

One is the presence of the Passover lamb's blood. As God has said:

> "The blood on the houses where you are staying will be a **distinguishing mark** for you; when I see the blood, I will pass over you. No plague will be among you to destroy you when I strike the land of Egypt" (Exodus 12:13 CSB).

Of course, at God speed, this is saying much more than having physical blood of a slain lamb on anyone's house. On the spirit level, it's saying the distinguishing mark of God is the blood of the true Passover lamb, the Lamb of God who is Jesus. The house is where people live (the human mind or body), and God will spare the eternal death penalty for anyone currently dwelling in the dark land of misery (spiritual Egypt) as long as he or she is covered by the bloody death sacrifice of the Lamb of God.

Another sign for the people of God is resting on the seventh day of the week, known as God's Sabbath day:

> "Be careful to keep my Sabbath day, for the Sabbath is a **sign** of the covenant between me and you from generation to generation. It is given so you may know that I am the LORD, who makes you holy" (Exodus 31:13 NLT).

> "The Israelites must observe the Sabbath, celebrating it throughout their generations as a **permanent** covenant. It is a **sign forever** between me and the Israelites, for in six days the LORD made the heavens and the earth, but on the seventh day he rested and was refreshed" (Exodus 31:16–17 CSB).

As we see today, millions of people defy this sign, having little problem working on the seventh day of the week, because they have been tricked by "Satan, the one who deceives the whole world" (Revelation 12:9 CSB).

Thus, people who keep God's instructions including the Sabbath and Passover have the mark of God upon them. By default, anyone opposing God has upon himself or herself the sign of man, the mark of the beast. Scripture actually specifies where this identifying sign is:

> "If anyone worships the beast and its image and receives a **mark** on his **forehead** or on his **hand**, he will also drink the wine of God's wrath" (Revelation 14:9–10 CSB).

Remember to think at God speed when reading words such as *forehead* and *hand*. We shouldn't think only about our physical body. Our forehead represents our thoughts. What we think is at the forefront of our minds. Our hands represent what we do, our actual deeds. Thus, the mark is the sign, the indicator, of what we *think* and what we *do*.

As noted, there are also signs, marks, and symbols for people obedient to God. And again, our hand and forehead are their locations:

> "Love the LORD your God with all your heart, with all your soul, and with all your strength. These words that I am giving you today are to be in your heart. Repeat them to your children. Talk about them when you sit in your house and when you walk along the road, when you lie down and when you get up. Bind them as a **sign** on your **hand** and let them be a **symbol** on your **forehead**" (Deuteronomy 6:5–8 CSB).

In addition to words such as *sign* and *mark*, Scripture also uses the word *seal*, which, of course, is a mark that identifies something:

> "They were told not to harm the grass of the earth, or any green plant, or any tree, but only those people who do not have **God's seal** on their **foreheads**" (Revelation 9:4 CSB).

> "Nevertheless the solid foundation of God stands, having this **seal**: "The Lord knows those who are His," and, "Let everyone who names the name of Christ depart from iniquity" (2 Timothy 2:19 NKJV).

> "Don't work for the food that perishes but for the food that lasts for eternal life, which the Son of Man will give you, because God the Father has set his **seal of approval** on him" (John 6:27 CSB).

When we connect the dots, we can see God's seal, the mark of God, is on the foreheads or minds of His people. In other words, the indicator that we're with God and approved by Him is our thoughts of obedience, instead of the mark of the beast, the mark of man, which is defiance toward our Creator by putting the will of physical man ahead of the will of the true Spirit God. When we defy God by putting our own will first, we violate the very first commandment instructing us to have "no other gods before me," the Creator (Exodus 20:3). When we rebel against our Maker, we're actually making ourselves out to be a sovereign god who refuses the will of the true God.

With this in mind, God blasted the serpent devil, who was "more cunning than any **beast**" (Genesis 3:1) about his arrogant attitude, for trying to put himself ahead of the Creator:

> "Your heart is proud, and you have said, "I am a god; I sit in the seat of gods in the heart of the sea. Yet **you are a man** and not a god, though you have regarded your heart as that of a god" (Ezekiel 28:2 CSB).

> "You will die a violent death in the heart of the sea. Will you still say, "I am a god," in the presence of those who slay you? Yet you will be only a **man**, not a god, in the hands of those who kill you" (Ezekiel 28:8–9 CSB).

This brings us full circle in our study of the beast. As we have just read, God has told a powerful spirit being, Satan the devil, the one who is tricking the whole world because he is more cunning and deceptive than any other "beast," that he is merely a "man," someone who is mortal and will be put to death, even though he thinks he's a god.

It is obvious at God speed that the Creator equates the beast with man, especially rebellious man. Whether it's the most cunning beast of the field in the person of the devil or the human dogs, pigs, wolves, jackals, vultures, and snakes who refuse to follow the instructions of the Maker, we the disobedient people are the beasts of Scripture who need to repent of our wicked thoughts and actions to get out of this place, this spiritual Egypt, this body of the beast, so we can be given immortal life as the literal children of God.

RAISING KIDS

There are numerous instances in Scripture of raising children, and when I use that phrase, I'm not referring to instructing kids on the proper way of living, though there's plenty about that, as you know. I'm talking about raising people from the dead.

I'm now going to present you with some of these events as an exercise to help your mind reach God speed and understand these accounts on the spirit level, because they're about much more than reviving physical corpses to a breathing state. They all refer to humanity being healed from eternal death and being restored to life, resurrected from the dead in the future. As we go through this, try to think not only about the physical event that took place but also the higher meaning being broadcast. Don't worry. I'll spell it out for you just in case you don't get it. Let's start with a widow's son being raised by Elijah.

> "After this, the son of the woman who owned the house became ill. His illness got worse until he stopped breathing.
>
> "She said to Elijah, 'Man of God, why are you here? Have you come to call attention to my iniquity so that my son is put to death?'
>
> "But Elijah said to her, 'Give me your son.' So he took him from her arms, brought him up to the upstairs room where he was staying, and laid him on his own bed.
>
> "Then he cried out to the LORD and said, 'LORD my God, have you also brought tragedy on the widow I am staying with by killing her son?'

> "Then he stretched himself out over the boy three times. He cried out to the LORD and said, 'LORD my God, please let this boy's life come into him again!'
>
> "So the LORD listened to Elijah, and the boy's life came into him again, and he lived.
>
> "Then Elijah took the boy, brought him down from the upstairs room into the house, and gave him to his mother. Elijah said, 'Look, your son is alive.'
>
> "Then the woman said to Elijah, 'Now I know you are a man of God and the LORD's word from your mouth is true'" (1 Kings 17:17–24 CSB).

Here we have a sick child who stops breathing and dies. This sick child, at God speed, symbolizes humanity, all people who are no longer breathing in the spiritual sense. They're dead in God's sight because they no longer have the spirit, the breath of the Creator, inside their minds. They're focused merely on physical lusts of the flesh, not the spirit.

Meanwhile, Elijah, a man of God whose name means "my God is Yah" or "God is Jehovah" stretches his own body over the boy **three times** and prays for his life to be restored. Does this three times sound familiar yet? It should, because it represents what's been mentioned numerous times here. It's the past, present, and future. Yesterday, today, and tomorrow.

The scene reveals that during all time periods (past, present, and future), the way to have life restored is to have the true man of God who represents the Creator come in full contact with the people who have been spiritually dead. This man of God symbolizes none other than Jesus, and another hint in the story to help you grasp this fact is the final statement that "the LORD's word from your mouth is true." As we've seen before, Jesus is known as the Word (John 1:1), the Word of God (Revelation 19:13), and everything He says is true because He is the truth (John 14:6).

A similar raising of a dead child is recorded in the time of the prophet Elisha, whose name carries the same meaning of Yeshua or Jesus, "God is salvation." Notice how Elisha raises the dead boy:

> "Then he lay down on the child's body, placing his mouth on the child's mouth, his eyes on the child's eyes, and his hands on the child's hands. And as he stretched out on him, the child's body began to grow warm again! Elisha got up, walked back and forth across the room once, and then stretched himself out again on the child. This time the boy sneezed seven times and opened his eyes!" (2 Kings 4:34–35 NLT).

Reading this at God speed reveals much more than just the singular event from Old Testament times. It is painting the spiritual picture of God bringing dead people to life. He stretches His mouth on the child's mouth, meaning He puts His words into our mouths, so we can say what He says. He places His eyes on the child's eyes, injecting Himself into what we see, so our spirit sees what He sees. And He puts His hands on the child's hands, causing us to do the very things that He does. All of this is another way of saying we become divine as He covers our entire being with Himself and we become filled with the Spirit.

A picture related to this child's resurrection is recorded in the New Testament, as believers were suddenly infused with the very presence of God Himself at Pentecost:

> **"And everyone present was filled with the Holy Spirit and began speaking in other languages, as the Holy Spirit gave them this ability" (Acts 2:4 NLT).**

Like the child's resurrection by Elisha, this amazing event is also forecasting the future time when people will be completely filled with God's own Spirit, returning them to life, and speaking words that originally seemed very foreign to them, because they are the words of God and not the words of rebellious mankind.

There's one other resurrection that puzzles many Bible readers about what it's really saying. It involves what happened after the Messiah was executed.

> **"And Jesus cried out again with a loud voice, and yielded up His spirit. Then, behold, the veil of the temple was torn in two from top to bottom; and the earth quaked, and the rocks were split, and the graves were opened; and many bodies of the saints who had fallen asleep were raised; and coming out of the graves after His resurrection, they went into the holy city and appeared to many" (Matthew 27:50–53 NKJV).**

On the physical level, it's obvious that after Jesus died and rose from the dead, a certain number of His believers were brought back to physical life and strolled into the holy city of Jerusalem to present themselves to many other people that they were alive again. Now let's make the jump to God speed. As we know by now, God declares the end from the beginning, so this event is not merely talking about the resurrection of those believers some two thousand years ago. It is also a prophecy for the future.

It alludes to the First Resurrection when the saints, the faithful people set apart by God, will come out of their graves, out of their dead bodies, and go into "the holy city, new Jerusalem" (Revelation 21:2). In other words, it's a foreshadow of the time they'll be transformed into their new spirit bodies and enter the kingdom of God.

Keep in mind that when Jesus died, those people who came out of their graves and went into the holy city did not do so the moment Jesus expired. The Bible specifically notes it was "after His resurrection, they went into the holy city and appeared to many." So let's connect some more dots from the Bible to understand more of what's being said on the spirit level.

When Jesus died, He did not come back to life instantly. In fact, there was a three-day delay:

> "For as Jonah was in the belly of the great fish for three days and three nights, so will the Son of Man be in the heart of the earth for **three days and three nights**" (Matthew 12:40 NLT).

> "God raised up this man on the **third day** and caused him to be seen, not by all the people, but by us whom God appointed as witnesses, who ate and drank with him after he rose from the dead" (Acts 10:40–41 CSB).

Do the words "three days" and "third day" ring any bells? It's what we keep hearing: yesterday, today, and tomorrow. And in this case, when Scripture says God's followers came out of the graves and went into the holy city, they, like Jesus, did so on the third day. In other words, at God speed, it's the spiritual "tomorrow," the future resurrection that has not taken place yet!

Everyone who rejects the wicked ways of man will come out of their dead bodies on the third day, which is tomorrow. Remember the order. Yesterday (the past) is the first day. Today (the present) is the second day. And tomorrow (the future) is the third day. So the true believers of God will be raised up to eternal life the third day, "the last day" as Jesus repeatedly calls it (John 6:39, 40, 44, 54). It is the day still ahead of us in the spiritual story being told by God.

With this in mind, other Scriptures suddenly will pop with fresh meaning when they're understood at God speed. Here are but a few:

> "Be sure they are **ready** on the **third day**, for **on that day the LORD will come down** on Mount Sinai as all the people watch" (Exodus 19:11 NLT).

> "On the **third day**, when **morning came**, there was thunder and lightning, a thick cloud on the mountain, and a **very loud trumpet sound**, so that all the people in the camp shuddered. Then Moses **brought the people out of the camp to meet God**, and they **stood** at the foot of the mountain" (Exodus 19:16–17 CSB).

> "Now it came to pass on the **third day**, that Esther **put on** her **royal apparel**, and **stood** in the inner court of the king's house" (Esther 5:1).

> "After two days will he **revive** us: in the **third day** he will **raise us up**, and **we shall live** in his sight" (Hosea 6:2).

> "Now the **temple was finished** on the **third day**" (Ezra 6:15 NKJV).

I pray that you're hearing the secret song by now and understand what's being sung. But if not, I'm here to help you comprehend these passages. So here goes.

The third day is tomorrow, the future time ahead of us. God urges us to be ready for His arrival by preparing ourselves right now, learning to do good and eliminating evil from our lives. Because tomorrow is when morning comes. It is when God, who is light, shines forth and conquers the darkness of our current evil time.

It is tomorrow when we're brought out of our fleshly camp to personally meet God, finally being able to stand in the presence of the Almighty, in the inner court of His house, wearing the new, royal apparel of our spirit bodies as we will be immortal kings, serving the King of kings.

It is after two days, after the past and present, that God revives us. It is on the third day, tomorrow, that He raises us up and elevates us to our new divine position, as we finally live forever in the kingdom of God.

It is on the third day, tomorrow, that the temple, the actual house of God, His dwelling place where He chooses to put His name, located inside all His faithful followers, is finally finished.

This all takes place tomorrow, on the third day. "It will happen in a moment, in the blink of an eye, when the last trumpet is blown. For when the trumpet sounds, those who have died will be raised to live forever" (1 Corinthians 15:52 NLT).

Yes, ladies and gentlemen, this is the very good news of your personal destiny. A major theme of the Bible is that God is raising His kids from death to life. End of story. And the beginning.

11TH GEAR:

God Speed Ahead: Keys *in* Reaching God Speed

THIS **BOOK** has been filled with many Bible verses that have hopefully opened your mind to the spirit meaning of what God has written in Scripture. And now I'm going to present you with some keywords and techniques to help you reach God speed quicker and make your understanding rocket to new heights. They help make the unseen suddenly visible, and often reveal the end game, the reason we're all here and the place to which we're heading.

PERSONIFICATION

From our earliest times as children, we learn about how things that are not human beings are personified as if they were actual people. When we read stories or see cartoons about animals that speak with human voices such as *Bambi*, *Horton Hears a Who*, *Charlotte's Web* or *Animal Farm*, they include characters that are personified with human thoughts and emotions. Scripture uses a similar personification technique in various ways, and becoming aware of this method will help you learn the hidden song being sung by God. Here are some examples.

KEYWORD: EARTH

We've seen many times already that the earth represents people, since that's the substance of human beings. We're made of the dust of the ground (Genesis 2:7). We're referred to as clay (Job 33:6) and mud that's stuck in the mire (Psalm 40:2 NLT). So when we read Scripture, let's keep in mind that in many cases, God is not actually focusing on physical dirt but *people*.

For instance, when Scripture says, "Let the whole earth shout joyfully to God!" (Psalm 66:1 CSB), it's not talking about piles of earth or physical land actually shouting out to God. It is personifying the earth and the lands because it's people who dwell in them, and the earth is the substance of which they consist. It is people who are able to shout joyfully to God. Here's more:

> "Listen, all you **peoples**; pay attention, **earth** and **everyone in it!**" (Micah 1:2 CSB).

> "Won't the **land** quake and all who dwell in **it** mourn?" (Amos 8:8).

> "The Lord, the GOD of Armies—he touches the **earth**; it **melts**, and **all who dwell in it** mourn" (Amos 9:5 CSB).

Again, God is equating the land and the earth with those who dwell in it: people. And when people are quaking, they figuratively melt with fear and trembling. This is the song being sung at God speed.

The same can be said about the heavens. The term refers not just to a place where God and the angels dwell, but it also alludes to the people who live in that place, usually referring to angels.

> "Therefore rejoice, **you heavens**, and **you who dwell in them!**" (Revelation 12:12 CSB).

It's no different from today's news reports. When we read or hear phrases such as "The White House said today," we obviously know that a solid, white building is not voicing audible sentences. The White House is merely a term to represent the person or power who dwells in that place.

Often, God combines personified items. Here's an example where He's talking to His children, both His angelic offspring and His human kids:

> "Listen, **heavens**, and pay attention, **earth**, for the LORD has spoken: 'I have raised **children** and brought them up, but they have rebelled against me'" (Isaiah 1:2 CSB).

Once again, God is not telling physical clouds in the sky and piles of dirt to listen up and pay attention. He's addressing His own rebellious children and says as much in the verse. It's a main theme of the entire Bible that many of God's own offspring—angels and physical human beings—don't wish to obey His instructions.

When we keep connecting Scriptures with this method, it's amazing to see what becomes visible:

> "Look up to the heavens, and look at the earth beneath; for the **heavens will vanish like smoke**, the **earth will wear out like a garment**, and its **inhabitants will die like gnats**. But my salvation will last forever" (Isaiah 51:6 CSB).

Don't think just physically when reading the above verse. Put together everything you've learned so far, and you'll understand the translation at God speed. The heavens are the wicked angels who will die, vanishing like smoke into nothingness if they don't repent. The earth is wicked people who are dying as well, in the process of withering, wearing out like a garment. The verse outright tells us this when it says **its inhabitants will die** like gnats! Remember, the wages of sin is death, not eternal life, even for angels, because Scripture says God "alone is immortal" (1 Timothy 6:16 CSB).

The more familiar we become with Scripture, the more we can recognize the pattern of personification and hear the song more clearly as we connect the dots. Let's stretch this concept a little more.

> "Let the **heavens** be glad, and the **earth** rejoice! Let the **sea** and **everything in it** shout his praise!" (Psalm 96:11 NLT).

In the above verse, the heavens represent God and the angels. The earth represents human people. And the sea and everything in it refer to people as well! We mustn't forget what we've seen in Scripture before.

> "You have made mankind like the fish of the sea" (Habakkuk 1:14 CSB).

> "'Come, follow me,'" Jesus said, "'and I will send you out to fish for people'" (Matthew 4:19 NIV).

> "The Lord said...I will bring my people again from the depths of the sea" (Psalm 68:22).

At God speed, the sea refers to the world and the people who dwell in it, since the sea is the place where fish—people, spiritually speaking—dwell. Yes, there's a reason beyond the obvious that a popular theme park is called SeaWorld. Because the sea represents the world. We even talk about a "sea of humanity" in regular parlance.

And when we open our spiritual eyes and ears, it's obvious that when God says He's going to bring His people again from the depths of the sea, He's talking about bringing dead human beings who once dwelled in the world to life again.

The more we read Scripture, the more it becomes obvious that person-ification is a very common tool. We've already seen many times how God refers to people as animals. Here are some more examples to bring you up to speed when these are understood on the spirit level, not just the physical.

> "But there is hope for whoever is joined with all the living, since a live dog is better than a dead lion" (Ecclesiastes 9:4 CSB).

Live dogs refer to people who repent of their unclean, sinful, vicious, doglike behavior and become alive to God. A dead lion represents some-one who was once royal and kingly, whether it be a human or an angel, but becomes spiritually dead to God by refusing to follow the divine com-mandments. When we're joined with all the living, we're joined to God, since God has life and gives life. Thus, a live dog, a repentant person joined with God, is better off than a dead lion, a rebellious person opposing God.

KEYWORD: TREES

Trees are another common item found in Scripture, and believe it or not, they are also used to represent people on many occasions. Here are some examples in which it's obvious they refer to people who can think, speak, and take action, be it good or evil:

> "A good **tree** can't produce bad fruit, and a bad **tree** can't produce good fruit. So every **tree** that does not produce good fruit is chopped down and thrown into the fire. Yes, just as you can identify a **tree** by its fruit, so you can identify **people** by their actions" (Matthew 7:18–20 NLT).

> "Either make the **tree** good, and his fruit good; or else make the **tree** corrupt, and his fruit corrupt: for the **tree** is known by his fruit" (Matthew 12:33).

> "The **trees** decided to anoint a king over themselves. They said to the **olive tree**, 'Reign over us'" (Judges 9:8 CSB).

> "Even the **trees** of the forest—the **cypress trees** and the **cedars** of Lebanon—sing out this joyous song: 'Since you have been cut down, no one will come now to cut us down!'" (Isaiah 14:8 NLT).

> "Let the fields and everything in them celebrate. Then all the **trees** of the forest will shout for joy" (Psalm 96:12 CSB).

God occasionally throws some playfulness into the mix, as in the case of Jesus healing a blind man. The gentleman whose sight was being restored noted: "I see **people**—they look like **trees walking**" (Mark 8:24 CSB).

With trees often symbolizing people, some Bible verses will jump off the page with new meaning, such as this one that equates people with all the terms we've just learned—earth, sea, and trees:

> "Then I saw another angel rising up from the east, who had the seal of the living God. He cried out in a loud voice to the four angels who were allowed to harm the earth and the sea: 'Don't harm the **earth** or the **sea** or the **trees** until we seal the **servants** of our God on their foreheads'" (Revelation 7:2–3 CSB).

This passage is not talking about four different items that get sealed by God, but just one: people. It is equating the earth, sea, trees, and servants of God. The individuals who are to be harmed are obviously people who are not God's servants. Learning the song at God speed will help you realize how often the Creator is saying the same thing over and over, with many prophecies coming to life.

It's not only trees, but branches, too, that symbolize people. How do we know? Jesus Himself said so.

> "**You are the branches**. The one who remains in me and I in him produces much fruit, because you can do nothing without me.

> "If **anyone** does not remain in me, he is thrown aside like a **branch** and he withers. They gather **them**, throw **them** into the fire, and **they** are burned" (John 15:5–6 CSB).

Knowing this will make your understanding of other passages soar.

> "But in that day, the **branch** of the LORD will be beautiful and glorious; the fruit of the land will be the pride and glory of all who survive in Israel" (Isaiah 4:2 NLT).

Many people already understand that the "branch" this verse mentions can apply to Jesus, and it does. But at God speed, it also applies to the people who obey their Master, since Scripture has identified each individual person as a branch. In other words, believers are the ones who will survive, who will be alive forever. They are the ones who will be beautiful and full of glory because they will have received their divine reward. Here's another example:

> "Behold, the days come, saith the LORD, that I will raise unto David a righteous Branch, and a King shall reign and prosper, and shall execute judgment and justice in the earth" (Jeremiah 23:5).

Yes, this is a prophecy about Jesus. But it's also a prophecy for anyone who gets his act together and becomes part of God's family who will reign with God on a king's throne and be a judge, administering justice and righteousness. Remember, Jesus is called the "King of kings" (Revelation 17:14). We are those kings of the future, ruling under the leadership of the ultimate King. And we'll be the saints, the people being sanctified, who will judge angels and the citizens of the world.

> "Or don't you know that the saints will judge the world?… Don't you know that we will judge angels…?" (1 Corinthians 6:2–3 CSB).

Yes, faithful believers are the righteous branches who shall reign and prosper, executing judgment because we will be sitting on the very throne of God, as promised by Jesus:

> "To him who overcomes I will grant to sit with Me on My throne" (Revelation 3:21 NKJV).

Personification in Scripture is more common than readers might think. Even words such as valleys, mountains, and hills can represent people.

> "Every valley shall be exalted, and every mountain and hill shall be made low" (Isaiah 40:4).

The same thing is said with the exalting of humble people while bringing down the arrogant:

> "Exalt him that is low, and abase him that is high" (Ezekiel 21:26).

Grass, flowers, and rivers can symbolize people as well.

> "The **grass** withers, the **flower** fades, Because the breath of the LORD blows upon it; Surely the **people are grass**" (Isaiah 40:7 NKJV).

> "**Clap your hands**, all you **peoples**; **shout** to God with a jubilant cry" (Psalm 47:1 CSB).

> "Let the **rivers clap their hands** let the **mountains shout** together for joy" (Psalm 98:8 CSB).

> "The **mountains** and the **hills** shall break forth before you into **singing**, and all the **trees** of the field shall **clap their hands**" (Isaiah 55:12).

Waters is yet another common term that can refer to people, and Scripture tells us that outright:

> "The waters...represent masses of people of every nation and language" (Revelation 17:15 NLT).

As we've seen, having this understanding unlocks other Scriptures, such as "the face of the waters" in Genesis.

> "And the Spirit of God moved upon the face of the **waters**. And God said, Let there be light: and there was light. And God saw the light, that it was good" (Genesis 1:2–4).

At God speed, this passage is not only talking about the beginning, it's revealing the end game as well. When God's Spirit moves on the face of the waters, in other words when God moves His personal presence into the faces of His people, that's when we shall become made of brilliant light, immortal and glorified spirit, instead of our current outer darkness in which we temporarily reside. It is then that God declares that we are good, just like He is good because we'll be on the divine level with Him. As Jesus famously declared, "There is none good but one, that is, God" (Matthew 19:17).

We get a much clearer picture of our own glorious destiny as God's children when we realize what the words of Scripture represent and then simply connect related passages. This is an essential and easy key to reaching God speed.

Staying with our personification study, there are times when objects not only represent human people but God Himself.

For instance, examining the wide scope of Scripture, God is described as all of these things:

Light	True drink	Witness
Water	Husband	Truth
River	Father	Way
Fountain	King	Life
Fire	Man	Resurrection
Rock	Man of war	God Almighty
Fortress	Strength	Lord
Lamb	Power	Master
Lion	Horn of salvation	Servant
Love	High tower	Son of God
Sun	Wonderful Counselor	Son of Man
Shield	Exceeding great reward	Root
Refuge	Deliverer	Offspring
Lamp	Your portion	Spirit
Hiding place	Your inheritance	Comforter
Song	Bright Morning Star	Your help
Door	Good Shepherd	Savior
Gate	Anointed	Teacher
Temple	The First	Holy One
Branch	The Last	Creator
Tree	The Beginning	Redeemer
Vine	The End	Word
Bread of life	The Alpha	
True food	The Omega	

There are probably many more, and while some of the items in the list refer to a person, such as Father, most are usually associated with inanimate objects, such as a door or a rock.

"I am the door" (John 10:9).

"That Rock was Christ" (1 Corinthians 10:4).

The point is, God is represented through the things He has created, and Scripture tells us that plainly:

> "For the invisible things of him from the creation of the world are clearly seen, being understood by **the things that are made,** even his eternal power and Godhead; so that they are without excuse" (Romans 1:20).

In other words, we as human beings can just examine the things in our physical world to find out who God is and what He is like. His hidden qualities and attributes become evident when we merely open our eyes. Thus, we don't have a single excuse for not following His instructions, because He has been broadcasting on all frequencies.

On occasion, there are things describing God which are not physical objects, but abstract nouns, describing intangible things such as emotions, concepts or ideas. An example is when Scripture says, "God is love" (1 John 4:8). That's very straightforward.

But then there are passages where we need to do a little detective work, connecting the dots to reveal the hidden message. I'll provide a simple example with a common word: Wisdom. Throughout the book of Proverbs, Wisdom is actually personified as if it were a person, having a mouth and voice and taking certain actions. Many Bibles even capitalize Wisdom. I'll now provide you a sampling of what is said about Wisdom, and see if you can figure out who it sounds like on the spirit level of God speed.

> "I call to you, to all of you! I raise my voice to all people.

> "You simple people, use good judgment. You foolish people, show some understanding.

> "Listen to me! For I have important things to tell you. Everything I say is right, for I speak the truth and detest every kind of deception.

> "My advice is wholesome. There is nothing devious or crooked in it.

> "My words are plain to anyone with understanding, clear to those with knowledge" (Proverbs 8:4–9 NLT).

> "I, Wisdom, live together with good judgment. I know where to discover knowledge and discernment.

> "All who fear the LORD will hate evil. Therefore, I hate pride and arrogance, corruption and perverse speech.

"Common sense and success belong to me. Insight and strength are mine.

"Because of me, kings reign, and rulers make just decrees.

"Rulers lead with my help, and nobles make righteous judgments.

"I love all who love me. Those who search will surely find me"
(Proverbs 8:12–17 NLT).

"I have been established from everlasting, From the beginning, before
there was ever an earth" (Proverbs 8:23 NKJV).

"I was there when he established the heavens, when he drew the horizon
on the oceans.

"I was there when he set the clouds above, when he established springs
deep in the earth.

"I was there when he set the limits of the seas, so they would not spread
beyond their boundaries. And when he marked off the earth's foundations,

"I was the architect at his side. I was his constant delight, rejoicing always in his presence.

"And how happy I was with the world he created; how I rejoiced with the
human family!

"And so, my children, listen to me, for all who follow my ways are joyful.

"Listen to my instruction and be wise. Don't ignore it.

"Joyful are those who listen to me, watching for me daily at my gates,
waiting for me outside my home!

"For whoever finds me finds life and receives favor from the LORD.

"But those who miss me injure themselves. All who hate me love death"
(Proverbs 8:27–36 NLT).

"Come, eat of my bread And drink of the wine I have mixed. Forsake
foolishness and live" (Proverbs 9:5–6 NKJV).

There's plenty more, but hopefully you're catching the drift concerning who this could be talking about. If you haven't been able to figure it out yet, the answer is God, perhaps Jesus specifically, the Architect at the side of God the Father. God is the One calling out to all people, urging us to listen, hating arrogance, and detesting every kind of deception. Kings rule because God puts them on thrones. Whoever finds God finds life, and if we hate God, we automatically love death. And we've already seen that Jesus is begging us to eat of His bread, because He Himself is the "bread of life" (John 6:48).

Thus, even simple words and concepts such as Wisdom can represent the Creator Himself, when we listen at God speed.

THE MEANING OF NAMES

Another fun way to help us reach God speed is to learn the meaning of names, because names carry important meaning and help unlock the hidden story embedded in Scripture. We've already talked about the meaning of some names. Jesus, or His Hebrew name of Yeshua, for instance, means "God saves," "God will save," or "God is salvation." *Michael* means one "who is like God." *Goshen* means "drawing near," *Sodom* means "flaming" and *Egypt* means "dark place of misery." But there are hundreds of names in Scripture, and it's quite eye-opening to learn not only what the names mean but how they tell the unseen story of God.

Let's start with a couple of names most people would recognize: David and Goliath. In Hebrew, *David* simply means "beloved." *Goliath* means "an exile." And, of course, Goliath was a fierce giant, a champion warrior of the Philistines.

Now here's where it begins to get interesting. The name *Philistine* literally means "dust-rollers," as in people who are intensely grieving and are rolling themselves in the dust. It derives from the Hebrew verb *palash* meaning to burrow in the ground or to agonize loudly. It's reminiscent of what Adele sings about in "Rolling in the Deep." Recall what the dust represents. It's people, the flesh, because that's what we're made of, the dust of the ground. And we're all in agony because we dwell in this dirty, physical condition instead of the glorious light of the spirit in which we're intended to exist.

So, when the Bible recounts the famous confrontation of David and Goliath, it takes on a whole new meaning at God speed. It's really depicting the spiritual battle between the **beloved** people of God (whether they be faithful angels or humans) versus the defiant giants (rebellious angels or humans) who are dwelling in **exile** from God's kingdom and who are **rolling in the dust**, dwelling and grieving in the flesh.

David famously asks: "who is this uncircumcised Philistine, that he should defy the armies of the living God?" (1 Samuel 17:26).

At God speed, here's the scenario: it's the beloved people of God boldly asking who is this rebellious dust-roller who dares to defy the obedient armies of the true God. Scripture uses the term "uncircumcised" for an important reason on the spirit level. Circumcision is the removal of the flesh both literally and figuratively. Therefore, if someone is uncircumcised, his heart is not obedient to God, and therefore he remains in the flesh, driven by the lusts of the flesh and never making the jump from mortal flesh to immortal spirit in the end. In other words, the dust-rollers never gain eternal life. They're stuck in the flesh, mired in the mud.

Many already know the outcome of the David and Goliath story. It was a smooth stone slung by a shepherd that sank into the forehead of the giant dust-roller in exile, killing him instantly (1 Samuel 17:49). Translation at God speed: Believers are the stones that have been prepared and polished by God. We are the weapons in the bag of the chief Shepherd who becomes King. The fearless Shepherd represents Jesus who uses His chosen weapons, His smooth stones, His prepared believers, to fight against the champion of the dust-rollers (people in the flesh), none other than Satan the devil. Remember:

> "Our struggle is not against flesh and blood, but against the rulers, against the authorities, against the powers of this dark world and against the spiritual forces of evil in the heavenly realms" (Ephesians 6:12 NIV).

The conclusion explains: "And when the Philistines saw their champion was dead, they fled" (1 Samuel 17:51).

Translation: And when the dust-rollers, those who are living in the flesh, realize their arrogant and wicked leader—the devil who defied the Living God—is dead, they no longer have a will to fight against the Sovereign Creator and subsequently leave the battle.

Interestingly, the Creator uses names as a tool to help us reach God speed, training us to pay attention to the meaning of people and place names right from the start. In Genesis, we see Eve given her name, meaning "life," and the Bible explains she was called Eve "because she was the mother of all **living**" (Genesis 3:20). And, as a matter of fact, people who are alive in the flesh today and will be made alive forever in the spirit have all had Eve as their mother. So her name declares the end, which is eternal life, right from the beginning.

Millions of people are familiar with the fallen angel who is called Satan, but many may not know that this name means *enemy* or *adversary*. It's someone who resists and opposes, and, as we all know, Satan is someone who resists and opposes God. But knowing the significance of the meaning of Satan allows us to realize the term can apply to anyone who opposes God, even people who claim to follow God. One famous instance recorded in the Bible features Jesus scorching His own beloved disciple Peter for being more concerned about human reasoning than the plan of God: "Get behind me, Satan! You are a hindrance to me because you're not thinking about God's concerns but human concerns" (Matthew 16:23 CSB). Jesus was not talking to the fallen angel called "the enemy," but His own chosen follower who was acting like His "enemy" at that moment.

This pattern of including reasons for names is plentiful. Here's another example.

After Jacob wrestled with the angel of God, his name was changed by God from Jacob, meaning "supplanter," to Israel, which can mean "one who wrestles with God" or "prince of God."

> "And He said, 'Your name shall no longer be called Jacob, but Israel;
> for you have struggled with God and with men, and have prevailed'"
> (Genesis 32:28 NKJV).

Not only was there a change in the man's name, but also the place got a fresh name as well, to Peniel or Penuel, both meaning "Face of God."

> "And Jacob called the name of the place Peniel: for I have seen God face
> to face, and my **life is preserved**" (Genesis 32:30).

At God speed, this again is telling us the conclusion of the story. After we struggle with God, once-treacherous human beings will undergo a name change, from supplanter to "Face of God," since we will become part of God's spirit family and bear the face of God on our face as our life is preserved. In other words, we get God's face on us when we receive immortal life. The very next verse confirms this when we hear the words at God speed.

> **"The sun shone on him as he passed by Penuel"** (Genesis 32:31 CSB).

This is really saying that when we see the face of God, we will become radiant with light like the sun shining from our faces! As we've seen: "Then the righteous will **shine like the sun** in their Father's kingdom" (Matthew 13:43 CSB).

The story of Jacob wrestling with God and changing his name is not merely a physical, historical event. At God speed, it's an embedded prediction of what will happen to obedient human beings who wrestle with God and ultimately become princes with God. We're meant to rule with Him in the brilliant family of God, made up of spirit instead of flesh.

KEDAR

Here's an obscure name most people would not recognize, but it's found about a dozen times in the Bible: Kedar. The name may mean nothing to you, but it's actually quite important. *Kedar* means "dark" or "darkness," and once we recognize this, we can understand what Scriptures mean at God speed.

> **"I am dark but beautiful, O women of Jerusalem—dark as the tents of Kedar"** (Song of Songs 1:5 NLT).

> **"What misery that I have stayed in Meshech, that I have lived among the tents of Kedar!"** (Psalm 120:5 CSB).

> **"All the flocks of Kedar shall be gathered together to you.... And I will glorify the house of My glory"** (Isaiah 60:7 NKJV).

With Kedar referring to something that is dark or in darkness, these Scriptures now leap off the page with enhanced meaning. Because we, the people, are dark, living in darkness, both physical and spiritual darkness. The physical darkness is our body of flesh, since we're covered by dark earth, as opposed to the brilliant light that God is in His true form. Plus, spiritually speaking, people in the flesh love to do dark deeds, as Jesus stated: "men loved **darkness** rather than light, because their deeds were **evil**" (John 3:19).

Now let's translate those three Kedar verses at God speed.

When the woman in Song of Songs 1:5 says she's dark but beautiful, dark as the tents of Kedar, she's talking about the dark tent of the human body. The woman represents all humanity, and we're all dark in our bodies yet still beautiful in God's sight when we're obedient. Human beings, even in their dark flesh, should be in love with the ultimate Man of Light, their Husband, who is God.

Psalm 120:5 talks about living among the tents of Kedar, and again, it's talking about dwelling in the darkness of our physical human bodies. It also makes note of the misery of staying in Meshech. That name *Meshech* means "departed" or "drawn out," as in departing from God or being drawn away from Him. So the verse in its entirety is describing how miserable it is to depart from God and remain in the flesh.

And Isaiah 60:7 is a prophecy about the future, when the flocks of Kedar, the dark, disobedient rebels, will finally come to God, and the house of God will be glorified when people arise and shine, as the start of the chapter so brightly announces: "Arise, shine, for your light has come, and the glory of the LORD shines over you" (Isaiah 60:1 CSB). It's talking about the future time when human beings will no longer be covered in the darkness of the earth but will be completely shining with the light of God as newly arisen children of God in His divine family.

At times, the use of names is not only meaningful but humorous as well. For instance: "Ekron shall be uprooted" (Zephaniah 2:4 NKJV). Chances are, you've never heard this verse explained, let alone heard of the word *Ekron*. It's a physical place, but when we know the meaning of its name, it all becomes clear at God speed.

Ekron simply means "uprooted." So when God says, "Ekron shall be uprooted," it's actually some comical wordplay: "The uprooted shall be uprooted." God is indicating on the spirit level that people who are not rooted or attached to Him will be uprooted, as in torn down and exterminated, not receiving eternal life. Plants in the garden don't live when they're uprooted, and neither do people when we're uprooted from our Maker.

Similar wordplay is found in the name of Noah's son: "God shall enlarge Japheth" (Genesis 9:27). The name *Japheth* means "enlarge" or "expand." So the verse is actually saying, "God shall enlarge those He's enlarging," or "God shall expand those He's expanding."

Another fun discovery is learning the meanings of pagan peoples' names, those spiritually far away from God, as they also broadcast the hidden story. Here's a passage that names a bunch of different nonbelievers. At first glance on the physical level, it just seems like a boring list of groups of people whose names are tough to pronounce:

> "When the LORD your God brings you into the land which you go to possess, and has cast out many nations before you, the Hittites and the Girgashites and the Amorites and the Canaanites and the Perizzites and the Hivites and the Jebusites...you shall conquer them and utterly destroy them. You shall make no covenant with them nor show mercy to them. Nor shall you make marriages with them.... For they will turn your sons away from following Me, to serve other gods; so the anger of the LORD will be aroused against you and destroy you suddenly" (Deuteronomy 7:1–4 NKJV).

The meanings of some of these nonbelieving peoples are enlightening, to say the least.

Hittites means "Terrible ones" or "Fearful ones"

Girgashites means "Dwellers in a clayish soil"

Amorites means "Talkers"

Canaanites means "Merchants" or "Global traders"

Hivites means "Villagers in tents"

Jebusites means "People who tread down"

As is obvious by the four verses of Deuteronomy 7, God wants His people to have absolutely nothing to do with these folks, and the meaning of their names spills the beans on the real reason when understood at God speed.

These people who reject the true Creator God are **terrible ones** in God's sight. They are **fearful** and **cowardly**. They **talk, gab, and complain** too much instead of listening. They treat other people without any respect, **treading down** on them. They're more interested in their **global trade** and **merchandising** of evil, rather than separating themselves from the worldly things of man to serve God. And they want to remain in their temporary **tents**, **dwelling** in their physical bodies of flesh, which are made of **clayish soil**.

It's one thing to know what words and names mean, but unless we take the next step and apply it to other Scriptures and their spirit meaning, we won't have a complete picture. It all comes to light, making total sense when we merely do a little digging into the names and then connect the dots to reach God speed. You now have the entire Bible before you to use this technique. You'll be amazed when the pieces are put together.

RELATED WORDS AND CONCEPTS

Another tool in reaching God speed is to study synonymous words and concepts and their opposites as well. This will help in understanding how to connect ideas throughout Scripture.

I've compiled two lists here to help you understand. The first list contains words and concepts that are positive in nature. All of these words and their synonyms are related to each other. For instance, God can be associated with things like life, Spirit, light, love, and glory.

The second list features words and concepts that are negative in nature, and each one is the direct opposite of the word in the positive list. For instance, God tops the positive list, and the devil tops the negative list. Then there's life and its opposite, death. And so forth.

POSITIVE:	NEGATIVE:
• God	• Devil
• Life, alive, awake	• Death, sleep
• Spirit, seed, presence of God	• Flesh, beast, animal, carnal
• Blessing	• Cursing
• Light	• Dark, darkness, outer darkness, misery, Egypt
• Day	• Night
• Morning	• Evening
• Good, righteous	• Evil, wicked
• Obedience	• Disobedience, sin, rebel
• Fine linen	• Sackcloth
• Joy, rejoicing, singing, dancing, celebration	• Weeping, sorrow, pain, tears, mourning
• Heavens, skies, land of the living	• Earth, dust, clay, ground, mud, ashes, the deep, the sea, the abyss, hell, Pit, Sheol, Gehenna, realm of the dead
• Glory, honor	• Shame, disgrace
• Seeing, hearing, understanding	• Blind, deaf, without understanding
• Heal, health, healthy, saved, redeemed, restored	• Sick, disease, dying
• Humble, meek, small, simple	• Arrogant, proud, pride, boastful
• Sweet, honey	• Bitter, wormwood
• Food	• Poison
• Clean	• Unclean
• Freedom	• Prison, captivity, bondage, slavery
• Profit, prosper, grow	• Wither, decay, uproot
• Faith, trust	• Fear, anxiety
• Wise	• Foolish, stupid
• Pure	• Defiled
• Build, assemble, edify	• Destroy, tear down
• Peace	• Violence
• Love	• Hate
• Fruitful, produce, valuable, worthy	• Vain, vanity, useless, unworthy, worthless, nothing
• Eternal, lasting, everlasting	• Temporary, temporal
• Rise, raise, arise, get up, awaken, lift up, resurrect, born again	• Fall, fall asleep
• Children of God, offspring of God	• Children of the devil

REPETITION, REPETITION, REPETITION

Another helpful tool in reaching God speed is to understand how God repeats His message constantly. There's a reason for the repetition, and it has to do with humans being thick in the head. In our flesh, we simply don't hear and understand that well the first or second time. We need things repeated in order to learn them, whether they be songs on the radio, multiplication tables in grade school, or phrases in a new language we're trying to master. It's why advertisers air the same commercials over and over, because the human mind needs to see or hear the message numerous times before it's absorbed and remembered. God uses the same technique of repeating examples through history, and says as much with Paul recounting historical events from the Old Testament:

> "These things happened to them as **examples for us**. They were written down to warn us who live at the end of the age" (1 Corinthians 10:11 NLT).

Thus, a key question to ask ourselves is: "Where else does the Bible mention these words or something similar?" Locating the same exact phrases or similar patterns then becomes a matter of connecting the dots to reveal the big picture that was previously unseen.

In Scripture, the repetition can be blatantly obvious in repeated phrases but also more hidden, employing themes or historical events that broadcast the same message. God's desire for us to keep His commandments, which are repeated well over one hundred times, is an example of overt repetition. Here are three instances:

> "Keep my commandments, and live" (Proverbs 7:2).

> "For this is the love of God, that we keep his commandments" (1 John 5:3).

> "If you want to enter life, keep the commandments" (Matthew 19:17 NIV).

The hidden Scriptures with repeated events require a bit more thought, and their patterns reveal dazzling truths when understood at God speed. Here are some examples to help you see what countless people have missed over the years.

ENTERING THE PROMISED LAND

Let's start with the repeated story of conquests by Joshua and the Israelites as they fought for and entered the physical Promised Land in ancient times. Numerous battles took place against a variety of pagan peoples, and Scripture sounds quite repetitious in recounting the outcome of these events. I'll try to keep this as brief as possible.

One of the cities the Israelites conquered was called Ai, which means, fittingly, "Ruin."

> "They struck them down until no survivor or fugitive remained"
> (Joshua 8:22 CSB).

> "Joshua burned Ai and left it a permanent ruin, still desolate today"
> (Joshua 8:28 CSB).

Other cities saw the exact same devastation:

> "That day Joshua took Makkedah. He put the city and its king to the sword and totally destroyed everyone in it. He left no survivors" (Joshua 10:28 NIV).

The city of Libnah:

> "He struck it down, putting everyone in it to the sword, and left no survivors in it" (Joshua 10:30 CSB).

The king of Lachish:

> "Joshua struck him down along with his people, leaving no survivors" (Joshua 10:33 CSB).

Hebron:

> "They captured the town and killed everyone in it, including its king, leaving no survivors" (Joshua 10:37 NLT).

Debir:

> "He captured the town, its king, and all of its surrounding villages. He completely destroyed everyone in it, leaving no survivors" (Joshua 10:39 NLT).

Even when numerous enemies banded together to fight God's people, the outcome was the same: "not one enemy warrior was left alive" (Joshua 11:8 NLT).

In case you were unsure who was orchestrating all these military engagements, it was God Himself:

> **"For it was the LORD's intention to harden their hearts, so that they would engage Israel in battle, be completely destroyed without mercy, and be annihilated" (Joshua 11:20 CSB).**

There are more examples, but the pattern is obvious: war rages, cities get captured, and all the enemy warriors and their evil king are completely annihilated. When most people study these events, they look only at the physical, historical battles. But the events happen over and over, with the same wording in Scripture for a reason. And now that you're getting better at understanding God speed, you'll be able to recognize the meaning of these repeated events on the spirit level.

All we need to do is apply the techniques we've been using through this entire book, including connecting the dots of related Scripture, applying the meaning of names, and see how it broadcasts the end of the story, since God constantly declares the end from the beginning.

Let's start with the meaning of Joshua, since he's the one leading the fight and bringing the people into the Promised Land. It's actually the same name as Jesus, Yeshua in Hebrew, and it means "Yah (God) saves," "God will save," and "God is salvation." There's a reason Joshua has the exact same name as Yeshua: because Joshua represents Jesus in the spiritual story being told. Jesus is the God who saves and is leading us into the Promised Land of eternal life, our intended destiny, and salvation.

Next, we're told that God intended there to be opposition to His people. Thus, the physical battles are merely a picture of the spiritual warfare (Ephesians 6:12 NIV) in which we must engage before we can enter the Promised Land of immortal life. We're meant to fight against enemy warriors, whether they be the enemy king named Satan or any of his fellow adversaries of God, the spiritual "children of the devil" (1 John 3:10), as Scripture refers to anyone not practicing righteousness.

The Bible repeatedly states there are "no survivors" among the enemies of God's people. It says it over and over to get the message through our thick skulls. And the message at God speed is that not a single person who fights against God will survive. They're spiritually dead and they do not make the jump to everlasting life. It's as simple as that. No one who fights against Yeshua (the God who saves) and against His followers can enter the ultimate Promised Land and receive eternal life.

THE REPETITION OF JONAH

One of the more famous stories in the Bible is that of Jonah, a man who ran away from God, got swallowed into the belly of a great fish for three days, and subsequently prompted others to repent once he was freed from the body of the beast. The details are found in the book of Jonah in the Old Testament. I'm bringing up this prophet because an important part of his story was repeated by Jesus in the New Testament, and its replication will spark new understanding once understood at God speed. So let's jump in and have a splash. In the Old Testament, we're told:

> "Now the LORD had prepared a great fish to swallow up Jonah. And Jonah was in the belly of the fish three days and three nights" (Jonah 1:17).

And in the New Testament, Jesus recalls this, saying the only miraculous sign He would provide regarding His identity was the sign of the prophet Jonah:

> "For as Jonah was in the belly of the great fish for three days and three nights, so will the Son of Man be in the heart of the earth for three days and three nights" (Matthew 12:40 NLT).

On the physical level, Jesus remained in the ground for three days and nights before exiting, but that's not what I wish to focus on at the moment. The story is repeated to amplify an incredible, hidden meaning I'm happy to reveal now.

Jonah was a man who was swallowed into the belly of a great fish, a creature in the sea, a beast in the depths. Perhaps at this point, you already know what I'm going to say next. Jonah represents all of mankind, since we all live in the body of a beast, as we learned earlier. The number of the beast is the number of man. We all dwell inside a physical creature here in the depths of the spiritual sea.

And Jesus noted that as Jonah was in the belly of the great fish for three days, so He would be in the heart of the earth. What does this mean on the spirit level? Well, what does the earth represent? We already know from countless verses that the earth, dust, ground, land, mud, and clay are all metaphors for people, since that's what we're made of and where we live. At God speed, when Jesus says He will be in the heart of the earth, He is saying that He is present in the hearts of *people*! He dwells inside us. Yes, it's that simple when we simply connect the dots of Scripture. And what do the three days represent? We already know the answer: yesterday, today, and tomorrow. God dwells inside people in the past, present, and future.

Moreover, Jonah was a man who initially ran away from God. He symbolizes all of humanity in rebellion against God in all time periods—past, present and future—dwelling in our watery grave, the human body, being slowly killed in the belly of our personal beast. If we examine the thoughts of Jonah from inside the fish, we get a clear picture of his affliction, his time of trouble in the depths of what Bibles call Sheol, hell, the grave, and the land of the dead, all of which mean the same thing spiritually:

> "I called to the LORD in my distress, and he answered me. I cried out for help from deep inside Sheol" (Jonah 2:2 CSB).

> "The waters surrounded me, even to my soul; The deep closed around me; Weeds were wrapped around my head" (Jonah 2:5 NKJV).

> "I was imprisoned in the earth, whose gates lock shut forever. But you, O LORD my God, snatched me from the jaws of death!" (Jonah 2:6 NLT).

Translation at God speed: We are all in distress here in our current hellish place of death, the human body, from which we cry out to God for help. The waters surrounding us are other people who live in the deep beside us, and the weeds wrapping around our head represent evil individuals wrapping themselves around us, trying to choke any life out of our minds. We are all imprisoned by the earth, our very flesh, and we cannot get out of this prison body unless God personally intervenes and yanks us out of the beast, out of this place of death.

Ultimately, God commanded the fish to spew out Jonah from its belly, which is merely a picture of our future resurrection. We leave the place of death, our locked prison with its solid gates in our body of the beast, to enjoy real life.

The rest of Jonah's story shows the people of an evil city actually repenting en masse when the man who was thought to be dead is alive again, urging them to obey their Creator for a change. At God speed, it's a veiled prophecy of the future, when the obedient followers of God exit their dead physical bodies and convince "the rest of the dead," (Revelation 20:5) all the wicked folks who didn't get with the program in the first round, to repent so that they, too, can leave their body of flesh and inherit eternal life.

DEATH OF A THIRD

An astonishing example of repetition is located near the end of the Bible in the Book of Revelation. I alluded to it earlier when talking about the famous commercial catchphrase of "I've fallen and I can't get up!" But it's worth a closer look, as it reveals how God can point to a singular event by constantly restating the same thing in veiled fashion. It has to do with the fraction of one-third.

Here's a passage of Scripture that is only six verses, and please take note of how often "a third" is mentioned:

> "The first angel blew his trumpet, and hail and fire, mixed with blood, were hurled to the earth. So **a third** of the earth was burned up, **a third** of the trees were burned up, and all the green grass was burned up.

> "The second angel blew his trumpet, and something like a great mountain ablaze with fire was hurled into the sea. So **a third** of the sea became blood, **a third** of the living creatures in the sea died, and **a third** of the ships were destroyed.

> "The third angel blew his trumpet, and a great star, blazing like a torch, fell from heaven. It fell on **a third** of the rivers and springs of water.

> "The name of the star is Wormwood, and **a third** of the waters became wormwood. So, many of the people died from the waters, because they had been made bitter.

> "The fourth angel blew his trumpet, and **a third** of the sun was struck, **a third** of the moon, and **a third** of the stars, so that **a third** of them were darkened. **A third** of the day was without light and also **a third** of the night" (Revelation 8:7–12 CSB).

That's a whole lot of thirds being discussed here. And there's likely a significant reason, if we just read a little further into Revelation, where a third is mentioned in a well-known passage we've talked about before:

> "There was a great fiery red dragon...Its tail swept away **a third** of the stars in heaven and hurled them to the earth" (Revelation 12:3–4 CSB).

This, friends, is the spiritual key to understanding all those previous verses, because they're all referring to the same, singular event: the fall of Satan and a third of the angels.

As we've seen, the dragon is Satan the devil: "So the great dragon was thrown out—the ancient serpent, who is called the devil and Satan, the one who deceives the whole world" (Revelation 12:9 CSB).

The dragon's tail sweeping away a third of the stars and hurling them to the earth refers to his constant spewing of lies that led to a third of the angels being kicked out of their heavenly home and sent to earth. When you see or hear the word "tail" in Scripture, think "tale," as in a lie. The Bible itself does this:

> "The **tail** is the prophet, the one teaching **lies**" (Isaiah 9:15 CSB).

> "With their **tails** they had the power to harm people" (Revelation 9:10 CSB).

It's the tails (tales), the incessant lies, that harm people, leading to spiritual death of individuals, whether they be angels in heaven or human beings on earth.

Now go back and read those six verses of Revelation 8:7–12 with all those fractions of a third repeatedly popping up, and you can understand what's being said at God speed.

The great star, burning like a torch that fell from heaven is the formerly obedient angel who rebelled against God and fell to the earth. It's none other than Satan the devil. Another name for that angel now is Wormwood, meaning "bitterness." The devil's character is full of bitterness, and he spreads his bitter spiritual poison to the minds of others through lying, since he is the father of lies. He poisoned the minds of a third of the angels, darkening these stars of heaven into their current spiritual condition of death. This is why a third of all those things mentioned are destroyed. He spiritually killed a third of the angels, represented by trees, living creatures, ships, rivers, springs of water, and so on. And the reference to "all the green grass was burned up" is a reference to all human beings being dead. Remember, "Surely the people are grass" (Isaiah 40:7 NKJV). While a third of the angels became dead to God, **all** human beings in the flesh are currently in that same dead condition, as we temporarily dwell in our mortal "body of death" (Romans 7:24 CSB).

There's a reason the final book of the Bible carries this name *Revelation*—because it reveals the answers, just like the answers to many math problems in school are revealed at the back of the schoolbook. Even the abbreviation for *Revelation* is "Rev," and that word means to excite, to increase, and to operate at high speed, like revving up your engine and making the jump to God speed.

KEYWORDS: HEAL AND HEALING

The words *heal* and *healing* are extremely important in Scripture, as they refer to more than just the healing of any physical ailment people suffer. At God speed, it means to be saved, as in given eternal life.

> "**Heal** me, O LORD, and I shall be **healed**; **save** me, and I shall be **saved**" (Jeremiah 17:14).

This helps in understanding other Scriptures, as when Jesus said: "The kingdom of heaven is at hand. Heal the sick, cleanse the lepers, raise the dead, cast out devils" (Matthew 10:7–8).

Not only was that an instruction for His apostles of that time to physically heal people, it is a prophecy for the future when the kingdom of God arrives in full force, when all sick people are healed, when all the lepers are cleansed, when all the dead are raised, and when all evildoers are cast out. Because without the presence of God, all human beings are sick, all are spiritual lepers, and all are dead to God.

Here's another example: "the leaves of the tree were for the **healing** of the nations" (Revelation 22:2).

At God speed, this verse simply indicates that people (the leaves) who are attached to the tree of life (God) will be helping to save (heal) people of all nations who did not get with the program. Every healing in the Bible is a picture of ultimate salvation.

KEYWORD: SHINE

The word *shine* is a beautiful term on its face, as it denotes an emission of bright light and has connotations of performing extremely well, as when someone shines, performing well at his or her job. At God speed, it illuminates a fantastic meaning concerning our future, if we get our act together and follow the divine instructions.

Here are ten examples, after which I'll connect the dots:

> "The LORD make his face **shine** upon thee.... And they shall **put my name** upon the children of Israel; and I will **bless** them" (Numbers 6:25, 27).

> "God certainly does all these things two or three times to a person in order to turn him back from the Pit, so he may **shine** with the **light** of **life**" (Job 33:29–30 CSB).

> "**Restore** us, God; make **your face shine on us**, so that we may be **saved**" (Psalm 80:3 CSB).

> "**Arise, shine**, for **your light** has come, and the **glory** of the LORD **shines over you**. For look, darkness will cover the earth, and total darkness the peoples; but the LORD will **shine** over you, and **his glory** will **appear over you**" (Isaiah 60:1–2 CSB).

> "I will not keep still because of Jerusalem, until her righteousness **shines** like a **bright light** and her **salvation**, like a **flaming torch**" (Isaiah 62:1 CSB).

> "If you are **filled with light**, with **no dark** corners, then your whole life will be **radiant**, as though a **floodlight** were **filling you with light**" (Luke 11:36 NLT).

> "For God, who commanded the **light** to **shine out of darkness**" (2 Corinthians 4:6).

> "Get up, sleeper, and **rise up from the dead**, and Christ will **shine on you**" (Ephesians 5:14 CSB).

> "The city does not need the sun or the moon to **shine** on it, because the **glory of God illuminates** it, and its **lamp** is the Lamb" (Revelation 21:23 CSB).

"Then the righteous will **shine like the sun** in their Father's kingdom"
(Matthew 13:43 CSB).

Some of these passages may be familiar to you, and some may not.
But they are all broadcasting the same message at God speed. They are all
talking about the divine destiny of obedient people who make the jump
from physical bodies to divine spirit. Once they exit the darkness of the
flesh that currently covers all human people, they will become flaming
torches of brilliant light and will shine with nothing short of the glory of
God. Because we will finally receive the ultimate blessing, gaining entry
into our Father's family.

This is when God's own name becomes our name, like when a bride
marries her beloved man, she takes his name as their family name. Or when
a man has children, they all bear the name of the father. Scripture says
numerous times that people who are saved have the name of Jesus "and his
Father's name written on their foreheads" (Revelation 14:1 CSB).

Once we are restored, as in resurrected from the dead and quickened
into our immortal state, the glory of God and the Creator's face will shine
on us. That means we actually will possess the face of God, because we'll be
on that new level, the level higher than the human level. We'll be on God's
level, completely illuminated like a floodlight fills a room with brilliant
radiance. We all need to wake up out of this nightmare of death in which
we're all asleep and come to the realization that we're not meant to be in
our body of death forever. Just as Jedi Master Yoda tells Luke Skywalker
in *Star Wars: The Empire Strikes Back*, "**Luminous beings are we, not this
crude matter**," God is revealing our final destination of becoming immortal members of His own brilliant and luminous family, set apart from our
crude, fleshly matter. So let's flip our personal light switch from off to on,
to shine out of the darkness and "Let there be light."

SAMSON'S RIDDLE

There are not many conspicuous riddles in the Bible, but one that has a
high profile is this puzzle from Samson:

"Out of the eater came something to eat, and out of the strong came
something sweet" (Judges 14:14 CSB).

The Bible doesn't hide the solution, as the answer is a strong lion that Samson had torn apart and inside whose dead body he later found sweet honey.

But when we examine the riddle and its answer at God speed, there's much more to be learned. Let's start with Samson. His name means "Sun Man" or "One like the Sun." He's a Nazarite, someone set apart for God, and his mission in life was to begin saving His people from the power of the Philistines, the dust-rollers. He can represent both Jesus, the Bright Morning Star, and any faithful follower of the Creator.

On his conflict with the beast, Scripture says:

> "Suddenly a young lion came roaring at him, the Spirit of the LORD came powerfully on him, and he tore the lion apart with his bare hands" (Judges 14:5–6 CSB).

Who might the young, roaring lion represent? There's actually more than one answer:

> "Your enemy the devil prowls around like a roaring lion looking for someone to devour" (1 Peter 5:8 NIV).

> "Do all these evildoers know nothing? They devour my people as though eating bread" (Psalm 14:4 NIV).

> "My chosen people have roared at me like a lion of the forest, so I have treated them with contempt" (Jeremiah 12:8 NLT).

Thus, the young lion who roars at Samson is any wicked individual—including the devil—who roars at God, defying Him to His face, and devours up the minds of decent people. The fact that Samson rips apart the beast is a picture of God or His faithful believers tearing apart the enemy in our body of the beast in which we temporarily dwell. The Creator actually says He rips apart people who forget Him:

> "Repent, all of you who forget me, or I will tear you apart, and no one will help you" (Psalm 50:22 NLT).

Once the strong beast is overcome, there is sweet food that is produced out of its formerly ferocious body. This is exactly the spiritual picture that happens to every true follower of God. Once we have fought against and overcome the devil, a sweet food, the true food, the pleasant presence of God Himself, is produced inside our bodies. Here are a few examples from Scripture:

> "I would satisfy you with honey from the rock" (Psalm 81:16 CSB).

> "Pleasant words are a honeycomb: sweet to the taste and health to the body" (Proverbs 16:24 CSB).

> "How sweet are Your words to my taste, Sweeter than honey to my mouth!" (Psalm 119:103 NKJV).

> "Truly the light is sweet, and a pleasant thing it is for the eyes to behold the sun" (Ecclesiastes 11:7).

Thus, the riddle of Samson can finally be understood at God speed. The powerful eater, the evil one who devours up people's minds, has to be overcome and defeated so that the true pleasant food, who is the sweet light, can be developed inside our bodies of the beast. It is then that our eyes will get the sweetest treat ever, beholding the Sun of Righteousness (Malachi 4:2 NKJV).

LOOK WHO'S TALKING

At times, it's important to consider who is doing the speaking and who is the person being spoken to on the spirit level, because Scripture is often multi-dimensional. Here's a simple example:

> "How happy is everyone who fears the LORD, who walks in his ways!...

> Your wife will be like a fruitful vine within your house, your children, like young olive trees around your table" (Psalm 128:1–3 CSB).

On the surface level, this obviously can be talking about any servant of God who is faithful and obedient. It is especially addressing a man whose wife will produce obedient offspring, children who are likened to young olive trees. When we make the jump to God speed, we can see this passage means more than initially meets the eye.

We already know how God declares the end from the beginning, so we should ask ourselves: "Who is the most famous wife the Bible talks about at the end of the story?" The answer is, of course, the wife of God Himself, which is the collective body of believers.

> "The marriage of the Lamb has come, and His wife has made herself ready" (Revelation 19:7 NKJV).

Thus, this song being sung in Psalm 128 can be heard as the voice of God the Father singing to His Son Jesus, the Lamb, who is marrying His bride, all faithful ones. The wife of Jesus will be a fruitful vine as the song says, because obedient people will produce fruit, additional faithful children who are like young olive trees. It's as simple as that. The words and songs of the Bible are not solely about God's voice to physical mankind. They are often being addressed to other individuals in the spirit dimension.

INSIDE THE MIND OF THE DEVIL

The "look who's talking" method can provide insight into what other individuals are thinking, even the devil himself. Here's a famous passage from the prophet Ezekiel, and when it's read at God speed, it becomes obvious the message can be seen as one to Satan the devil. The evil one is called the prince of Tyre, which means prince of the Rock, and we have to keep in mind that God Himself is the Rock and the devil was one of His obedient princes before rebelling against the Creator:

> "Son of man, give the prince of Tyre this message from the Sovereign LORD: 'In your great pride you claim, "I am a god!

> I sit on a divine throne in the heart of the sea."'

> But you are only a man and not a god, though you boast that you are a god" (Ezekiel 28:2 NLT).

> "Therefore, this is what the Sovereign LORD says: Because you think you are as wise as a god, I will now bring against you a foreign army,

> the terror of the nations. They will draw their swords against your marvelous wisdom and defile your splendor!

> "They will bring you down to the pit, and you will die in the heart of the sea, pierced with many wounds.

> "Will you then boast, 'I am a god!' to those who kill you? To them you will be no god but merely a man!

> "You will die like an outcast at the hands of foreigners. I, the Sovereign LORD, have spoken!" (Ezekiel 28:6–10 NLT).

At God speed, we're actually witnessing a message from God the Father to Jesus, the Son of Man, and to us as well, since each of us is also a son of man (or daughter of man), since we all descended from the first man, Adam. The message relayed through both Jesus and us informs the devil, the rebellious prince of the Rock who thinks he's a god, that he's not going to be an immortal god. Instead, he'll be a mortal man, dwelling in the same place the spiritually dead dwell, known as the pit, or the sea. The enemy, and anyone who thinks like the adversary, is an outcast who will dwell here in the land of the dead, where the walking dead (human beings) have their present existence.

APPLY THE ACCELERATOR

If we continue to apply the tools and techniques presented thus far, we finally can understand many more famous and not-so-famous portions of Scripture at divine velocity. So let's shift into overdrive and step on the gas pedal to translate more passages, illuminating astonishing, new meaning as we accelerate to God speed.

PEARLS BEFORE SWINE

> "Do not give what is holy to the dogs; nor cast your pearls before swine, lest they trample them under their feet, and turn and tear you in pieces" (Matthew 7:6 NKJV).

Translation: Don't waste what is sacred and holy, as in your pearls of wisdom, on vile people who are unholy and have no interest in repentance. Otherwise, they'll treat what you've given them with utter disrespect, and then they'll personally turn on you, intending to destroy you.

WITHERING HEIGHTS

> "Then all the trees of the field will know that I am the LORD. I bring down the tall tree, and make the low tree tall. I cause the green tree to wither and make the withered tree thrive" (Ezekiel 17:24 CSB).

Translation: In the future, all the people of the world will know that I am God. I humble arrogant people, and I raise up and exalt humble people. I make so-called "alive" people wither away in mortal bodies, and I also make people currently withering away in mortal flesh eternally alive if they obey Me.

THE NAGGING WIFE

> "Better to live on the corner of a roof than to share a house with a nagging wife" (Proverbs 25:24 CSB).

Translation: It's more pleasant to be alive and exist in the higher, spirit realm than to temporarily dwell in the physical, mortal bodies of people who incessantly complain.

FLAMING ARROWS

> "Like a madman who throws flaming darts and deadly arrows, so is the person who deceives his neighbor and says, 'I was only joking!'" (Proverbs 26:18–19 CSB).

God speed accelerator: To unlock this verse, simply connect the dots of flaming darts and deadly arrows to the New Testament, where it mentions "the fiery arrows of the devil" and "all the flaming arrows of the evil one" in Ephesians 6:16, depending on the version.

Translation: Just like the insane maniac known as the devil who's constantly attacking people, so is anyone who intentionally lies to someone and uses the excuse of "Just kidding!"

BREAD OF WICKEDNESS

> "For they eat the bread of wickedness, and drink the wine of violence" (Proverbs 4:17).

Translation: Evil people consume the devil's poisonous food and drink, his wicked ways of rebellion against God, and violence against others.

A STAR IS BORN

> "The LORD merely spoke, and the heavens were created. He breathed the word, and all the stars were born" (Psalm 33:6 NLT).

Translation: God spoke into existence the angels of heaven. The angelic host were born when God breathed into them the breath of life.

MORNING STARS AND SONS OF GOD SHOUTING FOR JOY

> "Where were you when I established the earth?... Or who laid its cornerstone while the morning stars sang together and all the sons of God shouted for joy?" (Job 38:4–7 CSB).

This is not only looking back at the ancient past when the physical earth was created and all the angels (the morning stars and sons of God) rejoiced, but it's also a prophecy for the future. We need to remember what Jesus said elsewhere:

> "I am the bright morning star" (Revelation 22:16).

> "They will have the same authority I received from my Father, and I will also give them the morning star!" (Revelation 2:28 NLT).

Thus, here are two possible translations at God speed for the passage from Job, and both can hold true:

1. When the people of earth are established with eternal life, the angels will be shouting for joy.

2. When the people of earth are established with eternal life, these newly born sons of God who have been given the morning star, the divine presence of Christ Himself, will be shouting for joy.

PASSOVER HIGHLIGHTS

The original Passover involving Moses leading the Israelites out of Egypt is quite famous, but there are numerous hidden nuggets that come to life when they're understood at God speed:

> **"And there was a loud wailing throughout Egypt because there wasn't a house without someone dead" (Exodus 12:30 CSB).**

Translation: There's plenty of pain, anguish, and weeping in the flesh—this dark place of misery in which we all dwell. Because every single person in the physical world is already spiritually dead in the sight of God.

> **"None of you shall go out at the door of his house until the morning" (Exodus 12:22).**

Translation: You shall stay in your current mortal bodies until the return of the morning light, until the return of God. It is in the morning, when the light overcomes the darkness, that we exit our current house and become the children of light.

> **"You must not leave any of it until morning; any part of it left until morning you must burn" (Exodus 12:10 CSB).**

Translation: The flesh is not meant to remain when the morning comes, when God returns. Human flesh is transformed into the Spirit of God at that point. If there is any flesh that remains, as in humanity remaining rebellious, it is fit for having heat reapplied in the second death. That means rebels will be raised to physical life in the Second Resurrection and have to be taught properly, coached and judged by the children of God, so they can exit the flesh as well and become spirit.

> **"Many other people went up with them, and also large droves of livestock, both flocks and herds" (Exodus 12:38 NIV).**

Translation: Many other people besides the Israelites also will be saved through the blood of the Passover. The mention of large numbers of livestock, flocks and herds merely repeats this fact, since animals symbolize people in Scripture. And "large droves," at God speed, suggest numbers that are so big, they're hard to grasp.

NO FLESH SAVED

> "And except those days should be shortened, there should no flesh be saved:
> but for the elect's sake those days shall be shortened" (Matthew 24:22).

This verse has been understood by many to indicate that no physical person would survive the horrific end-time events unless the time is shortened and Jesus comes back to intervene. And that very well may be true on the physical level. But there is an additional meaning at God speed.

The word *save* in that Scripture is the Greek word *sōzō*, and it means to save spiritually. It's the precise word the Bible uses when it talks about our ultimate saving, as in this example:

> "You are to name him Jesus, because he will **save** his people from their
> sins" (Matthew 1:21 CSB).

Thus, on the spirit level, when Jesus says in Matthew that no flesh would be saved unless the days are cut short and He intervenes, it's because people in the flesh will have become so far away from God spiritually that they could not be saved. They will have become so disobedient, rebellious, wickedly sinful, or even unknowing of the plan of God, they would remain in their dying physical state and never escape the flesh and receive everlasting spirit life. That's why the time has to be cut short. For the sake of the elect, those few believers who remain at that time, God will return to save His faithful ones, instantly transforming their bodies from flesh to spirit in the blink of an eye.

AFTER THE FORBIDDEN FRUIT WAS EATEN

> "He said to the woman: I will intensify your labor pains; you will bear
> children with painful effort. Your desire will be for your husband, yet he
> will rule over you" (Genesis 3:16 CSB).

Translation: God says to all humanity (the woman, the bride): You'll have to go through a painful process to give birth to the children of God. It won't be easy to gain everlasting life. There will be many trials and tribulations along the way. You will want to be with your husband, who is God Almighty, and He will always be the Supreme Ruler over all people.

"For you are dust, and to dust you shall return" (Genesis 3:19 CSB).

Translation: You rebellious, physical human beings are made of the dust of the ground at present. And, if you don't repent, you shall return to your dust-composed bodies of flesh. This return will take place in the future when you're raised back to temporary existence in the Second Resurrection to be coached and judged by the children of God.

THE CORRUPT EARTH

"The earth also was corrupt before God, and the earth was filled with violence" (Genesis 6:11).

Translation: People are corrupt because they rebel against their Creator. The people, who are made of earth, are filled with all sorts of wickedness and violent thoughts.

THE BEGINNING AND THE END

"In the beginning God created the heavens and the earth" (Genesis 1:1 NKJV).

Translation: In the end of the current age and the beginning of the next age, God will create and give everlasting life to the sons of God, known as "the heavens," and bring back to life those who dwell in the dust, the physical people made of flesh, known collectively as "the earth."

THE BREATH OF LIFE

"And the LORD God formed man of the dust of the ground, and breathed into his nostrils the breath of life; and man became a living being" (Genesis 2:7 NKJV).

Note: I realize this verse was mentioned earlier in the book, but I'm repeating it because of its extreme significance concerning everyone's future.

Translation: In the future, God will re-form every single man and woman out of their dust-composed bodies. When the Creator breathes His Spirit into our spiritually dead bodies, those who are saved will become a Living Being, a literal child of God who then will live forever. Others who have not believed during this first round will also have a portion of God's

Spirit breathed into them, and they will be raised to physical life as a temporary living being. These unbelievers will then be instructed on how they, too, can become an eternally Living Being.

LIGHT OF DAY SEPARATED FROM THE DARKNESS OF NIGHT

> "God divided the light from the darkness. And God called the light Day, and the darkness he called Night" (Genesis 1:4–5).

Translation: In the future, God will raise to eternal life faithful people who will be made of Light. These people are collectively known as the "Day." He will also raise to temporary life people who are unbelievers. They will exist in the flesh once again, in their state of darkness because they loved darkness rather than light. These people are collectively known as the "Night," as they will be covered in their outer darkness, their human flesh, having been separated from the people of the Light.

THE SEED IS IN ITSELF

> "And God said, Let the earth bring forth grass, the herb yielding seed, and the fruit tree yielding fruit after his kind, whose seed is in itself, upon the earth: and it was so. And the earth brought forth grass, and herb yielding seed after his kind, and the tree yielding fruit, whose seed was in itself, after his kind: and God saw that it was good" (Genesis 1:11–12).

> "God also said, 'Look, I have given you every seed-bearing plant on the surface of the entire earth and every tree whose fruit contains seed. This will be food for you, for all the wildlife of the earth, for every bird of the sky, and for every creature that crawls on the earth—everything having the breath of life in it—I have given every green plant for food.' And it was so" (Genesis 1:29–30 CSB).

Hint: "The **seed** is the **word of God**" (Luke 8:11).

> "Whoever has been born of God does not sin, for His **seed** remains in him; and he cannot sin, because he has been born of God" (1 John 3:9 NKJV).

Translation: God is bringing forth people (represented by grass, herbs, trees, and fruit) who have the Seed in itself. In other words, these people

have the Word of God, the very presence of Jesus Himself, inside their being. Upon given eternal life, they are ultimately born of God and cannot
sin because God's Seed, His personal presence, always remains in them, and
that's why God sees them as "good," because only God is good. These newly
divine children of God in His family will be food for every unbeliever, what
the Bible calls the wildlife of the earth. Just as God is our true food now
as He educates us, so those in God's expanded family, the Seed-bearing
plants, will be food for other people, teaching and nourishing them on how
to enter into life.

THE FUTURE EXPANSION

> "God shall enlarge Japheth, and he shall dwell in the tents of Shem; and
> Canaan shall be his servant" (Genesis 9:27).

Translation: In the future, God will enlarge those people whom He is enlarging. In other words, He will expand His family big-time, both in number and in the amount of spirit they have, since *Japheth* means "to enlarge"
or "expand." The enlarged divine family will live forever in the tents, the
housing, of the Name of God, since *Shem* means "the Name." They actually
will bear God's Name. They'll be enlarged and expanded, finally quickened
into divine spirit and no longer dwelling in the tents of Kedar, the tents
of dark flesh. Meanwhile, the people of the world, represented by Canaan,
whose name means "merchants" and "international traders," will be serving
these new additions to the divine family. The unbelieving people of the
world will be ruled by the faithful people who were granted eternal life in
the First Resurrection.

AVOIDING EGYPT

> "Do not go down to Egypt; live in the land where I tell you to live"
> (Genesis 26:2 NIV).

Translation: You won't find eternal life in the dark place of misery, the flesh.
So don't go there and seek the darkness. You will have eternal life in the
land I've promised you, which is the Spirit-filled life in the ultimate Promised Land, the kingdom of God.

WELLS FILLED WITH EARTH

> "Now the Philistines had stopped up all the wells which his father's servants had dug in the days of Abraham his father, and they had filled them with earth" (Genesis 26:15 NKJV).

Translation: While the servants of God our Father (Abraham means "Father of many") have been preparing people to be containers (wells) of God's spirit, the dust-rollers, evil people in the flesh who oppose the will of God, have been trying to thwart the Master Plan. They constantly try to prevent people from gaining eternal life by keeping them spiritually soiled, and thus, covered in dust.

PACKING PHONY GODS

> "If you find your gods with anyone here, he will not live!" (Genesis 31:32 CSB).

Translation: No one will receive the gift of eternal life if they're carrying—either secretly or out in the open—anything to do with false gods.

JOSEPH AND THE ADDITION

> "So Pharaoh asked his officials, 'Can we find anyone else like this man so obviously filled with the spirit of God?'

> "Then Pharaoh said to Joseph, 'Since God has revealed the meaning of the dreams to you, clearly no one else is as intelligent or wise as you are. You will be in charge of my court, and all my people will take orders from you. Only I, sitting on my throne, will have a rank higher than yours.'

> "Pharaoh said to Joseph, 'I hereby put you in charge of the entire land of Egypt.' Then Pharaoh removed his signet ring from his hand and placed it on Joseph's finger. He dressed him in fine linen clothing and hung a gold chain around his neck.

> "Then he had Joseph ride in the chariot reserved for his second-in-command. And wherever Joseph went, the command was shouted, 'Kneel down!' So Pharaoh put Joseph in charge of all Egypt" (Genesis 41:38–43 NLT).

God speed accelerator: While this can be a prophecy relating to the roles of God the Father and Jesus as rulers, it is also a prophecy about all true believers in God. The name *Joseph* means "he adds," "the addition," or "the increase." Joseph represents the **addition** or **increase** in the members of God's family.

Translation: When the above passage is read at God speed, it becomes obvious that the faithful believers are the intelligent and wise ones obviously filled with the spirit of God. Therefore, God makes them second-in-command, with only the King of kings higher in rank.

Being put in charge of the entire land of Egypt refers to the believers' divine rulership over the people in the dark land of misery, those still in the flesh. Those physical people will actually "bow down" to the additional members of God's family, as is also written in Isaiah 45:14 and Revelation 3:9.

The fine linen given to additional members of God's family is predicted elsewhere, as the bride of God in the future will be "'given the finest of pure white linen to wear.' For the fine linen represents the good deeds of God's holy people" (Revelation 19:8 NLT).

THE ABOMINABLE SHEPHERDS

"The Egyptians despise shepherds" (Genesis 46:34 NLT).

Translation: People living in the flesh, in the dark place of misery, utterly detest anyone who shepherds other people toward God and eternal life. Because they love the darkness and wish to be their own masters, rather than submitting to the true Master Shepherd.

DARKNESS TO LIGHT

"Even the darkness will not be dark to you; the night will shine like the day, for darkness is as light to you" (Psalm 139:12 NIV).

"The LORD turns my darkness into light" (2 Samuel 22:29 NIV).

Translation: The faithful believers presently dwelling in the darkness of fleshly, human bodies will be transformed into spirit beings on the divine plane, shining with the brilliance of the Day, which is the light of God. In other words, physical flesh becomes divine spirit.

THE SHEET REMOVED

> "On this mountain he will destroy the burial shroud, the shroud over all
> the peoples, the sheet covering all the nations; he will destroy death
> forever" (Isaiah 25:7–8 CSB).

Translation: In the coming kingdom of God, people's covering of flesh will
be removed, leaving them as spirit beings. The burial shroud or sheet that
covers the spirit within us refers to our physical bodies of flesh, and that
is what shall be taken off, leaving only eternally alive individuals made of
spirit. Hence, death is destroyed forever.

DARK STARS

> "I clothe the heavens with blackness, and I make sackcloth their covering"
> (Isaiah 50:3).

Translation: Rebellious angels who once shone with the amazing brightness of an obedient spirit will be clothed in blackness, transformed into a
darkened state, becoming covered with the outer darkness of flesh, sym-
bolized many times in Scripture by sackcloth. (It is then that they will
be coached and judged by former human beings who will have made the
jump to the spirit level.)

The same result is said using different words here:

> "Or who can tilt the water jars of heaven when the dust hardens like cast
> metal and the clods of dirt stick together?" (Job 38:37 CSB).

Translation: The water jars of heaven refer to angels, spirit beings
who dwell in heaven. But God can and will pour them out into the dust,
into beings of flesh, casting them into a more hardened form, like cast
metal or hardened clay, just as human beings have been cast in a physical
body of flesh.

THE GOOD NEWS IN A VERSE OR TWO OR THREE

Occasionally, there are brief passages that actually summarize the entire message of God in just a few verses. Here are some examples:

> "So Jesus stood still and commanded him to be called. Then they called
> the blind man, saying to him, 'Be of good cheer. Rise, He is calling you.'

> And throwing aside his garment, he rose and came to Jesus" (Mark 10:49–50 NKJV).

Translation: We human beings are all spiritually blind people. God calls us and instructs us to rise from our dead state. When we rise in the future, we'll cast off our garment of flesh, become spirit, and unite with our Creator.

> "He is like a tree planted beside flowing streams that bears its fruit in its season and whose leaf does not wither. Whatever he does prospers. The wicked are not like this; instead, they are like chaff that the wind blows away. Therefore the wicked will not stand up in the judgment, nor sinners in the assembly of the righteous" (Psalm 1:3–5 CSB).

Translation: Obedient faithful people will be like God, the ultimate Tree of Life. They will be planted right next to the living waters, consisting of the Spirit of God, always producing positive results and whose everlasting spirit body will never wither or decay, as in die. However, evil people who don't follow God will be blown away because of their worthlessness. They are debris, just as chaff is. They won't rise to eternal life and join those who have been assembled by God for divine life and rulership.

THE HUNT FOR REBEKAH

The search to find and marry Rebekah sums up the story of God through her name and actions in just a couple of verses. Keep in mind the name *Rebekah* means "firmly secured" or "tied securely."

> "The woman was very beautiful, a virgin; no man had ever slept with her. She went down to the spring, filled her jar and came up again" (Genesis 24:16 NIV).

Translation: The bride of God (faithful humanity) is beautiful in His sight because she keeps herself pure and spotless and has been firmly secured for eternal life. She fills herself, her personal container, with "the spring of the water of life" (Revelation 21:6 CSB) and then comes up again to everlasting life by resurrection.

And this beautiful, sought-for bride of Christ apparently has a desire to help others gain salvation, as she told her lord: "I'll draw water for your camels too, until they have had enough to drink" (Genesis 24:19 NIV).

Camels, as we've seen, represent people. They are servants, to be specific. So when the secured bride says she'll draw water for the servants of her lord, it's saying at God speed that the true believers, the sinless ones who are married to God, whose knot is securely tied to Him, have a strong desire to share the true drink, the water of life, the Spirit of God, with other people.

JEHU AND JEHONADAB

Jehu and Jehonadab are two ancient men in Scripture who are obscure, to say the least, in the minds of many but are seen summing up the message of God in two verses:

> "When he left there, he found Jehonadab son of Rechab coming to meet him. He greeted him and then asked, 'Is your heart one with mine?'
>
> "'It is,' Jehonadab replied.
>
> "Jehu said, 'If it is, give me your hand.'
>
> "So he gave him his hand, and Jehu pulled him up into the chariot with him.
>
> "Then he said, 'Come with me and see my zeal for the LORD!' So he let him ride with him in his chariot" (2 Kings 10:15–16 CSB).

Here's the translation at God speed:

Jehu means "Yah is He" or "He is Jehovah," as in, "He's God!" *Jehonadab* means: "The Lord gives willingly and spontaneously." *Rechab* means "Rider, driver, or controller." With this in mind, these two verses are broadcasting the entire Master Plan of the Creator.

Jehu represents God, and it is God who is asking us if our hearts are one with His. We human beings are all Jehonadab. We are the people to whom the Lord is giving His spirit willingly and spontaneously. Plus, we are all sons of the ultimate Rider, the top Driver, the Controller-in-chief, who is God.

God wants to know if we're united with Him in our hearts. If so, He reaches down from His heavenly chariot into our lower dimension of earth and pulls us up, raises us from the dead, to join him in His vehicle, being a rider or driver right beside Him. This is precisely what Jesus promised regarding our personal, glorious end: "To him who overcomes I will grant to sit with Me on My throne, as I also overcame and sat down with My Father on His throne" (Revelation 3:21 NKJV).

OIL INTO EMPTY JARS

> "Elisha said, 'Go around and ask all your neighbors for empty jars. Don't ask for just a few. Then go inside and shut the door behind you and your sons. Pour oil into all the jars, and as each is filled, put it to one side.' She left him and shut the door behind her and her sons. They brought the jars to her and she kept pouring. When all the jars were full, she said to her son, 'Bring me another one.' But he replied, 'There is not a jar left.' Then the oil stopped flowing" (2 Kings 4:3–6 NIV).

Hint: *Elisha* means "God is salvation," the same meaning as Jesus or Yeshua.

Translation: God is telling obedient human beings (the woman) to collect empty jars to be filled with oil. In other words, He instructs his faithful followers to collect their friends, relatives, and everyone else who are empty vessels so they can be filled with the Spirit of God, represented by oil being poured. As God repeatedly says, "I will pour out of my Spirit upon all flesh" (Acts 2:17).

Those who have God's Spirit poured into them are considered holy, which means "set apart" or put to one side as in the Elisha story. The process of pouring the Spirit into people continues until there are no more rebellious people (empty vessels) to be filled. Thus the Spirit is no longer poured out, since all people will know and obey God at some point far into the future, described in this prophecy:

> "And they will not need to teach their neighbors, nor will they need to teach their relatives, saying, 'You should know the LORD.' For everyone, from the least to the greatest, will know me already" (Jeremiah 31:34 NLT).

HOT STUFF

> "Then King Nebuchadnezzar was astonished; and he rose in haste and spoke, saying to his counselors, 'Did we not cast three men bound into the midst of the fire?' They answered and said to the king, 'True, O king.'

> "'Look!' he answered, 'I see four men loose, walking in the midst of the fire; and they are not hurt, and the form of the fourth is like the Son of God.'

> "Then Nebuchadnezzar went near the mouth of the burning fiery furnace and spoke, saying, 'Shadrach, Meshach, and Abed-Nego, servants of the Most High God, come out, and come here.' Then Shadrach, Meshach, and Abed-Nego came from the midst of the fire.

> "And the satraps, administrators, governors, and the king's counselors gathered together, and they saw these men on whose bodies the fire had no power; the hair of their head was not singed nor were their garments affected, and the smell of fire was not on them" (Daniel 3:24–27 NKJV).

Translation: The three men cast into the fiery furnace represent all people from all three time periods: the past, present, and future. The blaze is this physical life, this flaming Sodom, and "furnace of affliction" (Isaiah 48:10) to which we're all subject. With the divine presence and help of the Son of God (Jesus), obedient people who trust in God are no longer held in captivity. We're free from our chains to walk at liberty completely unharmed by all the flaming arrows of the devil fired upon us in this living hell. Additionally, the story is a prophecy for the future, signifying that once we are completely freed from our physical bodies, we "shall not be hurt of the second death" (Revelation 2:11) in what is called "the lake of fire" (Revelation 20:14) and "furnace of fire" (Matthew 13:42). There will be absolutely nothing that can harm us in our glorified spirit state, and there won't be a hint of the smoke of poisonous ideas, the pollution of the world, that permeates people still in the flesh.

THE LIONS' DEN

> "Daniel answered, 'Long live the king! My God sent his angel to shut the lions' mouths so that they would not hurt me, for I have been found innocent in his sight. And I have not wronged you, Your Majesty.'

> "The king was overjoyed and ordered that Daniel be lifted from the den. Not a scratch was found on him, for he had trusted in his God" (Daniel 6:22–23 NLT).

Translation: Daniel, whose name means "judge of God" or "God is my judge," represents all believers in this physical world, this den of vicious beasts, a place where "Roaring lions that tear their prey open their mouths wide against me" (Psalm 22:13 NIV). It's the place where our chief enemy the devil "prowls around like a roaring lion looking for someone to devour" (1 Peter 5:8 NIV).

Like the previous story of the men not harmed in the blazing furnace, the rescue of Daniel broadcasts the same message at God speed. By being obedient and putting our trust in God, we're found innocent in His sight and therefore can escape all harm and certain death in the den of lions, the realm of the devil, and his evil followers. Being lifted out of the deadly den is an illustration of being raised from this deadly place to our ultimate place of safety, eternal life with God.

VICTORY WITH GIDEON

> "The armies of Midian, Amalek, and the people of the east had settled in the valley like a swarm of locusts. Their camels were like grains of sand on the seashore—too many to count!
>
> "Gideon crept up just as a man was telling his companion about a dream. The man said, 'I had this dream, and in my dream a loaf of barley bread came tumbling down into the Midianite camp. It hit a tent, turned it over, and knocked it flat!'
>
> "His companion answered, 'Your dream can mean only one thing—God has given Gideon son of Joash, the Israelite, victory over Midian and all its allies!'" (Judges 7:12–14 NLT).

God speed accelerators: *Midian* means "strife;" *Amalek* means "valley dweller;" *Gideon* means "feller" or "one who cuts down"; *Joash* means "given by the Lord" and *Israelite* means "prince of God" or "one who prevails with God."

Translation: All the disobedient people of the world moved east of Eden. They moved away from God's presence and became full of strife, dwelling in the valley of the shadow of death, which is the flesh. There's now a whole lot of these rebels fighting against God.

Gideon, the feller, can represent both Jesus and His faithful followers, as both will be used to figuratively cut all evildoers down to size, felling their arrogance.

The loaf of barley bread is the true food, Jesus Himself, the bread who comes down from heaven and slams into the tents of flesh (human beings) to knock down mankind and overturn the rebellious human government. The dream is a vision showing that God has given his obedient warriors, the sons given by the Lord who are princes of God and have prevailed with Him, complete victory over all people who clash with God, who don't agree with Him and instead have strife, friction, and dissent.

On a side note, the story of Gideon concludes with a battle in which a small number of soldiers were armed with a clay jar containing a torch:

> "He divided the 300 men into three groups and gave each man a ram's horn and a clay jar with a torch in it....
>
> "Suddenly, they blew the rams' horns and broke their clay jars.
>
> "Then all three groups blew their horns and broke their jars. They held the blazing torches in their left hands and the horns in their right hands, and they all shouted, 'A sword for the LORD and for Gideon!'" (Judges 7:16–18 NLT).

Translation: The people divided into three groups represent all people from the past, present, and future (yesterday, today, and tomorrow). The clay jars with torches inside are merely an illustration of our human bodies. We are the jars of clay, earthen vessels carrying inside our physical bodies a light, which is the Spirit of God. When the horns get blown at the end of this age, our physical bodies (our jars) get removed to reveal the blazing Spirit of God concealed within. That's the moment we become transformed in the blink of an eye into our new, glorified bodies of Spirit. The sword mentioned is "the sword of the Spirit, which is the word of God" (Ephesians 6:17). The shout declares that the Word of God, the presence of Christ Himself, is now shared with all his fellow warriors from all time periods who have overcome the enemy and won the spiritual battle to become glorified.

THE WIFE OF NOBLE CHARACTER (PROVERBS 31 WOMAN)

When millions of people read this famous part of Scripture, they examine it at human speed only, thinking it refers merely to a virtuous, physical woman who can become a wife of noble character for her husband. But at God speed, it takes on much more meaning. Let's start with the Scripture:

"Who can find a wife of noble character? She is far more precious than jewels.

"The heart of her husband trusts in her, and he will not lack anything good.

"She rewards him with good, not evil, all the days of her life.

"She selects wool and flax and works with willing hands.

"She is like the merchant ships, bringing her food from far away.

"She rises while it is still night and provides food for her household and portions for her female servants.

"She evaluates a field and buys it; she plants a vineyard with her earnings.

"She draws on her strength and reveals that her arms are strong.

"She sees that her profits are good, and her lamp never goes out at night.

"She extends her hands to the spinning staff, and her hands hold the spindle.

"Her hands reach out to the poor, and she extends her hands to the needy.

"She is not afraid for her household when it snows, for all in her household are doubly clothed.

"She makes her own bed coverings; her clothing is fine linen and purple.

"Her husband is known at the city gates, where he sits among the elders of the land.

"She makes and sells linen garments; she delivers belts to the merchants.

"Strength and honor are her clothing, and she can laugh at the time to come.

"Her mouth speaks wisdom, and loving instruction is on her tongue.

"She watches over the activities of her household and is never idle.

"Her children rise up and call her blessed; her husband also praises her:

"Many women have done noble deeds, but you surpass them all!

"Charm is deceptive and beauty is fleeting, but a woman who fears the LORD will be praised.

"Give her the reward of her labor, and let her works praise her at the city gates" (Proverbs 31:10–31 CSB).

God speed accelerator: The key that unlocks this proverb is realizing that the wife, the virtuous woman of noble character, represents the wife of Christ, meaning all faithful believers. Remember, "the marriage of the Lamb has come, and His wife has made herself ready" (Revelation 19:7 NKJV). Reading all the verses a second time with this in mind allows you to get up to speed and understand its full meaning.

Translation: The bride of Christ, all faithful believers, is more valuable than precious jewels. God trusts His believers with everything, as they reward Him with good, pure thoughts, and righteous actions.

The faithful willingly work in the service of the Creator, receiving their true food, Jesus, from the faraway dimension of heaven.

Rising at night to feed others refers to people spiritually rising from the dead, as in becoming awakened to God while they are still in the flesh, then feeding other people with the truth, even before the next age of light and everlasting life commences.

The field the woman evaluates and "buys" is the truth (Proverbs 23:3) and believers grow the truth by expanding God's vineyard of obedient children.

The strength believers draw on is God Himself, since "God is my strength and power" (2 Samuel 22:33).

The profits that can be seen refer to our ultimate gain or valuable return, which is eternal life, and believers can see that good reward long in advance, just as all the heroes of faith saw the promises "afar off, and were persuaded of them, and embraced them" (Hebrews 11:13).

The lamp that never goes out at night is the very presence of God in us. "You, LORD, are my lamp" (2 Samuel 22:29 NIV).

The passages about extending her hands to the spinning staff and that her clothing is fine linen and purple refer to sewing together colorful, royal garments of fine linen, representing people's righteous actions (Revelation 19:8). They allude to the coat of many colors mentioned in the story of Joseph (Genesis 37:3) since our eternal garment of light is comprised of many colors, just as all colors are present in visible light. They're also tied to an earlier prophecy stating: "And all the women that were wise hearted did spin with their hands, and brought that which they had spun, both of blue, and of purple, and of scarlet, and of fine linen" (Exodus 35:25).

The making and selling of linen garments and delivering belts and sashes to merchants refer to believers teaching and offering righteousness to others, with earlier Scriptures mentioning "the sash of finely spun linen expertly embroidered with blue, purple, and scarlet yarn" (Exodus 39:29 CSB).

God's wife, which includes everyone in the divine household, is "doubly clothed" with both strength and honor.

The fact that she makes her own bed coverings or tapestry, as some Bibles render it, reflects the instruction to "work out your own salvation" (Philippians 2:12).

Her Husband is well-known, because she's married to God, and He's already situated in the kingdom of God with the elders, righteous angels who can be considered our elder siblings, since they were created before human beings.

The laughing at the time to come is believers rejoicing, singing, and laughing about what's to come in the everlasting kingdom.

Obviously, God's holy people speak wisdom, teaching love and kindness to others. They're actively engaged in everything good, not slackers who sit around doing nothing.

The mention of the woman's children rising up to praise her is a prophecy for the future, when other people who have been instructed by the woman (believers) will rise up in a resurrection from the dead and will praise everyone who got with God's program in the first round.

Believers will also be praised and glorified by their spiritual Husband, God, who will tell them collectively: "Well done, my good servant!" (Luke 19:17 NIV).

Because the true followers of God have excelled in righteousness during this physical life, surpassing what nonbelievers have done, they will receive the reward of eternal life, as Jesus said: "My reward is with me, and I will give to each person according to what they have done" (Revelation 22:12 NIV).

HIDDEN GEMS LOST IN TRANSLATION

Because the Bible was not originally written in English, occasionally there are passages that have had part of their meaning lost in translation. But once we dig into the original language in which it was inked, we can unearth hidden gems that sparkle with clarity once examined.

IT IS THE GLORY OF GOD TO CONCEAL
A MATTER (THE WORD)

Here's a verse mentioned earlier to help illustrate this fact:

> "It is the glory of God to conceal a matter and the glory of kings to investigate a matter" (Proverbs 25:2 CSB).

On its surface, the verse already says something compelling, that God conceals things, and He is prompting His people to probe and uncover the mystery He has hidden. But there is something extraordinary hidden in the Hebrew language, and it is not well known among those in the English-speaking world. The word that is translated as "a matter," or as some Bibles put it, "a thing," comes from the Hebrew word *dabar*. And what does *dabar* actually mean in English? It means "the word" and is translated as *word* more than eight hundred times in Scripture.

What's so significant is that even those first learning how to read Scripture understand that "the Word" is actually a name for the Creator God. As we've seen:

> "The Word was God" (John 1:1).

> "His name is called The Word of God" (Revelation 19:13).

In fact, in the Old Testament, many instances of the word *dabar* as "the word" are actually referring to the Person who is called "the word of the LORD." Here are two examples:

"Then came the word [dabar] of the LORD to Isaiah, saying..." (Isaiah 38:4).

"Then the word [dabar] of the LORD came unto me, saying..." (Jeremiah 1:4).

What's astonishing is that when we translate *dabar* as it should be rendered in the proverb about God concealing things, it broadcasts a message with incredible new life. Here's how it can properly be read:

"It is the glory of God to conceal **the Word** and the glory of kings to investigate **the Word**" (Proverbs 25:2).

Perhaps you can understand what's being said at God speed. Here's a translation that should shed even more light:

"It is the glory of God to conceal **Jesus** and the glory of kings to investigate **Jesus**" (Proverbs 25:2).

That's right, folks, this simple proverb about investigating things is not merely about probing into just any matter. It's about investigating the God who hides Himself. It is the Creator's glory to conceal Himself in pretty much everything, as we're learning in this book, and it is our duty, honor, and glory to investigate the Maker, to seek God's kingdom and search for His presence, even His personal presence that's hidden inside us.

"Now determine in your mind and heart to seek the LORD your God" (1 Chronicles 22:19 CSB).

"But from there you will search again for the LORD your God. And if you search for him with all your heart and soul, you will find him" (Deuteronomy 4:29 NLT).

"The wicked, through the pride of his countenance, will not seek after God: God is not in all his thoughts" (Psalm 10:4).

"Seek the Kingdom of God above all else, and he will give you everything you need" (Luke 12:31 NLT).

LOWER THAN THE ANGELS

Another hidden jewel can be found in the famous song that sings about what mankind really is, and why God made men and women in the first place:

> "For You have made him a little lower than the angels, And You have crowned him with glory and honor" (Psalm 8:5 NKJV).

On its surface, this verse appears to be saying that men and women were created as beings a little lower than the spirit beings called angels. And that's very true, so I don't wish to take anything away from that. But when we look at the original term in Hebrew that many Bibles render as *angels*, it's actually *Elohim*, the word for God!

So, the verse can and should be read in an additional way, and other Bible translations have figured that out:

> "Yet you made them only **a little lower than God** and crowned them with glory and honor" (Psalm 8:5 NLT).

> "You made him **little less than God** and crowned him with glory and honor" (Psalm 8:5 CSB).

Thus, when we understand the entire meaning at God speed, the verse is not only telling us our beginning position of being created a little lower than God and His angels, it's also forecasting our future. We're going to be raised to a higher level, the divine level as immortal children of God. It is then that we'll be crowned with glory and honor as we'll be judging and coaching rebellious angels and other human beings who didn't follow God.

SO?

There's one other important gem that has been lost in translation, and, ironically, it's in the most famous verse in the Bible:

> "For God so loved the world that He gave His only begotten Son, that whoever believes in Him should not perish but have everlasting life" (John 3:16 NKJV).

We mentioned this before in discussing the snake mounted on the pole, and the execution of Jesus replicating that picture. I just wish to take a moment now to focus on the word *so*, because many millions of people have misunderstood its meaning, usually due to improper teaching. Many take the phrase "For God so loved the world" to mean that God loves the world **soooo much**.

This is simply not true, as the author of John 3:16 also wrote this:

> "Do not love the world or the things in the world. If anyone loves the world, the love of the Father is not in him.

> "For everything in the world—the lust of the flesh, the lust of the eyes, and the pride in one's possessions—is not from the Father, but is from the world. And the world with its lust is passing away, but the one who does the will of God remains forever" (1 John 2:15–17).

Obviously, God can't be loving the world **so much**, and also instruct us not to love the world or things of the world. But there is a solution, and it resides inside the meaning of the word *so*.

There is another meaning for *so* that has absolutely nothing to do with quantity, as in "so much." It has to do with the way or manner something is done. It means "in this way," "in this manner," "thus," or "likewise." For instance, if an athletic coach is trying to teach his or her student to learn the proper way to ice skate, shoot a basketball, or perform any sport better, the coach would say, "Do it like **so**." In other words, do it this way, in this fashion, in this manner. This is exactly the meaning of the word *so* in John 3:16. In its original Greek, the word is *hoytō*, and it means "in this way."

Thankfully, some newer Bible translations have awakened to realize this important difference and have published the proper meaning. Now, the famous section reads:

> "Just as Moses lifted up the snake in the wilderness, so the Son of Man must be lifted up, so that everyone who believes in him may have eternal life. For God loved the world **in this way**: He gave his one and only Son, so that everyone who believes in him will not perish but have eternal life" (John 3:14–16 CSB).

Hence, it is not about God loving the world soooo much, but rather it is that during the execution of Jesus, God was loving the people of the world in a manner that gave them *a way* to escape their death penalty, *in the same way, in the same manner* as the ancient Israelites were spared the death penalty when they looked at the snake mounted on the pole. God is merely repeating the imagery, as we have seen that He is a Teacher who instructs us through repetition, as all good teachers do. So there.

12TH GEAR:

Conclusion: The End *of the* Journey Is Just *the* Beginning

NOW THAT you've been revved up to God speed and your mind is firing on all cylinders, I wish to share with you now a brief anecdote that helped prompt me to write this book. It might seem humorous and a little embarrassing, but it really happened this way. I was at a supermarket and needed to use the restroom. It was located at the back of the store, but a lady working there told me I needed to first fetch the key from the customer-service desk at the front of the store.

Once I had the key, which was attached to a giant golden baton, I marched back toward the restroom, and then stood there outside the facility. Since the door was locked, I presumed the restroom was occupied. So I just stood there and waited. Nothing happened, except for my remaining uncomfortable with a full bladder. That's when the same employee I had encountered earlier came back to the restroom area and asked me if I had used the facility.

"Did you go in yet?" she asked me.

"The door is locked," I said.

That's when the woman responded in a very pleasant tone with a phrase for the ages.

"That's what the key is for."

My wife burst out in laughter when I first told her this story, and I understand why. Of course. That's what the key is for! To unlock the door and have my rest. And I already had the key in my possession. That's when it hit me that the key to unlock the mystery of life and everything in it is already in our hands. As I said at the start of this book, it is the key to everything good. The key to life, success, happiness, peace of mind, and understanding beyond our wildest imagination.

That key is God. It is the divine knowledge He has revealed to us. His mind, His very presence is the key to everything, the divine tool that leads to complete understanding and eventually life that does not end. He has given us this key to unlock the door so we can enter into the truth and find the rest we all desire.

With this writing, I hope that I have opened your mind to realize you already possess the key as well. You just have to use it. Because God's presence is everywhere. He is all in all. And you have now been given the tools to see things that were previously invisible. You can now hear things that were previously inaudible.

God is a broadcaster, and He is broadcasting on all frequencies, so we have no excuse for not following Him. No matter where we look or what we listen to, His divine messages can be seen and heard at all times, if we have eyes to see and ears to hear. They are present in songs on the radio, the movies, TV shows, and commercials we watch, the stories we tell our children, the sayings we frequently use, our life activities, events in the news, and even nature itself. Everything is connected. And all those things I mentioned at the start have one thing in common: God.

The key that connects and unlocks everything is the Word of God. It allows us to "break on through," as the aptly named Doors would sing, to the other side so we can understand everything. It is the template for all that exists. The Bible actually represents the Creator in written form. Anything and everything can and should be compared to Scripture to understand the repeated messages. Because the song remains the same.

It is the song we have had from the beginning. It is God's message of goodness and life versus evil and death. If we choose the path of light, obedience, and the Spirit, we can have eternal life. If we choose the path of darkness, rebellion, and the flesh, we will have death. If we put into practice what we have learned here, we can come out of this dark and miserable place, this spiritual Egypt in which we dwell, and come to the light of everlasting life. Being aware of the divine template and patterns will go a long way in giving you the peace of God, which surpasses all understanding.

You now have the ability to comprehend the Bible on a level you probably have never had. So when reading Scripture, don't just read it to understand the physical, historical events of ancient times. Make the conscious decision to hunt for the unseen spiritual message being broadcast simultaneously. Because the invisible message is present, hiding in plain sight for anyone who has eyes to see and ears to hear it. It takes a little effort, but shifting gears to see the unseen can be accomplished with practice and God's help. I thank the Creator for revving my mind up to God speed, and I pray that this book can serve as a guide so you can make the jump as well.

There is no longer any reason for you to be operating at human speed. Because human speed is like trudging through mud, which you understand now on the higher level. We are intended to escape the mud, all that is associated with the flesh, and become clean, accelerating our thoughts and our existence to the spirit plane of incorruption and immortality. We simply have to open our minds to realize the presence of the Creator permeates all, and there is much more than meets the eye on the physical level. Once we come to this understanding, we can reach God speed and arrive at our intended end, which, of course, is our new beginning. Life.